Animism

A Cognitive Approach

An Introduction to the Basic Notions
Underlying the Concepts of the World and of Man
Held by Ethnic Societies, for the Benefit of Those
Working Overseas in Development Aid and in the Church

Textbook
to Robert Badenberg's Handbook
The Concept of Man in Non-Western Cultures

Lothar Käser

VTR
Publications

Bibliographic Information Published by the Deutsche Nationalbibliothek
The Deutsche Nationalbibliothek lists this publication in the Deutsche
Nationalbibliografie; detailed bibliographic data are available in the Internet
at http://dnb.d-nb.de.

ISBN 978-3-95776-111-8

VTR Publications
Gogolstr. 33, 90475 Nürnberg, Germany, http://www.vtr-online.com

© 2014 by Lothar Käser

Translated from German
by Derek Cheeseman of MissionAssist (http://www.missionassist.org.uk)

Printed by Lightning Source

Dedicated to my students, friends and acquaintances
among the members of SIL
(Summer Institute of Linguistics, Wycliffe Bible Translators)
worldwide,
and
in memory of Kenneth L. Pike,
Co-founder of SIL,
Honorary Doctor of the Albert-Ludwig-University Freiburg im Breisgau.

Contents

Preface

Books have a story behind them, long before their content takes shape. This story is usually told briefly in the foreword, at least those parts which are interesting and worth narrating.

There are books which are heralded by an announcement from the author. There can be various reasons for that. Some authors pen hints as to a sequel, because they want to keep their readership (and hence the purchasers) in tow, as it were, rather like television news broadcasts, at the end of which the viewers are recommended to watch the next programme in order to stop them hopping to another channel.

This book was also announced in advance, in my introduction to ethnology, which was published under the title **FREMDE KULTUREN** (Foreign Cultures) in 1997. At the end of chapter 14, entitled Animism, I had put the following note: "The theme of this chapter is dealt with here in the briefest fashion. In reality a discussion of animism demands a separate volume. It is being planned." (Käser 1997:233). One lady reviewer picked up on this statement with the comment, "Let's hope it appears soon!" (Wiesemann 1998:75). That sounded confident and was also something of a challenge for me, which accelerated the completion of this (extremely difficult) work.

And yet, with the passage of time I have several times regretted having made the attempt to write an introduction to the thought structures of the phenomenon of animism. It became apparent that the very term is disputed, and rejected by many as being irrelevant or out-of-date. Also it became evident that the animistic view of man and of the world was so complex in its various manifestations that again and again I feared being swamped by the plethora of detail; more than once I was on the point of giving up working on the manuscript.

Numerous ideas, arguments and examples used in the book are derived from reading hundreds of ethnological publications. Just as with the compilation of **FOREIGN CULTURES** I regret my unfortunate lack of success, despite intensive efforts, in pinpointing all my sources. I beg the indulgence of the authors. Since **ANIMISM** is likewise conceived as a *textbook* I have once again, as far as possible, dispensed with annotations in the form of footnotes and other attributions such as is customary in scholarly publications, so as not to overload the text. However, I could not do without them altogether.

Not long ago I had a conversation with a missionary working in a rural part of Europe. He complained that the Christianity practised by the people he was working amongst was nothing more than a shell, empty of meaning, reduced to a "religion of festivals". They only turned up in church at Christmas and Easter, or on the occasions of the "rites of passage" such as baptisms, confirmations, weddings, funerals etc. Yet at the same time they studied their horoscope, laid tarot cards, used the pendulum, wore amulets and carried talismans around with them, tried to contact deceased relatives and were involved with neo-shamanism. His conclusion: "Wherever you look, animism, animism, animism!"

I pricked up my ears. Had he really meant animism, or was he talking about occultism?

The fact that he considered both terms identical, or simply confused the two, is unfortunately not at all unusual. In the context of European-Western culture one is always meeting people who share this false opinion. But as a missionary he must be able to keep animism and occultism apart from each other. Admittedly working in Europe while holding this opinion would not cause too many problems or create confusion, but that would not be the case outside Europe, where he would have to deal with people who draw on an animistic view of the world and of man when they reflect on and shape their existence. This became one of my reasons for writing this book.

One particular difficulty was how to make the comprehensive and complex material understandable, its structures often being so alien to European-Western thinking, how to avoid overloading it with unnecessary detail and how to break it down into manageable study units.

Textbooks are abbreviated presentations of mostly complex material, and their authors are always under pressure to keep things brief. There is a hidden danger here of creating a false picture of what is being described. The continual dealing with evaluating what is important and what is not, having to find the answer in every single section as to which facts to include and which to omit, all this slowed down the completion of the manuscript considerably.

It arose out of a myriad of activities. At the beginning stood five years of work on Chuuk, an atoll in Micronesia, where from 1969 to 1974 (and again later on) I undertook extensive field research, becoming familiar with the language and pre-Christian religion of the islanders. The insights I gained then were intensified and extended in over twenty-five years as a college teacher with students of ethnology, philosophy of religion, missiology, general linguistics, on preparatory courses for medical and technical personnel in the Third World, during numerous lecture and research tours in Oceania, South-East Asia, Africa and South America. It was principally the move towards practical application and the opportunities for relating the material in a concrete way to the work among the societies of the Third World which guided me in sifting the contents of this introduction and tailoring it to the needs of the target groups named in the subtitle.

It was precisely in those situations where I was striving to sift, select, and put into a sequence of lessons the wealth of material, in such a way that it would be understood by lay ethnologists, that the fundamental structures of animistic forms of thought opened up to me. Much that is essential in this introduction owes a lot to those situations.

In earlier times, the so-called "good old days", one liked to address forewords to the "sympathetic reader". Before I conclude I would like to address myself to the critics, to the "sympathetic" ones, but also to the others whom I must face with the publication of my perceptions of animism. Critical discussion of hypotheses, theories and research results is a basic principle, essential for securing their soundness. This must also apply to my ideas.

In presenting and developing the ideas and connected matters in the following pages I have taken care to argue neither unscientifically, ideologically nor normatively. However that may be, my intention was to approximate to the (unattainable) norm. In reality no one who thinks and writes can be free of ideological constraints, for the grammar alone of the language one is working in directs the searching and discerning eye in certain directions, quite apart from personal perspectives of world view orientation. However, this kind of restriction of freedom characterizes not only authors, but also their critics.

I am not a (Christian) fundamentalist. However, it is possible that in some passages my own Christian perspective will be recognized, bearing in mind that the book as a whole was written for readers with precisely this perspective. Hence it is possible – as has happened – that established experts, reading critically, will find that my ideas should be "appreciated with caution", whatever that may mean.

The guarantee of scholarly work, among other things, is that all conditions under which an assertion could be disproved should be laid bare. I hope that I have achieved this with reference to the orientation of my own world view.

For the rest the following must be true. If one concedes that the declarations of the adherents of foreign religions are not invalidated because they display the signs of their religious convictions, then that must also apply to my own statements.

At this point there may be some authors who thank their wives for numbering the pages and for not disturbing them further in their work of writing. Such an imputation is far from my intention. Instead I thank my wife sincerely for all the support she has given during the creation of this manuscript, for her readiness to postpone or even forego many other things which ought to have been done during this time. Above all I thank her for her continual and alert checking of each part as it was completed. Without her as a "sympathetic critic" quite a lot of inconsistencies and errors would not have been picked up.

I must also thank a number of others, especially those mentioned in the dedication. There are three who should be particularly selected. I am grateful to my son Matthias Käser, who always had the right advice when the computer programs were not behaving as they should; my daughter, Dr. Beate Engelen, und her husband Oliver for their careful perusal of the manuscript and their most stimulating "marginal notes"; finally my colleague and former student Robert Badenberg, whose own research and publications on the topic of animism have made significant contributions to this volume.

Schallstadt, Winter 2012
Lothar Käser

Introduction

The introduction explains how to approach this book as a textbook, how it is set out, to whom it is addressed and how to engage with its content.

What this Book Is, and What It Is Not

This book is a *textbook*. Hence it is neither an exhaustive treatment of the topic of animism, nor a description of a particular regional or ethnic manifestation of animism. As a textbook it considers the commonalities and differences which characterize animistic systems of thinking throughout the world, extracts those elements regarded as of the essence, and seeks to present them in a systematic way. The aim is to help readers to find their way conceptually among the plethora of detail of the various forms of animistic religion and enable them to engage with the relevant literature.

The abundance of manifestations, emphases and concepts in which animism reveals itself, and within the most diverse human societies, is indeed impressive, making it difficult to comprehend its essential nature. To the outside observer the sheer flood of detail conveys the impression that the animisms of the countless ethnic groups are almost perfectly disparate entities impossible to systematize. The ensuing disappointment causes many of those working in such societies to give up all too soon in their attempts to discover the systematic understanding available. The cause of this paralysis is the fact that over a long period of time the study of animism was unable to uncover any clear *underlying structures* with the help of which some conceptual order could be given to the above mentioned abundance of manifestations, emphases and concepts, thus enabling them to be learned systematically. Such underlying structures do exist, but in reality not only in each individual manifestation of animism; as underlying structures they are similar and comparable in all animisms found in human societies.

An awareness of underlying structures is rather like owning a compass. A compass helps you to hold your course in the ocean of facts and data. This textbook is to be regarded as such. In addition it aims to provide a *framework of recognition* within which individual manifestations with animistic background can be interpreted. This in turn will enable an understanding of their functions and significance for those who shape and manage their existence with the aid of an animistic view of the world and of other people. However, the aim is not only to create a framework of recognition, but in addition a *framework for research* which will help readers to initiate their own investigations in their particular field of work, and if possible contribute to filling the enormous gaps in research that still exist, gaps which reveal the incompleteness of our knowledge of animistic systems of thought and limit our understanding of them, at least in part.

In what follows there are many references to *perceptions*. This relates to a prominent feature of the content of animistic thought structures. Their perceptions are not 'real' in the sense of a material reality. Souls and spirit beings are only visible in a qualified sense. Hence they are hardly or not at all accessible to direct and controlled observation. For the most part there are only indirect pointers to their existence. This is particularly the case with the presence of a 'soul' in or with human beings. It is primarily a matter of effects which one assumes emanate from the soul and lead one to infer that there exists something that can be understood as soul. Hence we are dealing by and large with perceptions. However, since these do appear plausible in many respects, they are assumed to be a reality, mostly in a surprising matter-of-fact way.

Who Needs to Know about Animism?

My observations are directed to a particular *target group*: (Christian) development aid workers (nurses, doctors, teachers, agronomists etc.), overseas church workers (missionaries, lecturers etc.), those training them, and also lay people who have an interest in foreign cultures, societies, religions and any work being done by the above groups. Their concerns and the problems associated with the animistic way of thinking which are very much part of their working environment determine the standpoint on which my presentation is based.

There is an important feature of my approach to this target group. I do not consider the work of missionaries and church workers to be in blanket terms destructive of culture, nor am I of the view that the work of the development aid worker is to be evaluated without hesitation as positive or even as totally separate from that of the missionary and church worker. *Both missionaries and development aid workers are basically and in the same ways participants in intrusions into other societies and cultures*. This is evident from situations like the following:

The Bayaka pygmies in the Central African Republic are hunter-gatherers. In order to secure their existence through this economic system they have developed comprehensive rituals over the centuries, e.g. for hunting the elephants in the forest. Among other things these rituals regulate the roles of the hunters in their group, the authority structures between old and young, and allocate to each member his position in Bayaka society according to his aptitude.

For some time there has been a sawmill in their region for processing the big rainforest trees to make timber for construction and furniture. The Bayaka men find work here, for which they receive payment and which they are also keen to do because with the money earned they can buy things that interest them and which also help the security of their livelihood (metal tools etc.). Now, sawmill, paid work and the monetary economy that comes with it are part of a quite different culture, simply technologically overpowering. No hunting rituals are needed to earn one's living. Overnight they lose their meaning, and wherever things become meaningless people turn away from them. In the culture of the Bayaka the complex rituals are an important part of their religion. *It became meaningless not as a consequence of a Christianizing process, but because of technological and economic intrusion.* The factors which caused a culture change, in this case the decline of forms of religion, were the result of development aid, not of the work of missions, which usually exclusively get the blame.

A further example: In South-East Asia (e.g. in Sumatra) there are ethnic groups who had been cultivating traditional dry land rice for centuries. In parallel with this method of agriculture there developed a number of rituals of an animistic nature, based on perceptions of how the harvest yield could be protected and increased. Changes in the rituals had already been brought about through the influences of Hinduism, Buddhism, and above all the Islamisation of the old Indonesian cultures which occurred some centuries ago. But these rituals, together with their attendant annual festivals and all their customs, were not endangered and threatened with extinction until the introduction of wet rice cultivation and modern agricultural technology (threshing machines!). This was followed by school teaching, which naturally transmitted to the young farmers a scientific world view which had no room for the old perceptions and which changed their way of thinking (Psota 1996; Schneider 1995). *In this case also cultural change, independent of any influence from the process of Christianization, led the ethnic groups to give up their rituals, and with them eventually their religions too, which had developed over thousands of years and produced forms of culture of impressive aesthetic value.*

There is no doubt that every intrusion changes the culture, and there is no sure way of telling whether the change will be advantageous or damaging. It follows that one cannot simply label the intruder in advance as either a destroyer or a sustainer of culture without getting entangled in discrepancies.

Hence this book always refers to *agents of change*, whether the context is the doctor, the missionary, the teacher or the tropical agronomist. This expression was proposed a long time ago by the American ethnologist Ward Hunt Goodenough in his book (1963 and still worth reading) on this topic.

My assertion that medical practitioners also need to know about animism may surprise some, but the reason is clear, for in animistically oriented societies spirit beings, for example, are regarded as the main agents of disease. In my experience doctors and nurses have little or no knowledge of it beyond the elementary, nor are they clear about what animism is in terms of a system of thinking, or what it signifies for people who have to make use of it in coping with the basic issues of their lives. This probably stems from the fact that they were not (were not able to be) informed about it in the course of their education, since there is no need for it in European-Western cultures and societies. In medical science illness is not recognized as being caused by spirits. And later on, when they are working in an animistic environment, they are so occupied with the familiar structures of European-Western medical practice that they are not able to perceive the quite different concepts of their animistically oriented patients about medical matters. With the passage of time most of them probably notice that the latter react to their diagnoses and remedies with incomprehension, mistrust and occasionally also with refusal. However, most of them never find out why that is so.

Prospective missionaries and other church workers are probably at an advantage. In the course of their training they are clearly confronted more intensively with the problem of animism. However, the image of it that they construct is for the most part so overlaid with Christian and at the same time European-Western models of thinking that it rather resembles an ideology conveying what animism must be rather than showing things as they really are. Consequently such people enter "the field" with false expectations. The next chapter will look at this in detail.

Two Ways of Looking at Animism

Since the appearance of Tylor's epoch-making volumes of 1871 (more about that in the next chapter) ethnological research and religious studies have generated a considerable number of works on the theme of animism. Most of their authors were and are representatives of the European-Western sciences, presenting and evaluating the subjects of their research – and how could they do otherwise – from their own cultural perspective. In contrast it is my declared intention to describe the phenomenon of animism from the perspective of those who themselves indeed employ animistic thought forms in shaping and coping with their lives. My approach is therefore to be not *etic*, but *emic*[1], although I am aware that in this I can be only partially successful.

It is this limitation to the emic perspective that also demands (certainly to begin with) that statements of biblical or theological origin are not adduced in order to comment on, interpret or evaluate animistic phenomena. Such statements are not part of their world views, any more than the thought categories of the European-Western cultural circle are. *In concrete terms this means that I intend to describe animism exclusively as it is portrayed by the people who use it, in whose heads it exists in the form of concepts and conceptual structures*. Only when this framework of thinking has been grasped will it be appropriate to compare and broaden it with statements from the Bible, theology, psychotherapy and pastoral ministry, drawing best on the approach of Burnett (2000).

Describing it in this way will surely have the result that animistic phenomena will appear less dark, fearful and demonic than some of my readers most probably expect. It could be that I may be suspected of casually playing the whole thing down. *This would be not only regrettable but also wrong, because trivializing it could not be further from my intention.*

Hence in studying this book the reader must always bear in mind that it is not portraying animism as it appears and is assessed from the point of view of the foreign observer, but (as far as is possible) in the way so-called animists themselves understand, evaluate and experience animism. For the most part they do this differently from the way the foreign observer presumes. Above all they start from the premise that their way of looking at, evaluating and experiencing animism can be understood in and of itself, and is therefore self-evident to the foreign observer, needing no special clarification. By contrast the foreign observer believes that his very own view of (animistic) things is closest to reality. In trying to understand the complexity of animism he is liable to distort things considerably, particularly in his evaluation. *Hence it is vital to have a clear understanding of how so-called animists themselves perceive that complex system which European-Western oriented observers refer to as animism.*

---

[1] The terms "etic" (not to be confused with "ethic"!) and "emic" originate from general linguistics and were adopted by ethnologists; "etic" is used to describe linguistic or cultural phenomena independently of any reference to their function within a system; "emic" on the other hand takes account of this reference.

Two Examples of Animism Systems

Any and every particular form of animism presents an extraordinarily complex structure. This means that it is extremely difficult to explain it in purely theoretical terms. In my experience those who have not spent at least some time living among people who think animistically have the most difficulty in understanding it. In every culture in which animism is present it consists of thousands of individual aspects. At the same time there is no single culture which reflects all conceivable individual aspects in its system. Also it is in effect out of the question to find two cultures which are identical in terms of all individual aspects of its animism. Each cultural system selects and practises only a limited number out of the plethora of possibilities. Under these circumstances how is one to describe animism in general terms in order to produce a model applicable to all cultures in which it occurs?

In this situation I see only one possible way of dealing with the enormous difficulties arising for me. I will proceed not theoretically, but pragmatically. In concrete terms this means that I will start from two animistic systems which I myself have investigated in detail. These will be the animism of the Micronesian Islanders of Chuuk[2] (Käser 1977, 1989), a group of islands in the Pacific Ocean, and of the Asheninca Indians (Campa) of the Gran Pajonal in the Amazonian region of Eastern Peru (Käser 1995).

There is a bibliographic issue as regards the name "Chuuk". Until the 1970s the island group was called "Truk", and that is how it remains in the published literature to this day. In looking for references one should always use both names.

In this I am aware that I am limiting my observations to the conditions in Oceania and South America. Animism in Sub-Saharan Africa, for example, presents numerous other aspects and emphases. This is apparent from the outstanding description provided by Mbiti (1974). But it is clear that everywhere the basic structures of animistic thinking reveal such extensive commonalities that much of what I extract and generalize from my examples in Oceania and South America is also valid for other regions and can be carried over and applied to them. The deviations and differences, which are of course to be expected, and which readers of other material will inevitably come across, should be understood as *mental stimuli* and as offering the

---

[2] As an introduction into the world and culture of the Chuuk Islanders I recommend Gladwin/Sarason 1953, Goodenough 2002, Käser 1972 und 1990(a), Müller 1975. Information about the Asheninca (Campa) can be found in Mehringer 1986, Käser 1988, 1989, ²1990(b) and 1995.

opportunity of extending one's own knowledge. The reader should in no case proceed on the assumption that the characteristics of animistic concepts and structures of any arbitrarily selected culture are basically present in the same or similar form. By contrast he should be prepared to discover that in some places they are missing, or that other cultures employ features of animism that do not exist among the animists of the Chuuk Islanders and of the Asheninca. Hence the phenomena described here should only serve the engaged reader as points of reference. He should therefore, in the context of the particular culture he is working with, only take them reservedly at face value. He cannot avoid the need to examine them and compare them with the realities of the situation in which he is placed. Only under these conditions can the statements in the following chapters lay claim to do justice to the actual facts.

Compared with other systems of animism that of the Micronesian Islanders of Chuuk reveals a certain coherence and hence consistency, not only with regard to its concept of the person, but also with reference to its *perceptions of the nature of things*. In its basic structures it demonstrates virtually a didactically reduced model and hence provides an especially good example.

Both systems of animism on which I have chosen to rely in what follows can also be appraised in another respect. They embody

Two Main Types of Animism

Despite the extensive commonalities displayed by basic animistic systems worldwide, they reveal one *fundamental difference* by which one can classify animism into two main types: *there are systems of animism with and without ancestor veneration.*

The structure of the animism of the Chuuk Islanders is arranged in such a way as to enable veneration of ancestors. By contrast in the animism of the Peruvian Ashenica veneration of ancestors is not possible. More details in chapter 13.

Basic Knowledge of Ethnology

Occasionally the reader will notice that certain areas of knowledge of ethnology and its special terms are not more closely explained or are simply used as if they are generally known or self-evident. Unfortunately an introduction to such a specialized topic as animism does not permit an explanation of all the basic ethnological terms necessary for understanding. The lucidity of the text would suffer. I have covered this background knowledge in a special textbook mentioned briefly in the preface. The English translation of this book will soon be available, entitled **FOREIGN CULTURES. An introduction** to **Ethnology for development aid workers and church workers abroad.** In order to help readers without the necessary information to find the relevant places quickly I have appended in each instance the abbreviation "(**FC**, ch. ...)" throughout the following pages. There is also a glossary of important words which should easily clarify the meaning of special terminology etc.

❑   Suggestions for own investigations: In the following chapters there are notes, designated as such, containing suggestions and methods of procedure with the help of which one can do one's own research into animism (and other aspects of culture) in one's own field of work. The best way to do this is to query the statements and assertions of this book and put a question to a competent member of the relevant society or community, i.e. to an informant (cf. **FC** ch. 19).

The following works contain more on the theme of this introduction:

Burnett, David: World of the spirits. A Christian perspective on traditional and folk religions. London (Monarch Books) 2000.

Gladwin, Thomas; Sarason, Seymour B.: Truk: Man in paradise. Viking Fund Publications in Anthropology Nr. 20. New York 1953.

Goodenough, Ward Hunt: Cooperation in change. New York 1963.

Goodenough, Ward Hunt: Under heaven's brow. Pre-Christian religious tradition in Chuuk. Philadelphia 2002.

Käser, Lothar: ... und bliebe am äußersten Meer. Bad Liebenzell 1972.

Käser, Lothar: Der Begriff "Seele" bei den Insulanern von Truk. Diss. Freiburg 1977.

Käser, Lothar: Die Besiedlung Mikronesiens: eine ethnologisch-linguistische Untersuchung. Berlin 1989.

Käser, Lothar und Gisela: Die Campa-Indianer. ethos (Berneck/Schweiz) 3.1988:6-13.

Käser, Lothar: Durch den Tunnel. Die Geschichte der Übersetzung des Alten Testaments in die Sprache der Truk-Inseln in der Südsee. Bad Liebenzell 1990(a).

Käser, Lothar: Pauti. Mit einer Missionarin der Schweizer Indianermission unterwegs bei den Campa-Indianern in Peru. Berneck/Schweiz 1989, [2]1990(b).

Käser, Lothar: Kognitive Aspekte des Menschenbildes bei den Campa (Asheninca). *asien afrika lateinamerika* 23.1995:29-50.

Käser, Lothar: Fremde Kulturen. Eine Einführung in die Ethnologie für Entwicklungshelfer und kirchliche Mitarbeiter in Übersee. Nürnberg 2014.

Mbiti, John S.: Afrikanische Religion und Weltanschauung. Berlin, New York (Walter de Gruyter) 1974.

Mehringer, Jakob: Pajonal-Asheninca (Campa-Indianer). Ihre kulturelle Stellung im Rahmen der ostperuanischen Proto-Aruak-Stämme. Hohenschäftlarn 1986.

Müller, Klaus W.: Kurs 330 – Südseemissionare unterwegs. Bad Liebenzell 1975.

Psota, Thomas: Waldgeister und Reisseelen: die Revitalisierung von Ritualen zur Erhaltung der komplementären Produktion in Südwest-Sumatra. Berlin 1996.

Schneider, Jürg: From upland to irrigated rice. The development of wet-rice agriculture in Rejang Musi, Southwest Sumatra. Berlin 1995.

Tylor, Edward Burnett: Primitive Culture. Researches into the development of mythology and philosophy, religion, art and custom. 2 vols. London 1871.

Chapter 1
The Term Animism

This chapter explains which diverse phenomena of the past were labelled as animism, which ones in the present, and where the term comes from. It further explains how European-Western observers perceive animism, why they in the process arrive at false judgments, and why animism, because of its function as a framework of the mind, constitutes a stable element in the societies in which it occurs.

1.1   Breadth of Meaning and History of the Term

In current language usage *animism* refers to one of the oldest and most basic concepts of *theoretical ethnology* (Bird-David 1999:67), more precisely of the *ethnology of religion*, i.e. the branch of study which deals with religions and the forms of belief and worship of human societies who have no form of writing or not until recently. In addition animism forms one of the central topic areas of the *study of religions*[3]. The term is also found in other contexts, imbued sometimes with similar meaning but also with quite different ones.

Doctor (and Professor of Medicine) Georg Ernst Stahl of Halle (1660-1734) used the term animism to describe his speculative doctrine of the immortal soul as the supreme principle of the living organism, its non-material movements directing all organic processes of the human body via the brain and nervous system.

The origin of the term animism goes back to the beginning of the modern age, entering the European languages from the Latin *anima* or *animus*. In the spirit world of the Romans it signified a being regarded as personal which accompanied each human being during his or her lifetime, its presence being indispensable for the maintenance of the vital functions of the living body, and which, surviving the death of the body, perpetuated the human personal-

---

[3] As a rule of thumb the difference between theology and the study (or philosophy) of religions is as follows: theology is concerned with God (in ethnological terminology 'the Supreme Being') as the focal point of religious matters; the study (or philosophy) of religions on the other hand is concerned with those forms of culture and their contents which human beings have created in the course of their history to shape their relationship with God (with the 'Supreme Being').

ity in a "beyond". (Issues around the meanings of *anima* und *animus* are considered in more detail in ch. 11.9).

The Swiss psychologist Jean Piaget (1896-1980) introduced the term animism into *developmental psychology* (1926, 1978). He called the behaviour of children "animistic" when they attributed psychic qualities (awareness, recognition, knowledge or consciousness, will, etc.) to inanimate objects, in order to experience them as 'personlike' beings (Buggle; Westermann-Duttlinger 1987). In this the children somehow imagined that one could hurt a stone by kicking it, or that the sun shines with the declared intention of warming us. This is described as psychic animism.

This has some similarity with the so-called doctrine of *animatism*, an early concept in the ethnology of religion which has now lost its meaning. It was Robert Ranulph Marett (1866-1943), an English expert in the ethnology of religion, who coined the term after the Latin *animatus* ("vitalised, ensouled"). Animatism is the perception that inanimate things in the natural world are viewed as alive in the sense that they possess their own will, emotions and mind, e.g. volcanoes, storms etc. Such perceptions are found in many systems of animism, but they tend to be the exception. For a time animatism was regarded as a stage in the development of the history of human culture, preceding animism itself. Hence it is also called *pre-animism*. Marret's view that the 'liveness' of inanimate natural phenomena can be attributed to that force named in ethnology *Mana* (cf. ch. 5) has been disproved by later findings.

The childlike perceptions described by Piaget as animistic are in fact rarely found in animistic religions and thought forms. Among people who lived at earlier stages of cultural development there may certainly have been a tendency to explain the world in the way Piaget described. It could have been the origin of the variety of those animistic perceptions which can at present be observed in all the world's religions.

In comparative studies in the ethnology of religion and the study (philosophy) of religions animism is understood as the *belief in the existence and activity of anthropomorphically (human-like) and theriomorphically (animal-like) conceived spirit-like beings (souls and spirits)*. From this the English ethnologist Edward Burnett Tylor (1832-1917) developed a theory which saw in animism the origin of the religion of so-called primitive peoples and one of the original forms of religion itself (1871, II:2).

According to Tylor (1871) animism originated from the experience of *dreams* (cf. ch. 12), in which human beings are unconscious and yet experience themselves as living in the real world. From this, argued Tylor, man concluded that along with his body there belonged to him a further being (at least one), in whose experience he could participate. He claimed that this conclusion led to the notion of a soul (Lat. *anima*), which complemented the body and through its presence formed an indispensable prerequisite for the life of the body. In his view the concept of the soul arising in this way, together with the belief in the existence and activity of spirit beings, were the starting point of human religious behaviour in general. He suggested further that when someone died his soul was venerated as an ancestral spirit and later as a divine-like being. From a plurality of high ranking spirit beings man would conceive of one as raised to the rank of an almighty divinity and from then on venerated as the *Supreme Being*. In this way, in a later phase of the emergence of human culture, the doctrine of a single God developed, *monotheism*.

Tylor was not the first to think in this way. His ideas of the emergence of animistic thought forms through the experience of dreams can already be found in the 16th century, e.g. in John Spark 1564 (Shaw 1992:36).

Tylor's theory of animism as the origin of religion was influenced by the evolutionary approach of Darwin (1809-1882) and was supported in psychological terms by *Wilhelm Wundt* (1832-1920) in a ten-volume work ("Völkerpsychologie"). However, it is regarded today as at least superseded, and has thus become part of the history of the theory and science of ethnology. Also animism is no longer considered as a blanket term for the religions of preliterate or so-called primitive peoples.

1.2   The Problems of the Term Animism

As explained above, the term animism was derived from the Latin *animus* or *anima*, which can be rendered, depending on the context, by *soul* or *spirit*. In popular science literature and sometimes also by writers on the ethnology of religion this has led to animism being labelled as *belief in souls or spirits*. I accept that this is not completely wrong, for in one particular aspect it gets to the heart of the matter fairly accurately. But it also leads to considerable misunderstandings, for by "soul" and "spirit" people of animistic background possibly comprehend things essentially somewhat differently from Europeans, as is yet to be shown (cf. 3.7).

There is disagreement on the use of animism as a term in the ethnology of religion. Some recent authors have rejected it as unemployable (Hauschild 1993: 318, 323), or have asserted that it "no longer has any role in the literature and in the debate" (Schlatter 1988:473). I agree with this view if what is meant by animism is a general term for the religions of pre-literate societies, as often happened in the second half of the 19th century. It is also correct that

Tylor's ideas on the *development of religion*, compiled with the help of his concept of animism, can no longer be considered as valid today.

1.3   On the Issue of the Term "Animism"

Certainly it is wrong to assert that today "the word and term animism has vanished from the literature on anthropology" (Panoff/Perrin 2000:27). It continues to be used in the debate (Bird-David 1999, Harvey 2000). Schlatter has stated that for a long time now scholarship has had sufficient reasons for dispensing with the term animism (1988:476), but I consider this also to be premature. The phenomenon that has been and can still be referred to as animism undoubtedly exists, and the term, taking into account its origin from the Latin, is a suitable one for this purpose, provided the above mentioned problems are put to one side. Animistic thought structures such as the belief in the existence and power of spirit beings are also at present much more prevalent than we are inclined to accept. That which Edward Burnett Tylor in his epoch-making work of 1871 referred to as animism is clearly a phenomenon of global occurrence in (until recently) pre-literate societies, and is also evident as a *basic concept* in the so-called high religions, at least in their popular expressions, such as *Folk Islam*, the corresponding forms of *Buddhism*, *Shintoism*, the simpler forms of *popular Catholicism* in Central and South America, in the Philippines, and also in a good number of European regions, particularly in the countryside with its agrarian economy.

These arguments seem to me to be sufficient and valid reasons for my conviction that the term animism both now and in the future is not only justified, but also *indispensable*, because there is simply no better term. However, this does not preclude the question of how accurate a designation it can really be.

1.4   What Animism Is Not

As already explained, if it is no longer possible today to attach the label of animism to all the religions of "primitive peoples" across the board, then it is not just problematic, but untenable simply to categorise the religious behaviour patterns and forms of thinking of non-Christians ("heathens") in overseas regions ("developing countries") as animism (Sautter 1992). Such crude generalisations lead to a distorted perception of religious reality and in the final analysis to false judgments on the total way of life of ethnic groups and their needs. The tendency to one-sided approaches and simplifications when attempting to explain and understand animism from the perspective of European-Western societies cannot, however, be ignored.

In his introduction to the ethnology of religion Laubscher (1983) limits himself to the occasional mention that animism equals veneration of ancestors (238, 246 und 250). In my opinion this is to reduce animism to just one of its numerous aspects.

In their treatment of this topic theological and missiological training centres lay particular emphasis on the demonic aspect, undoubtedly part of the animistic system. This gives prominence to the widespread fear of evil spirits, their involvement with the spirits of the dead, the related phenomena of demon possession and the resulting problems of pastoral care among people of animistic orientation. The result of this learning experience is to strengthen the students' impression that animism is predominantly something threatening, and not just for those involved. In turn this impression considerably impairs one's perception of the reality of animism in which the graduates will later find themselves, whether working in the church or in development aid.

Another reason why such people tend to perceive the reality of animism in this characteristically distorted way has to do with a *methodic error* which they often make on the basis of their understanding of the Bible.

It is apparent that the Bible has a lot of important things to say about involvement with the occult and the demonic. But the animistically structured cultures themselves, and especially the thought forms of those human societies, do not have, or do not yet have, any connection with the declarations of the Bible. Hence animistic thinking, existing unseen in the heads of those involved, contains ordinarily only a tiny amount or indeed none of the elements which can readily and from the outset be compared with biblical statements and their contexts. One cannot therefore expect that a missionary or teacher trying to communicate the latter will be understood by his animistically oriented listeners in the way he intends. Possibly he will not be understood at all, unless he has studied carefully the animistic cognitive framework of his listeners, including omitting what the Bible has to say about it. *Only someone who understands the cognitive and explanatory framework employed by those who hopefully are to accept and grasp new knowledge will succeed in imparting biblical and Christian ideas.*

Communicating in a methodically correct manner also means that Christian teaching must be formulated in such a way that the foreign explanatory framework cannot or is not permitted to distort it. Only thus can the statements be at all comprehensible. Hence, *if new knowledge is to be conveyed rightly in terms of method and content, an unconditional prerequisite is a detailed awareness of this foreign explanatory framework, just as it is, i.e. free from all that the Bible has to say about the matter.*

In fact one can only understand any particular manifestation of animism if one first investigates it in and of itself, without any theology, simply from the way this particular expression of animism reveals itself from the perspective of those who practise it. Only then indeed, only then can one expect that the intrusion from outside that one is about to undertake, whether as a church worker, doctor, midwife or teacher, will happen in a purposeful and constructive way. Only so can one also be recognized as acceptable by those involved.

The lack of separation of Christian teaching from animistic theory is a methodic error, and we commit it not just because as normal people we are inclined to start from our own framework of thinking as the measure of all things and as an instrument of cognition. In my opinion the error is in reality consolidated by the failure of the preparatory theological and missiological places of training to require this separation, and indeed to communicate it as at all necessary. In fact they do the opposite. Instead of highlighting the separation of Christian teaching and animistic theory as an essential prerequisite for a proper working method, the teaching on the so-called "primitive natural religions" too often blurs the dividing line between the European-Western way of thinking with its theological aspects and the animistic way, a line that must remain recognizable and be maintained if the participants on both sides wish to understand each other rightly and be understood.

I say this without any sense of gloating or condescension, for I am aware of how difficult it is to teach in theory such a complex topic as animism without ever having had any practical experience of it. Certainly it is only rarely possible to find teachers in training institutions who also bring with them pertinent ethnological experience, which would necessitate working for several years in an animistic environment and acquiring in connection with that the corresponding knowledge of the language.

The result of not properly separating the animism of an ethnic group from the European-Western oriented foreigner's perception of it is for the most part a variously distorted picture. The very fact alone that animism is without due thought equated with occultism is a serious misunderstanding, leading to a false estimate in relation to the people among whom one is working. In addition (prospective) church workers tend to overestimate the significance of this area of the culture, usually considerably, and the effect of this on the reality of their working situation is that those involved see demonic forces at work at every turn. Also, when they return from the "field" and are travelling "on furlough" they are in danger of explaining the complexities of animism in their location with the aid of "ghost stories". This is surely partly due to the listeners, who are expecting something real and are mostly overtaxed in trying to understand such a difficult topic within the brief length of a missionary report. Churches who feel obligated to support development aid and mission often have the same perspective and have a corresponding expectation from e.g. a report on a project they are supporting or from a missionary address. My general impression is that the interest particularly of evangelicals in the demonic, fear-ridden aspects of animism is disproportionately large, and clouds their view of reality. Those who have lived and worked for any length of time within social structures with an animistic background know from their experience of meeting the people that they are not simply sinister characters oppressed by the occult, but are full of the joy of the good things of life in the best sense.

However, in saying this I am in no way implying that there is no harm in these things. *In societies with an animistic view of man and of the world individuals incur situations of duress and fear of which non-animists as a rule have no knowledge, and can have no inkling of, and from which those affected wish to see themselves released, if necessary in a forceful way.*

I consider that one of the essential aims of this introduction is to adjust the biased understanding of animism which Europeans tend to show, and to convey to those working in animistic societies a perspective that will enable them to develop a right perception of the realities, or at least facilitate it.

Those who set about trying to understand the animistic view of the world and of the person from this biased European perspective usually gain the impression that these ethnic groups have confused and vague perceptions of the world, and of the spirit beings whose existence and power they reckon with. From my experience this impression derives from two wrong notions which are usually the starting point for investigating and explaining animism, but which only lead to misunderstanding, to a one-sided evaluation, and to an under- or over-interpretation of details. These (wrong) notions are 1. Animism equals religion, and 2. Animism equals occultism.

1. *Animism is not actually a religion*, but more.

Animism must be regarded as a *world view,* in the most general sense of the word. It is equipped with a characteristic picture of the structure of the world, which is composed of spirit beings, humans, animals, plants and inanimate things. In addition animism is a *natural science*, for among other things its view of the world has ready explanations of how physical and chemical phenomena arise. There are ethnic groups who see meteors as shining spirit beings flying through the night sky, and there are people who are convinced that the rainbow is the work of a demon, causes illness, and is therefore to be feared. The Nharo of the South African Kalahari desert de-

clare that stars are the campfires of the souls of the dead, which sounds virtually poetic (Guenther 1983:96).

But animism is also a *philosophy*, for it provides answers to the question
of how all things, including man, are constituted according to their own na-
tures, where they come from, where they are going to, and what their final
destiny is. This will be explained in later chapters.

Of course it is also indisputable that animism is also a *religion*, or at least
has religious features, for animists feel that they are dependent on beings
which they assume are more powerful than humans, influence their lives, and
to whom they must therefore either subordinate their will, or whom they must
rather resist, persuade, appease or manipulate.

2. Animism cannot be equated with occultism[4].

As already mentioned, this false assessment is prevalent among Christians
in European-Western societies, and in practical situations can lead an observer unfamiliar with the culture to completely wrong conclusions and attitudes. Certainly phenomena which Europeans understand to be occult are of
considerable importance in animistic systems of thought, but they should not
at all be exclusively used to equate animism with occultism. We will see that,
alongside the occult aspect, animistic world views contain a considerable
complex of non-occult perceptions, and these need to be known if both the
whole and its constituent parts are to be rightly understood.

Hence those of my readers who regard themselves as Christians should
recall that the epistemological value of their explanatory framework with
reference to animistic phenomena is in all probability impaired by the fact
that they equate animism with occultism. Such an equivalence is actually not
possible, because otherwise every individual of an ethnic group with an animistically oriented culture would appear like those people of our European-
Western world who are oppressed by the occult, severely disturbed in their
personalities, handicapped in their dealings with others, with all the signs of
incapability in their lives, depression, periods of despair, tendency to abnormal behaviour patterns and suicide. An ethnic group consisting predomi-
nantly of such individuals would be a lunatic asylum and would surely crum-
ble and perish within a very short time.

Admittedly it cannot be denied that anyone working in an animistic environment can be confronted more readily than in his own world with events

---

[4] Occultism is understood to refer to those world views, teachings and practices
which are involved with the awareness of extra-sensory powers and occurrences.
More detail in Ruppert 1990.

behind which there lies more than he can rationally explain. But experience shows that animists are by no means the grim figures that Christians are inclined to imagine, not even those they most presume to be such, the mediums and shamans, who actively seek and cultivate contact with spirit beings. It may be true in individual cases, but not necessarily or exclusively to do with involvement with spirit beings.

1.5 Boundaries between the Animistic and the Occult

There is a theological issue here, which affects Christian psychology, psychiatry and pastoral care. *Members of European-Western societies recognize that the occult has a relatively clear boundary, but people of animistic background are as a rule not aware of any*. For them the crossing over is fluid, a kind of continuum. Psychologists, psychiatrists and pastoral carers who do not know this are unable to diagnose patients with this orientation correctly, nor give them therapy, and therefore they also cannot give them the counsel they need.

Moreover when people with an animistic framework of thought become Christians they do not immediately become conscious of the occult boundary. Missionaries often become concerned and disappointed about this. There are many causes of the tenacity with which occult thinking and behaviour is retained (e.g. contact with the spirits of deceased relatives). Most generally it is because the change which an animistic system of thought has to undergo if it is to give up such basic conceptual structures is so fundamental that it can only ensue over a long period of time.

Occult phenomena, no differently from all other individual aspects of such systems, are embedded in conceptual fields which to a great extent are active in the unconscious and supported by correspondingly attuned language structures. Hence they are secured against (rapid) change.

Systems of culture and thought patterns are so in line with each other in their individual aspects that they fit together like the parts of a watch. If one individual feature changes, it must allow the others time to adapt. If it changed more quickly there would be tension and distortion in the system. For example, if a few speakers of a language suddenly made fundamental changes to the rules of word order, the exchange of ideas and communication would be considerably disturbed and hampered. In its function as a strategy for shaping the process of living the system would be impaired. So one should not be surprised if animistic thought patterns also show themselves capable of resistance in their forms of occult phenomena.

The following sources contain more on the theme of this chapter:

Bird-David, Nurit: "Animism" revisited. Personhood, environment, and relational epistemology. Current Anthropology 40. Supplement.1999:67-91.

Buggle, Franz; Westermann-Duttlinger, Hilde: Animismus als alternative Weise des Welterlebens. Theoretische Überlegungen und empirische Forschungsergebnisse. Forschungsberichte des Psychologischen Instituts der Albert-Ludwigs-Universität Freiburg i.Br. Nr. 41. Freiburg 1987.

Burkhardt, Helmut; Swarat, Uwe (Hrsg.): Evangelisches Lexikon für Theologie und Gemeinde. Wuppertal et al. 1992.

Cancik, Hubert; Gladiger, Burkhard; Kohl, Karl-Heinz (Hrsg.): Handbuch religionswissenschaftlicher Grundbegriffe. Stuttgart et al. (Band 1) 1988; (Band 2) 1990; (Band 3) 1993; (Band 4) 1998; (Band 5) 2001.

Fischer, Hans (Hrsg.): Ethnologie. Eine Einführung. Hamburg 1983.

Guenther, Matthias G.: Buschmänner (Nharo). In: Müller 1983:75-107.

Harvey, Graham (ed.): Indigenous religion. A companion. London, New York 2000.

Hauschild, Thomas: Religionsethnologie: Dekonstruktion und Rekonstruktion. In: Schweizer, Thomas et al. 1993:305-330.

Jędrej, M. C.; Shaw, Rosalind (eds.): Dreaming, religion and society in Africa. Leiden, New York, Köln 1992.

Laubscher, Matthias: Religionsethnologie. In: Fischer 1983:231-256.

Müller, Klaus E. (Hrsg.): Menschenbilder früher Gesellschaften: ethnologische Studien zum Verhältnis von Mensch und Natur. Gedächtnisschrift für Hermann Baumann. Frankfurt/Main 1983.

Panoff, Michel; Perrin, Michel: Taschenwörterbuch der Ethnologie. (Hrsg. v. Justin Stagl) Berlin ³2000.

Piaget, Jean: Das Weltbild des Kindes. Stuttgart 1926 und 1978.

Ruppert, Hans Jürgen: Okkultismus. Geisterwelt oder neuer Weltgeist? Wiesbaden und Wuppertal 1990.

Sautter, Gerhard: Artikel "Animismus" in Burkhardt/Swarat 1992:75-76.

Schlatter, Gerhard: Artikel "Animismus" in Cancik/Gladiger/Kohl 1988:473-476.

Schweizer, Thomas; Schweizer, Margarete; Kokot, Waltraud (Hg.): Handbuch der Ethnologie. Berlin 1993.

Shaw, Rosalind: Dreaming as accomplishment: Power, the individual and Temne divination. In: Jędrej/Shaw (eds.) 1992:36-54.

Tylor, Edward Burnett: Primitive Culture. Researches into the development of mythology and philosophy, religion, art and custom. 2 vols. London 1871.

Chapter 2
Ways of Accessing an Understanding of Animism

This chapter explains which basic functions an animistic system of thought fulfils for those who draw on it for managing their lives. This will lead to showing how a European-Western observer should learn to understand such a system of thought, which problems make this understanding difficult for him, which methods are available to him for penetrating and learning animistic ways of thinking, for integrating them into the overall framework of the relevant culture, and thus making them conceptually available and applicable.

2.1   Animism as a Strategy for Shaping Existence

One of the most important functions of animistic systems of thought is the *provision of* (culturally overlaid) *knowledge*, which serves those who possess it as a *directive of action* in satisfying the needs of daily life and solving the problems of existence. One might add that all other areas of any culture have this function.

Here is a simple example of such culturally overlaid knowledge: hunters (hunter-gatherers) know the behaviour of certain animals which provide their society with food. They know tools and procedures which are so crafted that they kill these specific animals and so make them available to eat. This characteristic knowledge determines all actions which are necessary if a hunt is to be carried out successfully.

A further simple, this time animistic example, which shows the form in which a culture holds its knowledge ready as a directive for action: if a healer from an ethnic society is sure that certain illnesses originate because certain spirit beings have penetrated a human body, then he will focus his action as a healer on removing (exorcizing) such spirit beings from his patient, using suitable methods to keep them away, banish them etc.

Both examples reveal two things. First: using the totality of their culturally overlaid knowledge the people in question have at their disposal strategies for dealing with all possible situations of their existence and for solving corresponding problems. Secondly: this knowledge determines the intentions, the motives which underlie human actions and makes them appear intelligible and justified. Without knowledge of the motivation underlying human actions we are unable to understand correctly why someone acts in a particular way, and it makes no difference what kind of action it is (hunting, gathering, healing, sacrificing, fighting etc.) (For the mechanisms involved one can consult **FC** ch. 17). It follows that as foreigners our access to understanding a culture and society is blocked or at least hampered, because we do not have available the (motive-forming) background knowledge which is indispensable for comprehension.

This is indeed a fairly big barrier, hindering us in our actions and making our work less effective, particularly at the outset of our presence and involvement in a different society. But the barrier is not insuperable. We simply need to acquire the necessary knowledge. It can be learned, for even the members of that different society have acquired it through a learning process (cf. **FC** ch. 9).

2.2   Learning to Understand Animism

Learning how to handle the various forms of manifestation of a different society and culture happens to a large extent first by *living with the people*, finding out how they work, eat, celebrate, in short how they shape their existence. In this phase of learning we acquire *cultural competence*, which means that we learn how to conduct ourselves more and more like a member of the society we are living in, and can eventually shape our lives (roughly) as if we were one of them.

Learning in this way, through the sharing in daily life, certainly has many advantages, but there is also an incidental or haphazard nature about it. At times one learns certain areas of a culture in this way only in extracts. If you only meet the postman on his delivery round you will never be able to find out all that he has to do beforehand in order to be able to deliver the letters.

This is particularly true of the store of knowledge which characterizes the animistic world views. Living alongside only enables one to understand them in a piecemeal fashion. Hence the impression is often given that an animistic system of thought consists of a conglomeration of crude notions, that it is a mishmash of absurd ideas devoid of any logic. This impression is wrong. It can only be avoided by approaching such a world view systematically. This means painstaking detailed work. But the real learning process that results is all the more fruitful and is combined with personal satisfaction.

Learning systematically means first of all: *learning methodically*. Ethnologists whose attitude in their research is focused totally on learning, work with an approach called *participant observation*. For example, the simplest way to study (learn!) what happens in a Turkish wedding ceremony and which elements during the procedures are especially significant is to take part as a guest, and carefully observe what goes on. Observers who participate diligently consolidate things afterwards in their memory by writing up an exact report. If you have the good fortune to be invited to a wedding a second time you can by a *comparison* of the two events ascertain *commonalities* and *differences*, and so gain insights which will then help you to conduct yourself no longer like a foreigner but like a Turkish guest.

This method of participant observation – described in more detail, and to enable replication, in **FC** ch.19 – is particularly suitable for events such as weddings, folk festivals, football matches and similar events. On the other hand, if you want to succeed in grasping the fundamental concepts of animistic perceptions, you will have to supplement it through one or more different methods.

2.3   The Significance of Language Structures

The reason why the basic concepts of animistic world views are so little known is clearly to be sought in the fact that animistic ways of thinking generate an area of culture whose individual manifestations are not accessible to direct observation. This is because we are dealing with notions which are concealed in the heads of the people who are employing these ways of thinking to shape their lives. The only approach which really enables one to gain fundamental insights into the nature of the animism of an ethnic group is via their *language*, more precisely via painfully and closely conducted investigations of the meanings of words, lexical and conceptual fields and their structures, for it is these that shape systems in which animistic ideas are present, in a more or less encrypted form, and which for the most part can only be comprehended with their help.

2.4   An Important Challenge, and what One Must Know about It

Anyone who wants to learn to understand a particular animistic world view must therefore, at any price, learn the language belonging to it, for it is in its structures and vocabulary that the concepts according to which those people think and act lie encrypted, and yet at the same time are accessible.

The technique for getting to grips with other conceptual systems and thought patterns via language structures was developed from the so-called *Sapir-Whorf-hypothesis* and its *principle of linguistic relativity* from about the middle of the 20th century onwards. The new ethnological scientific paradigm arising from it was for a time called *ethnoscience*, sometimes also *new ethnography*. In the literature on ethnology it later came to be called either *cognitive anthropology* or (better) *cognitive ethnology*. Introductions to its methodology can be found in Whorf (1997 and later), Tyler (1969), Renner (1980), D'Andrade (1995), Wassmann (2003), also summarised in **FC** ch. 12.

The Sapir-Whorf-hypothesis or principle of linguistic relativity just referred to claims, in brief, that *the structures of a language give the concepts in which the speakers think a characteristic form, and thereby also determine their perception of reality.*

The fact that human thought and its resulting ability to grasp, handle and manage reality is to a large extent determined by the language and its structures in which the thoughts are formulated has two further implications. On the one hand it means that in many instances the concepts that are preset for us by our Indo-European languages block our view of how basic animistic concepts and ideas are conceived and understood by those who employ an animistic view of the world as the mental framework for coping with their lives. On the other hand this fact is an imperative challenge, to those who want to investigate and learn to understand animistic perceptions of the world and the related view of man of any ethnic group, *to learn the language*, and not just the usage in everyday situations, but so as to be in the position also to grasp and analyse its finer *grammatical structures*.

For this even linguistically gifted people and those with a special interest in learning languages need several years. Ethnologists working in the field (i.e. in a different society) rarely have so much time at their disposal. Presumably that is also a reason why fundamental concepts of animistic thought patterns have until now been so little researched and described in a thorough way.

By contrast church workers, above all missionaries, are clearly better placed in this regard. I venture to maintain that they work under almost ideal conditions. As a rule they spend several years, indeed often decades in the field, so their knowledge of the language is well above average. At all events the long period of their stay places them in the position of acquiring a thorough knowledge of the language in the above-mentioned form. However, most of them tend to disregard this important aspect, and are content just to master everyday usage. (How to learn a language consistently and with reference to the respective culture can be found in Brewster/Brewster 1977 or newer edition, and in Wiesemann 1992).

Among the most elementary foundational concepts one must start from is the recognition that *at the centre of animistic world views there lies in each case a characteristic view of man*. I would therefore maintain that development aid workers and church workers from European-Western cultures best begin by investigating the view of man which typifies the ethnic group whose animistic framework of thought they desire to learn.

2.5   In the Next Chapter

Anyone undertaking the attempt to understand animism in this way must certainly first have a conscious grasp of what their own view of man looks like, including especially both unconscious and preconscious aspects. What this view of man looks like and in what way it can lead to problems of perception when one experiences and investigates the view of man of other societies will be discussed in the next chapter.

The following sources contain more on the theme of this chapter:

Brewster, Thomas E.; Brewster Elizabeth S.: LAMP. Language acquisition made practical. Colorado Springs 1977 (or later).

Fischer, Hans, Beer, Bettina (Hg.): Ethnologie. Einführung und Überblick. Neufassung. Berlin 2003.

D'Andrade, Roy: The development of cognitive anthropology. Cambridge University Press 1995.

Renner, Egon: Die kognitive Anthropologie. Aufbau und Grundlagen eines ethnologisch-linguistischen Paradigmas. Forschungen zur Ethnologie und Sozialpsychologie 12. Berlin 1980.

Tyler, Stephen (Hrsg.): Cognitive anthropology. New York 1969.

Tylor, Edward Burnett: Primitive culture. Researches into the development of mythology and philosophy, religion, art and custom. 2 vols. London 1871.

Whorf, Benjamin Lee: Sprache, Denken, Wirklichkeit. Reinbek 1997 (and later).

Wassman, Jürg: Kognitive Ethnologie. In: Fischer/Beer 2003:323-340.

Wiesemann, Ursula (Hrsg.): Verstehen und verstanden werden. Praktisches Handbuch zum Fremdsprachenerwerb. Lahr 1992.

Chapter 3
Concepts of Man in Different Societies

This chapter explains what should be understood by a concept of man, why human societies possess such a concept, how they use it in terms of a goal, and how concepts of man can be classified into types. A fairly large section is devoted to showing how the concept of man of European-Western societies is constructed (body, soul, spirit), and which deviations from this are to be expected in other societies. At the end of the chapter there is a brief survey of the treatment of this theme and its sub-areas in ethnological research and literature.

3.1   What Is Meant by a Concept of Man

It is not easy to describe in simple words what a *concept of man* comprises. Wolters defines it as "Beliefs concerning the being and position of man in the cosmos, society, state and family, together with the meaning of his life and actions" (1999:96).

This broad and fairly abstract definition does indeed do justice to the term concept of man, but at the same time creates a problem of perception by giving the impression that man's position in the cosmos, society, state and family is of particular importance within the concept. In this way the first part of the definition, which speaks of the *being of man*, is pushed to the margins of our field of vision or vanishes completely from it. This has, as the available results of ethnological research have shown to date, not only yielded incomplete and wrong descriptions of concepts of man obtained from ethnic groups, but has also led to wrong evaluations of their primal religions.

The nature of man includes to begin with elementary things such as the *anatomy* and *physiology* of the body as viewed by that particular society and culture. If an ethnic group's perceptions of the human body are not taken into account one cannot draw up a complete picture of the forms of their animistic religion. It is clear from the example of the Chuuk Islanders in Micronesia (Käser 1977/1989), the Asheninca in Peru (Käser 1995) and the Bemba in Zambia (Badenberg 1999/2002/2003/2008) that their concept of man is characterized in a very special sense by their perceptions of the body. Without knowing this it is not possible to fully comprehend their ideas of the position of man in the cosmos and in society.

3.2   Functions of Concepts of Man

It is evident that the cultures of all societies and communities, whether they belong to the past or the present, possess their own concept of man in the above mentioned sense, and for quite everyday reasons. In all societies the children have to be encultured, i.e. imbued in such a way as to behave eventually in the way that the other members of their respective societies expect. Only when this objective has been attained do they regard themselves later as adults, equipped with those strategies for coping with existence that are attuned to their particular environment, and only in this way are they themselves accepted as members of their society. Hence concepts of man entail a *sense of objectives*, to which pedagogical considerations and procedures are directed. They thus provide *normative models* for what it means to be 'truly human', models which also have a part to play in daily life together, by specifying, among other things, what constitutes accepted social behaviour.

3.3   Typology of Concepts of Man

Concepts of man can be classified according to their characteristic features. Wolters (1999:96) distinguishes four types: 1. artistic, 2. metaphysical, theological and ideological, 3. concepts of man in the form of the combined experiences of life and the everyday, and 4. scientific concepts of man.

The form in which animistic concepts of man can be characterized using this typology can in individual cases only be assessed after careful examination of the data. For example, the concept of man of the Chuuk Islanders can be allocated fairly clearly to type 3 ('combined experiences of life and the everyday'), but this does not exclude the fact that it also contains traits of type 2 ('metaphysical, theological and ideological').

3.4   An Important Imperative

A European who wants to investigate and learn to understand the concepts of man of other societies must first be quite clear about the basic structure of his own concept of man, because this will pre-structure in a decisive way his perception of the way other societies see things. The history of the research into the concept of man provides clear proof of this.

3.5   The Characteristic European-Western Concept of Man

As I have noted, all human societies have their very own concepts of man, including also the European-Western ones (comprising also the English-speaking societies of North America, Australia etc.). Despite their dense complexity and considerable deviations in the details these concepts of man are composed of just a few basic elements.

In European-Western thought there are *two ideas of the nature of* man: 1. A fairly simple one, which I will call the popular one, and 2. a more complex one, rather more intellectually tailored, mainly to be found in philosophy and theology.

1. The popular or established form of the European-Western concept of man is bipartite: man consists of *body* and *soul*. This can be diagrammed as follows:

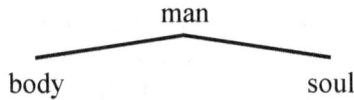

man

body   soul

The most important characteristics of man in this conceptual model are the *mortality of the body* and the *immortality of the soul*. What is meant by the term body needs no further elucidation. On the other hand the term soul, on closer examination, presents difficulties. In fact, two meanings lie behind it.

In this simple model the soul is on the one hand taken to be the place where fear, joy, longing etc. are felt. It is the *seat of the emotions*, of the 'soul-like experiences', the 'psyche' in the sense that one thinks that the psychic phenomena are located here. The term frequently used for this by the Indo-European languages of the European-Western cultural sphere is the 'heart'.

On the other hand the soul in this simple model is taken to mean *a being conceived as spirit-like*, allocated to each individual for the length of his life as a kind of 'inner person', which by its presence first enables the actual life of the body, finally departs from the body at death, and then perpetuates the personality of that individual in some kind of a beyond. This can be expressed in the following extended diagram:

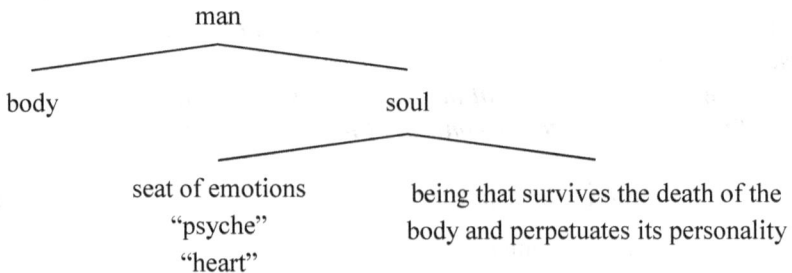

man

body   soul

seat of emotions   being that survives the death of the
"psyche"   body and perpetuates its personality
"heart"

In this simple model the intellectual ('mental') faculties of man are present, if at all, in a covert form. They are either understood as being allocated to that aspect of the soul which survives death and continues to exist as a personal being, as expressed particularly in the philosophy of the ancient world and the Middle Ages, and into the early modern period, or they are taken to be simply elementary functions of the brain.

2. The other, more complex form of the European-Western concept of man, rather more intellectually tailored, mainly to be found in philosophy and theology, adds a further component to body and soul, the *spirit*:

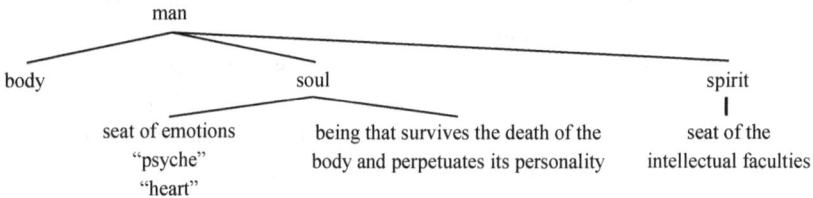

```
                          man
        _____/  _____
       /                |                                    \
    body               soul                                spirit
               _____/_____                          |
              /                    \                    seat of the
       seat of emotions   being that survives the death of the   intellectual faculties
          "psyche"        body and perpetuates its personality
          "heart"
```

In this more complex concept of man the soul is still viewed by most people and in countless language idioms as the seat of the emotions, and at the same time as a spirit-like being that survives the body and perpetuates its personality. By contrast the *spirit* of man is identified in the European-Western cultural sphere as his *intellectual* ('mental') *faculties*.

What the diagram does not convey with regard to the term spirit is the fact that we also regard it, too, as an immortal spirit-like being, if not with the same conceptual incisiveness and intensity as is the case with the soul. The question as to whether the spirit also survives the death of the body and perpetuates the personality of the individual is usually answered by members of European-Western societies in the affirmative.

To do this is to make *an extremely contradictory statement*. If both the soul and the spirit of man survive the death of his body, then two beings have emerged as continuations of man's personality in the beyond, a statement which presents a theological dilemma, as yet unsolved, and probably unsolvable. European-Western notions of this kind are indeed remarkable, and lead to remarkable forms of expression: we speak both of the *souls of the departed* and the *spirits of the dead*. I will be saying more about this below (under 3.7) in another connection.

It is of importance for theologians, and a point of doctrine, that the more complex, typically European-Western concept of man, with its characteristic tripartite division, as depicted in the above (third) diagram, is also the *New Testament concept of man*: according to 1 Thessalonians 5:23 man consists of body, soul and spirit.

This relatively simple formula is neither suitable as a basis for a scientific concept of man in general terms, nor can it be employed in modern psychology and psychiatry[5]. Rather, body, soul and spirit constitute the notional basis of a concept of man which is to be understood in *popular, everyday* terms, a concept of man postulated correctly by Wolters as a type 3 ('combined experiences of life and the everyday'). This is the concept of man which members of European-Western societies accept today without much thought, enabling them to make simple decisions about the nature of man, but with the restriction that, by means of the formula 'body, soul and spirit', they are led into expressing assertions and judgments which result in *a rough and ready concept of man*.

If we wish to use this imprecise concept of man as a starting-point or point of reference for understanding the concepts of man in other societies, we must be quite clear that, as already mentioned, it is neither a comprehensive and universally valid one, nor a scientific one, but a popular, Eurocentric one, formed by the European-Western cultures and their Indo-European languages, its notional basic structures present unconsciously in everyday speaking and thinking. These basic structures are not questioned, but presupposed as self-evident in their simplifying form, and are called on for understanding other unfamiliar concepts of man.

Hampered as it is by these features, it is not really of much value as an instrument of awareness for exploring a different concept of man. However, in our attempt to do such an exploration, we have at first no option but to draw on the help of precisely this (our own) concept of man, for without any basic concept as a compass we would find ourselves, at least in the initial phases of our own investigations, situated in this other, unfamiliar system of thought and concept of man with no means of orientation, especially in the animistic one. So there is nothing for it but to begin with the formula 'man equals body, soul and spirit'. In this, too, there is a problem.

When a European-Western observer investigates other concepts of man he takes the three components of body, soul and spirit, together with their special meanings, as his starting-point, and assumes that they not only determine his own, but also the other, unfamiliar concepts of man, both on a high level of abstraction and also in its countless aspects. This assumption is wrong.

Anyone who makes this the foundation of his investigations will only be given an incomplete or distorted picture of the unfamiliar concept of man that

---

[5] This can be compared with what Wulf (1991:5-12) writes about it. Since the end of the 18th century the term 'soul' has been losing more and more of its meaning in psychology. Outside of the scientific context the related notions have retreated and possibly only exist in fixed expressions of the language.

he is looking for. In order to avoid this error one must be quite clear about how a European-Western observer comprehends body, soul and spirit, and how for him they are knit together in his concept of man. Hence I will now describe these three components in the way they are understood in European-Western societies and then compare them with the corresponding concepts in other societies and languages, with the aim of recognizing and appreciating both commonalities and variations.

3.6   The European-Western Term 'Body' and Its Possible Variations in Non-European Societies

From the European-Western perspective all living things have a *body*, especially if they have a shape that can be recognized, but also objects all around which we perceive in a restricted form. We talk of geometric bodies such as cubes and spheres, but also of antibodies, foreign bodies, political bodies, bodies of knowledge, celestial bodies etc. (Müller 1985:392).

In societies using non-Indo-European languages the term may sometimes have quite different features. Only humans and animals may have a body. In these cases plants do not have bodies, and geometric shapes such as cubes and spheres are not bodies, but if need be are described with the word for *things*, a word whose meanings also include among others (unformed) matter. There are a few non-living things which are in some contexts spoken of as having a body, if they show forms which are similar to human or animal bodies (bottle, boat, aeroplane, shirt). Sometimes the term body is applied to things if the material form of their existence is linked with their *spirit double*. Hence the Chuuk Islanders of Micronesia say of a sacrificial meal in which the spirit double of the meal is consumed by an ancestral spirit, that only 'its body' was present. (More in ch. 7 ff. on what a 'spirit double' is).

Spirit beings are a special case. In animistically oriented societies it is usually said that they only have form. A body in the European-Western sense is therefore denied them.

Sometimes the term body is used for the *'I'* or the *self*. Hence on Chuuk, if one wants to describe someone as an egoist, one says 'he only thinks of the welfare of his body'.

On the whole it is clear that the term body presents the speakers of European-Western (Indo-European) languages with no particular difficulties of understanding when they are investigating unfamiliar (animistic) concepts of man. This is presumably because the human body is easily and tangibly accessible to our perception. You can see it, feel it, point directly to its parts etc. By contrast it is totally different with the terms soul and spirit, which mainly rest on notions with structures hidden in the heads and in the thinking of human beings, and can only be comprehended via statements from informants and an analysis of the language structures. In addition both concepts are characterized, in each case, by two very different and complex aspects.

3.7   The European-Western Terms 'Soul' and 'Spirit' and Their Possible Variants in Non-European Societies

In 3.5. we have seen that in the context of European-Western culture the *soul* is on the one hand the *seat of the emotional (psychic) faculties and processes* in human beings, and is hence the location in the body of joy, fear and countless other 'soul-like' experiences, and is on the other hand *the being that survives the death of a human being (of the body) and perpetuates the personality*.

By contrast *spirit* is understood to be on the one hand the *site of the intellectual faculties and processes* in human beings, i.e. the location in the body of thinking, remembering and countless other mental activities. On the other hand, and this was not yet mentioned in 3.5, spirit signifies a being which as a rule remains invisible and hence exists not in bodily form but in 'spirit-like' form, e.g. as a fairy, guardian angel, goblin, ghost, demon etc. (For the sake of completeness one simply must also mention here expressions such as 'the *spirit of wine* which awakens our *spirits*', which show how expansive the spectrum of the term 'spirit' is in reality.)

I must emphasize again that these definitions relate to popular everyday meanings, which furthermore are not and do not have to be identical in all European-Western societies and cultures.

This problem has been variously pointed out in connection with the term soul. Haekel writes, "that there is no unified Western concept of the soul as a basis for comparison. It differs according to philosophical orientation and world view [...]. Frequently the ethnographer is guided by a more 'common' concept of the soul" (1971:81). However, he does not proceed to explain what he means by a more 'common' concept of the soul. Fischer expresses similar thoughts in speaking of the difficulties surrounding any attempt to arrive at a clear definition of the term (1965:52 ff.). Moreover the issue is no different when it comes to the term spirit (cf. also Baumann 1955[1980]:82).

The fact that both soul and spirit contain two very different semantic[6] features has in the past triggered countless arguments and discussions as to how

---

[6] Semantics is the study of the meanings of the words of a language. Thus a semantic feature refers to a characteristic feature of meaning. For example: the word 'cow'

they are to be understood. These have spilled over into a wealth of literature, especially in theology. But there is no solution on the horizon, and it is probably not possible to find one, for the semantic features of both terms, soul and spirit, are so different that they are of no help in arriving at clear concepts. Finally the problem is made the more acute by the fact that both terms are apparently occasionally used to mean the same thing, and not only in pertinent references in the New Testament (e.g. in Philippians 1:27: '... that you stand in one spirit and one soul'). In ethnological publications as well there is a blurring of the concepts, which has its roots in the (Indo-European-affected) semantic structures. Thus Walter Hirschberg's dictionary of ethnology (Wörterbuch der Völkerkunde) contains the wording: '... of *spirits of the dead* (the *souls* of the *deceased*)' ... (1965:143), similarly also in Bleibtreu-Ehrenberg 1991:75-93.

In comparing the semantic features of both terms, soul and spirit, it is apparent that in European-Western thinking they are both spirit-like beings. But it is not possible to define spirits in terms of souls nor vice versa.

In the last analysis the difficulties with these semantic features of the terms soul and spirit are seen to be insuperable when in 3.5 we raised the (theological and general human) question of what happens to both when a person dies. How do we imagine the form of the after-life? As a dual existence? How else?

In the history of philosophy the term 'spiritual soul' keeps cropping up, both early and late. It is a linguistic oddity, which really brings home the dilemma, yet at the same time hints at a way out of it, for one way of solving the problem could lie in the recognition that two linguistic terms need not necessarily represent two different meanings. For example: the words 'morning star' and 'evening star' may seem to someone with little knowledge of English to stand for two completely different stars. In reality both refer to the planet Venus. The difference lies in the semantic feature 'time of day'. The same could apply to the words soul and spirit, although in essentially more complex dimensions. The history of the two terms, from antiquity to the present, justifiably permits this assumption (Bremmer 1983, Hasenfratz 1986 [a] and [b], Holzhausen 1988, Jüttemann/Sonntag/Wulf 1991).

One of the consequences of this difficult conceptual configuration is the discovery already established in 3.4 that soul and spirit with their characteristic European-Western overtones of meaning are not, or only in a very limited capacity, suitable as a starting-point and basis of comparison for investigating

---

has three basic semantic features: 1. cattle (as opposed e.g. to horse), 2. female (as opposed to steer or bull), 3. adult (as opposed to calf).

and understanding the concepts of man of other societies. However, because the formula 'body, soul and spirit' is at first the only starting-point available for someone working in a different society and culture and researching their concept of man, the foreigner, be he teacher, doctor, church worker or ethnographer, has no choice but to fall back on it.

In contrast to the term body, the way other people perceive the soul and spirit deviates to a considerably greater extent from what European-Western thought understands by them. *One of the most important and consequential differences lies in the assertion that the two semantic features of the terms soul and spirit, which in Indo-European languages can be comprehended in a single term, are frequently divided into two different terms in other languages, especially in animistically oriented cultures.* To put it more simply: when we are talking about the soul as the site of psychic faculties and processes it is given a different word from when we are referring to the soul as the being which survives the death of a person (of the body) and perpetuates his or her personality. The same applies to the term spirit. When the talk is of the seat of the intellect or mental faculties it is allocated a different word from when the reference is to a being which possesses no material body, or no longer does so, e.g. ghosts or spirits of the dead.

For this there is an abundance of examples. E.g., for the soul as the seat of the human psychic faculties and processes, i.e. for the location in the body of joy, fear and countless other emotions, the Chuuk Islanders of Micronesia say *neenuuk* or *neetip*; by contrast, for the soul as the being that survives the death of a person (of the body) and perpetuates his or her personality they use *ngúún*. The Iraya on the island of Mindoro in the Philippines use the corresponding terms *puso* and *gisarem*, the Peruvian Asheninca *rajancane* and *ishire*, and the Bayaka pygmies in the Central African Republic *ngbôngbô* and *efelô*.

When it comes to the spirit as the seat of human intellectual faculties and processes, i.e. the location in the body of thinking, remembering and countless other activities of the mind, other societies may possibly have no term. As a rule in this situation the term used is the same as the one for soul as the seat of human psychic faculties and procedures, i.e. for the location in the body of joy, fear and countless other emotions. This means that spirit is used exclusively to describe a being that remains as a rule invisible, and hence exists not in bodily form but in a 'spirit-like form', e.g. as a fairy, guardian angel, goblin, ghost, demon etc.

For the rest we can safely say that in countless cases man possesses not just a single being that survives the death of the body and perpetuates the personality, but two or more. Hence animistic concepts of man can be diagrammed in the following (conceptually European-Western) way:

man

body　　soul 1　　soul 2　　soul 3　　etc.

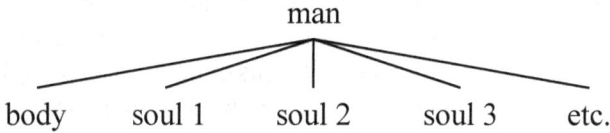

3.8　The Concept of Man in Different Cultures in Ethnological Research

Up till now the main analyses and investigations relating to the concept of man were to be found in philosophical and theological studies, and in the literature on the languages and cultures of the European and Near Eastern ancient world, where access to manuscripts reveal numerous indications of the corresponding conceptual terms.

The question as to what perceptions of man other societies have, particularly pre-literate ones, is certainly as old as ethnology itself as an independent scientific discipline, and the latter has meanwhile contributed comprehensive ethnographic material towards answering the question. However, titles of ethnological publications which show that their subject is the whole person are rare and of more recent date, e.g. Laufer (1957), or they describe things only metaphorically or figuratively, like Heintze (1973). An exception is the collected works of Müller (1983), whose contributions contain examples of concepts of man according to Wolters' type 3, along with extensive inclusion of perceptions of the body in very diverse pre-literate societies.

But if one is looking for relevant information in comprehensive descriptions of individual pre-literate societies, it is only to be found in those chapters dealing with partial aspects of the concept of man, such as body, soul, spirit, but also death, veneration of ancestors etc.

It is noticeable that the authors of the older ethnographic literature showed far more interest in the term soul than in the terms body and spirit. This is easily apparent, for example, in the relevant publications on African ethnic groups (Dieterlen 1941, Hochegger 1965, Mendonsa 1975, Willoughby 1928 and 1970). This imbalance could be due to the fact that in all known ethnic groups European-Western notions of what is meant by the soul are to be found much more clearly, albeit in very diverse forms, than phenomena which we would describe as spirit (in the sense of the intellect)[7]. It is still remarkable that concepts of the body only rarely appeared on the horizon of

---

[7] The original form of this sentence, which I have broadened, can be found in Haekel 1971:80.

researchers in the field, and hardly ever in any close connection with perceptions of soul and spirit, but were described separately. This resulted in a one-
sided and incomplete description of concepts of man, hampering their inclusion in the classification of related world views and often hardly permitting
one to draw any further conclusions.

Concepts of the body as the object of ethnological study, without taking
into account the overall concept of man, can also frequently be found in the
older literature. The best survey is provided in Blacking 1977.

One can also gather from the ethnographic source material that the concept of the soul, for example, can consist of very many different individual
perceptions, which are never actually realised all at the same time in any one
concept of man, with the result that from one ethnic group to another there
are considerable differences. In order to be able to do comparative work ethnologists were therefore faced with the necessity of creating types, based on
particularly characteristic and frequently occurring features of concepts of the
soul in the source material.

Hirschberg (1965, partly also 1988) proposes the following types: external
soul, image soul, bisexual soul, ego soul, free soul, function soul, breath soul,
bones soul, body soul, organ soul, shadow soul, dream soul, vital soul and
growth soul. In drawing up this typology of concepts of the soul there is
clearly a factor at work which has already made its disturbing presence felt in
the ethnographic primary source material: the concept of the soul characteristic of the European-Western approach with its two very different semantic
features.

The ethnographers who were trying to comprehend the concept of man of
a society and culture unfamiliar to them proceeded mostly according the following method. They started out from those features which defined their own
concept of man, among them in particular the features of their own notions of
the soul, and looked for something comparable in the unfamiliar culture. In
this way they did indeed find data which when assembled produced something which had some similarity to their own concept of man. But they were
mostly blind, at least to begin with, to the features which went beyond that in
defining unfamiliar concepts of the nature of man. Many aspects that they
discovered they found just by accident. At all events they were in danger of
overlooking essential areas of these unfamiliar concepts, particularly *when
the length of their stay in the field was short and their knowledge of the
language limited*. The result was very often a description containing very
significant gaps, possibly contributing only non-essentials, wrongly evaluating essentials, and in extreme cases leading to a conclusion which claimed
that the unfamiliar concepts of body, soul and spirit were identical to the

corresponding European-Western ones. Only with difficulty and with limited validity could viable typologies of the soul be acquired on the basis of such sources.

The fact that ethnographers started out from the features of the European-Western concept of man, looked for something comparable in the unfamiliar culture and thereby arrived at an incomplete picture of the object of their research is very apparent in the above-mentioned research undertaken by Fischer (1965) using the corresponding sources on Oceanic cultures. Here are two examples:

In certain contexts European-Western perceptions of the soul point to a connection with the concept of breathing [8], for example in the notion that in a person's final breath the soul leaves the body. In Oceania this connection is so rare that where it does occur it must be described as untypical. Despite this, ethnographers have tried to prove this connection in Oceanic societies as well (Fischer 1965:314-320).

A further feature of the European-Western concept of the soul has to all appearances produced a prominent gap in research on concepts of the soul and hence on the concept of man in Oceanic cultures. For Europeans the soul is not only the being which survives death, but is also the site of one's emotions. *In Oceania (and clearly also in many other regions) these two perceptions are largely separate or else linked with each other in a totally different way.* Consequently any attempt to understand them from the European-Western perception of the soul had inevitably to come to nothing. Fischer came to this conclusion: 'The investigation of this matter, the characteristic psychology of Oceanic peoples, is for the time being the area most poorly dealt with [...] In order to do comparative work here, it is necessary to undertake more precise philological study of the languages involved and/or take a stronger interest in the ethnographic field work on these issues' (1965:324). We are still faced with this challenge (even decades later).

Fischer also concluded that in Oceania there were four fairly large complex areas relating to these perceptions, and that to some extent they could be understood as corresponding to the European-Western concept of the soul: 1. the spiritual (spirit-like) double or dream ego, 2. the spirit of the dead, 3. the life force and 4. the centre of the psychic faculties.

---

[8] The Latin word for breath is *spiritus*, which could also be used in ancient Rome for soul and spirit. In English, and in the modern Romance languages derived from Latin, its meaning has become limited to 'spirit (being)', e.g. French *esprit* etc.

In addition the work contains a detailed survey of publications by ethnologists and religious studies scholars on the concept of the soul up to 1965,
from Adolf Bastian to Carl August Schmitz.

The view that the concept of the body and its manifestations in the language play an essential role in the symbolism of the primal religions of Oceania was investigated some time ago, and emphatically, by Barthel
(1964:920-26). Admittedly his dissertation limits itself to the circumstances
in Polynesia. However, I am convinced that mutatis mutandis his observations are pertinent for most of the other regions. He first draws attention to
the possibility of 'determining cultural models more precisely using ethno-
linguistic methods'(1964:920). After a brief comment on the problems arising from trying to determine the meanings of words from purely lexically
presented language data he addresses research with the following challenges,
objectives and procedural proposals for obtaining useful data (my italics): '…
A truly comprehensive and critically deepening study should […] as far as
possible analyse indigenous texts, in order to apprehend all semasiological
nuances (including emotional valences and any associated meanings) *in the
medium of the language itself* (924). […] We are looking for definitive cognitive models and culturally specific prevalences which are reflected *in the
language*'[…] How can one find the 'symbolic rules of classification' in
Polynesian? A technique for collecting and ordering material would proceed
according to the rules of onomasiology. This would apply to constructing
particular word groups (e.g. *parts of the body*) (925)'.

Following this Barthel sets out the (admittedly provisional) framework
which in his view would guarantee the results of research, called the 'main
principles of symbol formation in Polynesian'. He begins with 'biomorphic
models', which include '*anthropomorphic* symbolisms', i.e. the "figurative
meanings of 'conception, birth, growth, maturity and death' from the vocabulary of both *anatomy* and *physiology* …" (925-926).

The terminologically embedded European-Western concept of man with
its characteristic perceptions of body, soul and spirit as the starting-point for
investigating comparable perceptions in different societies has also led to
wrong conclusions with regard to other conceptual fields of animistic thought
systems, and left behind considerable gaps in research. Only so, for example,
can one explain the remarkable fact that notions of the 'souls of objects',
non-existent in the cognitive framework of European-Western societies but
without doubt present in the cognitive framework of animistic forms of society and religion, in some cases in pronounced fashion, has so far been given
only brief mention, and mostly completely overlooked or ignored. I find this

remarkable because there are obviously clear indications that it is particularly the *perceptions of the nature of objects which form the actual foundation of some of the perceptions of the soul and hence of the concept of man in animistically oriented ethnic groups, and without these the latter cannot be meaningfully represented or understood.* In the case of Oceania this gap has been proved (Fischer 1965, Käser 1977, Cain 1979); in other regions it must be presumed.

It can be further ascertained in the relevant studies that the soul as the centre of the psychic faculties is only mentioned in passing or not at all. The reason for this could be that this essential aspect of the European-Western notion of the soul forms such a different concept in non-European and ethnic societies, so that for a long time it remained concealed from any investigation emanating from the perspective of the European-Western concept of the soul. A further factor is the vocational and world view perspective of the authors of early reports. They were zoologists and medical practitioners, or missionaries imbued with the New Testament concept of man as they understood it.

In addition insufficient knowledge of the indigenous languages has hindered ethnographers in their efforts to connect with such a completely invisible area of culture as the concept of man and the related perceptions of the soul. In most cases there was no phonologically devised orthography available, and without this a whole range of linguistic categories which contribute to how the groups they were investigating conceive their world must have remained hidden from them. As a rule the time for any detailed research was far too short, as is particularly evident in Oceania in the "Findings of the South Sea Expedition 1908-1910" (Krämer 1932, 1935; Hambruch, Sarfert [Damm] 1935).

Finally, mention should be made of an opinion frequently represented in many relevant studies – the *mistaken opinion that soul and shadow are identical notions because they are given the same appellation.* More detail on this in ch. 11.4.

3.9   In the Next Chapter

So far we have looked at concepts of man. At the end of the second chapter I had observed that they form the centre of animistic *world views.* The basic structures of these will be described in the following chapter.

The following sources contain more on the theme of this chapter:

Badenberg, Robert: The Body, Soul and Spirit Concept of the Bemba in Zambia: Fundamental Characteristics of being human of an African Ethnic Group. Bonn 2002. 2nd rev. ed. (edition iwg – mission academics, Bd. 9. Verlag für Kultur und Wissenschaft).

Badenberg, Robert: Sickness and Healing. A Case Study on the Dialectic of Culture and Personality. Nürnberg 2008. 2nd rev. ed. (edition afem – mission academics, Bd. 11. Verlag für Theologie und Religionswissenschaft).

Barthel, Thomas S.: Ethnolinguistische Polynesienforschung. Anthropos 59.1964: 920-926.

Baumann, Hermann: Das doppelte Geschlecht. Ethnologische Studien zur Bisexualität in Ritus und Mythos. Berlin 1955 [Neudruck 1980].

Blacking, John (ed.): The anthropology of the body. New York 1977.

Bleibtreu-Ehrenberg, Gisela: Der Leib als Widersacher der Seele. Ursprünge dualistischer Seinskonzepte im Abendland. In: Jüttemann/Sonntag/Wolf 1991:75-93.

Bremmer, Jan: The early Greek concept of the soul. Princeton University Press 1983.

Cain, Horst: Aitu. Eine Untersuchung zur autochthonen Religion der Samoaner. Wiesbaden (Franz Steiner) 1979.

Dieterlen, Germaine: Les âmes des Dogons. Paris 1941.

Fischer, Hans: Studien über Seelenvorstellungen in Ozeanien. München 1965.

Hasenfratz, Hans-Peter: Seelenvorstellungen bei den Germanen und ihre Übernahme und Umformung durch die christliche Mission. Zeitschrift für Religions- und Geistesgeschichte (Köln) 38.1986/1.2:19-31. [a]

Hasenfratz, Hans-Peter: Die Seele: Einführung in ein religiöses Grundphänomen. Zürich 1986. [b]

Hambruch, Paul; Sarfert, Ernst; (Damm, Hans): Inseln um Truk. Ergebnisse der Südsee-Expedition 1908-1910. II. Ethnographie: B. Mikronesien, Bd. 6. 2. Halbband. Thilenius, Georg (Hrsg.) Hamburg 1935.

Haekel, Josef: Religion. In: Trimborn 1971:72-141.

Heintze, Dieter: Bilder des Menschen in fremden Kulturen. Stuttgart 1973.

Hirschberg, Walter (Hrsg.): Wörterbuch der Völkerkunde. Stuttgart 1965.

Hirschberg, Walter (Hrsg.): Neues Wörterbuch der Völkerkunde. Berlin 1988.

Hochegger, Hermann: Die Vorstellungen von "Seele" und "Totengeist" bei afrikanischen Völkern. Anthropos 60.1965:273-339.

Holzhausen, Jens (Hrsg.): Psyche – Seele – anima. Festschrift für Karin Alt zum 7. Mai 1998. Stuttgart und Leipzig 1998.

Jüttemann, Gerd; Sonntag, Michael; Wulf, Christoph (Hrsg.): Die Seele. Ihre Geschichte im Abendland. Weinheim 1991.

Käser, Lothar: Der Begriff "Seele" bei den Insulanern von Truk. Diss. Freiburg 1977.

Käser, Lothar: Die Besiedlung Mikronesiens: eine ethnologisch-linguistische Untersuchung. Berlin 1989.

Käser, Lothar: Kognitive Aspekte des Menschenbildes bei den Campa (Asheninca). In: asien afrika lateinamerika 23.1995:29-50.

Krämer, Augustin: Truk. Ergebnisse der Südsee-Expedition 1908-1910. II. Ethnographie: B. Mikronesien, Bd. 5. Thilenius, Georg (Hrsg.). Hamburg 1932.

Krämer, Augustin: Inseln um Truk (Centralkarolinen Ost). Ergebnisse der Südsee-Expedition 1908-1910. II. Ethnographie: B. Mikronesien, Bd. 6, 1. Halbband. Thilenius, Georg (Hrsg.). Hamburg 1935.

Laufer, P. Carl: Das Wesen des Menschen im Denken der Gunantuna (Neubritannien). Wiener völkerkundliche Mitteilungen 5.1957.2:127-160.

Mendonsa, Eugene. L.: The journey of the soul in Sisala cosmology. Journal of Religion in Africa (Leiden) 7.1975.1:62-70.

Müller, Klaus E.:(Hrsg.): Menschenbilder früher Gesellschaften: ethnologische Studien zum Verhältnis von Mensch und Natur. Gedächtnisschrift für Hermann Baumann. Frankfurt/Main 1983.

Müller, Wolfgang (Hrsg.): Duden Bedeutungswörterbuch. Mannheim, Wien, Zürich (Bibliographisches Institut) 5 1985.

Reichardt, Anna Katharina; Kubli, Erich (Hrsg.): Menschenbilder. Bern et al. 1999.

Trimborn, Hermann (Hrsg.): Lehrbuch der Völkerkunde. Stuttgart 1971.

Willoughby, W. C.: The soul of the Bantu. A sympathetic study of the magico-religious practices and beliefs of the Bantu tribes of Africa. Garden City, N.Y. 1928, reprinted 1970.

Wolters, Gereon: Darwinistische Menschenbilder. In: Reichardt/Kubli 1999:95-115.

Wulf, Christoph: Präsenz und Absenz. Prozess und Struktur in der Geschichte der Seele. In: Jüttemann/Sonntag/Wolf 1991:5-12.

Chapter 4
Concepts of the World in Different Societies

This chapter explains what is meant by a concept of the world, what distinguishes it from a world view or ideology, and in what ways people can make use of it in their thinking. It will also explain how an animistic concept of the world is constructed, and which of its basic principles require special consideration if they are to be understood from the perspective of a European-Western observer.

4.1   What Is a Concept of the World?

Describing in simple terms how a concept of the world is to be understood is similar in difficulty to describing a concept of man. As a rule it is to be distinguished from a world view or ideology, which certainly forms part of what a concept of the world is.

A concept of the world signifies the totality of perceptions with the help of which man explains the universe (the cosmos), its structure and its functions. This includes the perceptions by which he seeks to comprehend his own existence in the world, his origin, his destiny, and especially the possibility of a life following his bodily death.

Concepts of the world can take on a great variety of forms, depending on the culture (and the language!). Even within one and the same society there is no necessary uniformity. In Europe and the West there are groups of people outside of formal education who are content with a simple, closed model, considerably different from the so-called scientific concept of the world, highly complex, not self-contained, and open to new knowledge.

4.2   Functions of Concepts of the World

Put very simply: concepts of the world present strategies for explaining the world. In general terms they enable one to make judgments or speculations about the cosmos, the natural world, the essence of man and of things etc.

In addition concepts of the world, especially those of simple character, serve as a foundation for social and economic conditions inside communities. They explain, for example, why the religion of an ethnic group requires the worship of the sun or the moon as a deity, or why one's genealogy has to be calculated through the mother's line (matrilineal) or the father's (patrilineal) (cf. **FC** ch. 8). This gives rise to certain ideals and value notions, which in certain circumstances serve as guidelines of action for changing existing conditions if they are not found to be satisfactory. It follows that concepts of the world create and support ideologies which in turn form the foundation of the world view contained in that concept. Such ideologies are normative, i.e. they prescribe how one should be in one's society and in the world, and what one has to do in it. In this connection concepts of the world have a part to play in the way concepts of man originate and persist.

In the world view of a community the cosmos appears basically as an ordered entity. The cosmic order, which enables one to make statements about the nature of things and of man, thereby provides that society with the principles of their religion. The latter is also to be regarded as part of that concept of the world which helps to shape one's existence. This applies in special measure to animistic concepts of the world of pre-literate (or until very recently pre-literate) ethnic societies.

4.3   Animistic Concepts of the World

People whose thinking is shaped by animism possess mostly fairly simply structured notions of how the physical world around them is put together. Their concept of the world is basically quite similar to that which held sway in ancient Europe until well into the Middle Ages. In concrete terms this means that in many pre-literate societies it is accepted that the earth is a flat disc, below it the underworld, above it, like an upturned bowl, the arc of the sky. Where one lives is at the centre of the disc. The proof of this, such people would say, is that from where they live the distance to the horizon is the same in all directions, or that the sky is highest over their place of habitation.

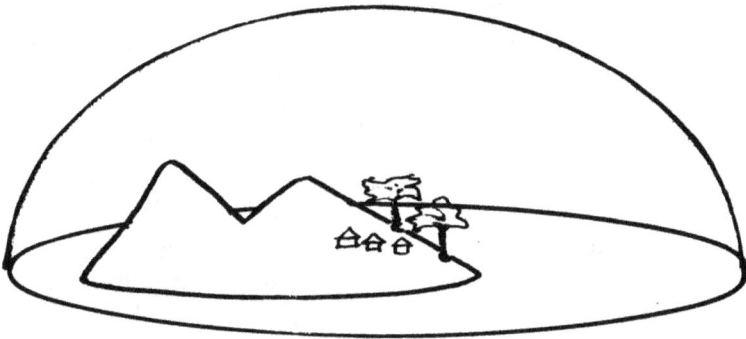

Simplified concept of the world in pre-literate societies

Concepts of the world in this form are usually found in flat landscapes where one can see the whole sky and horizon, hence in Oceania, and in large parts of Africa or America. Ethnic groups such as the Bayaka pygmies of Central Africa who live in the rain forest and therefore do not see the horizon, and only see the sky through the foliage of the tall rain forest trees, conceive of the world rather as a disc with an upturned cylinder over it. In this model of the world they themselves also form the central point.

The Bayaka concept of the world according to Bahuchet/Thomas
1991:108

Common to both models is the fact that the sky is not conceived as being far away from the earth, as in popular European-Western thought, but begins either no higher than the top of the trees or immediately at the earth's upper surface. Hence there can be no proverb about trees not reaching into the sky in such cultures. However, that needs to be qualified.

In prehistoric times, in the cultures of North Eurasia and the Near East, there was the notion of a tree which connected the three realms, with its roots in the underworld, and its branches in the heavens. Among the Germanic tribes or Teutons it was the world ash tree Yggdrasil. Also in the surviving shamanistically oriented concepts of the world in Siberia there is the so-called *world tree*, often in the form of a birch. In many ethnic groups one finds the idea of a *world pillar* or *column* instead.

sky/heaven
gods

earth
men

World tree as the centre of the Teutonic concept of the world
(http://nl.wikipedia.org/wiki/Yggdrasil)

In each case the sky, animistically understood, is not something 'beyond' the blue firmament, but 'this side', so it follows that the sky is to be regarded as a phenomenon inside this world.

Despite its simplicity such a concept of the sky can indicate very complex aspects in the details. During my ethnological and linguistic field work in Micronesia I looked for a term for the concept of the sky, and found a whole string of words that can be used for it. This was confusing at first. In answer to my questions one informant explained that the whole space under the hemisphere of the sky was 'sky', beginning immediately at the earth's surface. It further emerged that this whole space is divided into various layers, each with its own name, e.g. 'air-sky', 'spirits-sky', 'cloud-sky', 'star-sky', rather like a tower-block. The Iraya on the island of Mindoro in the Philippines have a complex model of the world with eight layers of sky, the lowest one beginning at treetop height. Particular features are allocated to each of these layers: meteorological events such as cloud formation and rain, bird flight, astronomical phenomena such as sun, moon and stars.

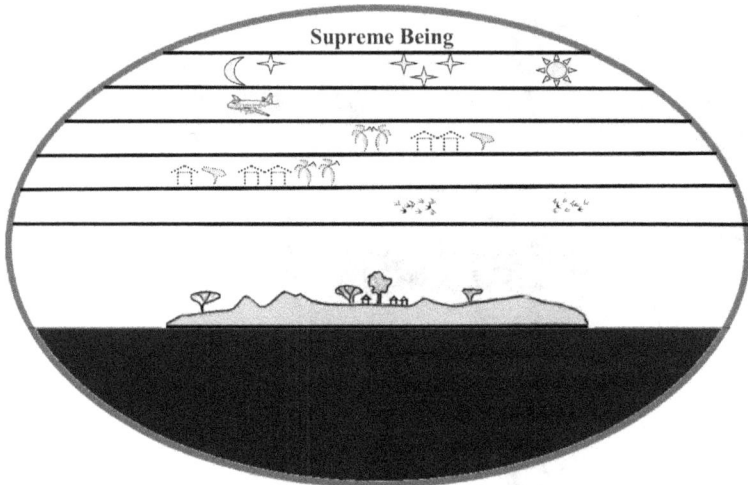

Irayan concept of the world with stepped sky

A linguistic and conceptual pattern of this kind can present difficulties when one is trying to convey and translate Christian concepts into such a cognitive framework, particularly bearing in mind which of the various words for 'sky' should be used in each case in Bible verses. (On the problems pertaining to this which arise in the Austronesian[9] languages cf. Käser 1998.)

Each of these levels or 'storeys' in the sky – and this is typical of an animistic concept of the world – can be the habitation of spirit beings. As a rule these are spirits which are kindly disposed towards man. The notion prevails that here there are houses, villages, landscapes with rivers, lakes, trees and mountains, as in the above illustration, not in material form, but *spirit-like*, just like the inhabitants. Such scenarios are most frequently described in the myths of the relevant ethnic groups. It can be regarded as a kind of *mythical geography*.

It is noteworthy that the Iraya do not regard the large airplanes they now see flying here as being in any danger. Neither they nor the spirit inhabitants of the various levels need to worry. The planes traverse these spirit regions without either pilots or passengers having the slightest inkling.

It is by no means rare to find that the towerblock-like structure of the space under the arc of the sky is perpetuated in the space under the earth, which is frequently the habitation of spirits which by contrast tend to be ill-

---

[9] Austronesian refers to the overwhelming number of languages in Oceania and South-East Asia between Madagascar and Easter Island.

disposed or indeed evilly disposed towards men, and where, in many forms of animism, the spirits of the dead also dwell.

The Yanomamö of Brazil have developed a particularly impressive model of the world, with various levels. In it the underworld is fully finished in form (level 4 Hei tä bebi). Above it is the level of men (3 Hei kä misi), and then two layers in the sky.

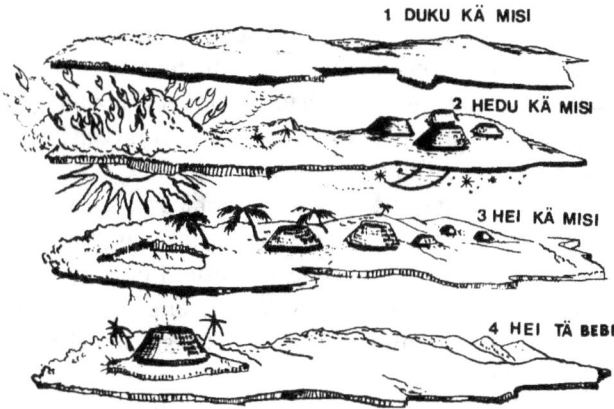

The Yanomamö concept of the world (taken from Chagnon 1992:100)

These details, although few, are sufficient to enable us to define *animistic concepts of the world as comprehensive concepts of the nature of the cosmos and of the visible and invisible elements it contains, including its inhabitants, both visible (humans, animals) and invisible (spirit beings).*

This definition furnishes the background for the following description and appreciation of the astonishing amount of detail which makes up each individual animistic concept of the world and of man. These details can be summarized under five points.

4.4   Basic Principles of Animistic Concepts of the World

In order to understand animism and the corresponding traces found in literate religions, it is best to bear in mind the following basic principles:

1. The world consists of material things and beings,

2. of spirit objects and beings,

3. which cannot be neatly separated from each other in space and time, and hence together constitute the real world of existence,

4. which have a mutual and deeply pervading influence on each other, with indications that greater conceptual weight, greater effects and effective opportunities are attributed to the spirit objects and beings.

5. In a world of this nature there also exists a principle called (in ethnology) mana, which achieves extraordinary effects.

Point 1 needs no special elucidation. The perceptions of the world of material things and beings constitute an area which seems comparable to the way Europeans think, and are as such easily understandable. However, one should be prepared for surprises, for the physical world can be structured and conceived in extremely different ways.

Point 2, however, contains a difficulty, or at least a surprise. Many Europeans are quite ready to conceive of the existence of spirit beings. But *spirit-like objects* are foreign to the European-Western cognitive framework of thought, or indeed unknown altogether. We either dispute that they exist, or at least we doubt it. Not so animists. For them the spirit realm is as real as the material realm, although with the limitation that as a rule spirit beings and spirit-like objects are not visible, except in dreams, under the influence of drugs, or in a trance-like (ecstatic) state.

For example the Chuuk Islanders explain everything they see in dreams either as the spirit doubles of things and living beings (*ngúún*), as the spirits of deceased relatives (*énú*), or as demons (*soope*), if their appearance arouses fear (Käser 1977). The Asheninca of Peru are alert to the possibility that evil spirit beings (*camari, peiari*) shoot arrows at people, spirit-like arrows admittedly, but none the less deadly. Their shamans have encounters with strange carnivores and dragons while they are under the influence of drugs (or in a trance or ecstatic state, cf. chs. 12 and 13), and these are believed to be experiences of the soul of the shaman on its journey into the spirit-world (Käser 1995).

If Christians are asked about their perceptions of spirit-like objects, their answers are at best hesitant. Most of them have rather fewer problems with spirit beings. They can quite well imagine the deceased, angels, demons and God as spirit beings. But the notion that things, such as those named in the Revelation of John, e.g. trumpets, bowls (of the wrath of God), books, (white) garments, and many other things, are not simply material, but must also be conceived as spirit-like if one is not to be entangled in contradictions, remains rather blurred.

There are patterns of thinking in European-Western folk medicine which also seem to be animistic in this way. Back pain in the area of the shoulder blades is graphically described as a "witch's arrow". Earlier generations believed that the (invisible) arrow released misfortune, and those hit by it could only conceive it to be spirit-like, shot by the witch from a spirit-like bow.

The knowledge of such specifically shaped notions of the nature of things and living beings provides explanations of many individual aspects of animistic concepts of the world, aspects which cannot be understood without this knowledge, for example astronomical events like phases of the moon, physical events like thunder and lightning, chemical events like the nightly phosphorescence of certain kinds of fungi, and biological events such as the activity of plant pests invisible to the naked eye. More on this in later chapters.

Points 3 and 4, which refer to the reality of the (double) world with its co-existence of matter and spirit, spatially and temporally inseparable and mutually inter-acting, can only be expounded in more detail after other facts have been clarified.

Point 5 (mana, 'the agent of extraordinary effects'), deserves a chapter of its own where it can be dealt with more comprehensively, bearing in mind its significance. And of course points 1 and 2 will receive more detailed examination in the following chapters.

4.5 The Hierarchy of the Occupants of the Cosmos in Animistic Concepts of the World

The five basic principles characteristic of animistic concepts of the world are supplemented by a *hierarchy in which a location and a status are allocated to all material and immaterial beings populating the world*. On the lowest rung are the animals and evil spirits. Above them are human beings and their spirit companions ('souls'), then come the good spirit beings, especially the spirits of the ancestors, and finally at the top the so-called 'Supreme Being', who as a rule created the world.

This *hierarchy* is determined by the mana ('the agent of extraordinary effects') conferred on them and the status which they possess thereby:

Supreme Being
high-ranking good spirits
good spirit beings, especially spirits of the ancestors
human beings and their spirit companions ("souls")
animals and evil spirits

4.6   Concepts of the World in Ethnological Literature

It is not easy to indicate clearly what is available in German ethnological literature, in books and journals, whether on concepts of the world or of man. Exceptions are e.g. Laubscher 1977, Lehmann (1976) and Müller (1970). Descriptions of concepts of the world are mostly provided in studies on the religions of ethnic groups. Frequently they are to be found under the heading *cosmology* (Köhler 1984, 1990[10]), which is more suitable as a search term than *concept of the world* when researching the literature for pertinent book titles and journalistic articles.

4.7   In the Next Chapter

It would seem obvious to continue with a description of the occupants of the cosmos listed in 4.5. However, for reasons of clarity a different procedure is to be preferred.

One aspect of central significance for understanding everything that happens in the world, especially the activity of spirit beings of all kinds, is the principle named in point 5 of section 4.4 above, i.e. *mana*. All the later chapters presuppose a knowledge of this concept, and so it must be given precedence in deciding what should be discussed in the next chapter.

The following sources contain more on the theme of this chapter:

Bahuchet, Serge; Thomas, Jacqueline M. C. (sous dir.): Encyclopédie des Pygmées Aka. Paris (SELAF) 1991.

Chagnon, Napoleon: Yanomamö. Fort Worth et al. (Harcourt Brace College Publishers) 1992 (4. Auflage).

Hasenfratz, Hans Peter: Die religiöse Welt der Germanen: Ritual, Magie, Kult, Mythus. Freiburg (Herder) 1992.

Holthaus, Stephan; Müller, Klaus W. (Hrsg.): Die Mission der Theologie. Festschrift für Hans Kasdorf zum 70. Geburtstag. Bonn 1998.

Käser, Lothar: Der Begriff "Seele" bei den Insulanern von Truk. Diss. Freiburg 1977.

Käser, Lothar: Kognitive Aspekte des Menschenbildes bei den Campa (Asheninka). *asien afrika lateinamerika* 23.1995:29-50.

---

[10] I am grateful to my colleague Ulrich Köhler, Freiburg, for information on literature dealing with concepts of the world.

Käser, Lothar: Der Begriff "Himmel" als Bibelübersetzungsproblem in den austronesischen Sprachen Ozeaniens und Südostasiens. In: Holthaus/Müller 1998:152-161.

Köhler, Ulrich: Das Modell des Kosmos im zeremoniellen Leben der Tzotzil von San Pablo. Indiana 9.1984:283-303.

Köhler, Ulrich: Kosmologie und Religion. In: Köhler 1990:221-240.

Köhler, Ulrich (Hrsg.): Altamerikanistik. Berlin 1990.

Laubscher, Matthias: Iban und Ngaju. Kognitive Studien zu Konvergenzen in Weltbild und Mythos. Paideuma 23.1977:221-253.

Lehmann, Albert: Auswirkungen des balinesischen Weltbildes auf verschiedene Aspekte der Kulturlandschaft und auf die Werthaltung des Jahresablaufes. Ethnologische Zeitschrift Zürich 2.1976:27-65.

Müller, Werner: Glauben und Denken der Sioux. Zur Gestalt archaischer Weltbilder. Berlin 1970.

Chapter 5
Mana: the Agent of Extraordinary Effects

This chapter explains what is understood by mana, how it operates and what it can effect, how it connects with rituals, amulets, talismans, fetishes, masks, medicine, witchcraft and the concept of the holy. The Folk Islam term *baraka* and its special meanings are discussed.

5.0   Introduction

People whose lives are shaped in a world with the form and structure described in the previous chapter need to have a strategy for explaining the *principle of cause and effect*. They proceed from the assumption that there are two different explanations for conditions and events that can be observed in their kind of world: they can have either a *usual* or an *unusual* cause.

Among the normal causes would be e.g. the fact that things fall to the ground, that plants, animals and human beings grow and pass away, or that the world looks just the same as it did a year ago. An abnormal causal connection would be when someone discovers that after drinking from a particular spring he no longer feels ill, when after visiting a place of pilgrimage he wins the lottery, or when the careful performing of a ritual before the start of a journey has clearly guaranteed a safe return.

Such notions of causality, the relationship of cause and effect, are common in many societies, including European-Western ones, although the latter understand them to be not usual and unusual, but *natural* and *supernatural.* *Societies with an animistic cognitive framework do not make this distinction, because for them everything that exists and happens in the cosmos is seen as natural.*

Hence it is of no significance whether an object or a being exists in material or spirit form, whether an event can be traced back to a usual or an unusual cause.

If it is clear that an event could not occur in the expected form, the cause, according to the conviction of people who think animistically, must derive from *mana as the agent of unusual effects.* However, from now on I will not use this description, but revert to the term *extraordinary* as in the title of this chapter, and as used by the most important German researcher of mana from an earlier period of ethnology, in his studies of 1915 and 1922.

5.1　The Term Mana

The names that ethnic groups who are familiar with this notion use to describe these extraordinary effects are not at all uncommon. The North American Iroquois call it *wakonda*, the Sioux and Oglala *wakan* (Bolz 1983), the Algonquin *manito* or *manitu* (Neumann 2001, Feest 1998). Among the African pygmies the term is *megbe*, and for many Bantu ethnic groups it is *ndoki* with other derivations (Herrmann 1961:33). The most well-known term for it is *mana*. It became the typical name for all phenomena of this kind. The word is taken from the Austronesian (Oceanian) language group. It became the accepted term in ethnology because it was the subject of a famous ethnographic study.

In 1891 the missionary R. H. Codrington published a work entitled "The Melanesians. Studies in their anthropology and folklore". It enjoyed a wide distribution and eventually came to be accepted in ethnography as a classic. In it he defines mana as follows: "this power, though itself impersonal, is always connected with some person who directs it ..." (119). Today we know that this definition is somewhat too narrow, but it gets to the essence of the matter.

❑ Suggestion for own investigations: the word for mana has a variety of linguistic forms. It can behave as an adjective or a noun; this means that a being, an object, or an event can be or possess mana. It is important to ascertain how the concept manifests itself in the language where you are working, and collect as many contexts as possible, i.e. phrases used by indigenous speakers.

5.2　The Concept of Mana in Detail

The following individual aspects of the concept are drawn mainly from Oceania. One should not expect that in other places it will reveal all the features typical of that region. In the world view of any one of the various cultures only parts of the possible range of meanings of mana are in fact realized.

Mana denotes a *particular characteristic of events, objects, places, times* and *beings*, revealed in its unexpectedness or extraordinary effectiveness. This quality cannot simply be translated as *force*[11] or *power*, as often happens, for this only serves to limit the spectrum of meaning of the mana con-

---

[11] Arnold van Gennep (1873-1957) employed the word "dynamism", derived from the Greek, for the various notions of a force emanating from the holy. This term is only rarely used today.

cept, for *mana is not only active in the religious sphere but also in secular or rather everyday contexts*. As well as power or force mana can also sometimes indicate, depending on the situation and cultural context, *authority, status, good fortune* (as opposed to the "bad luck" that one can have), *miracles* and even *validity* (e.g. of a document).

In and of itself mana is a value-free concept. However, viewed subjectively it is ambivalent. There is *good* and *evil mana*, depending on whether its effects are experienced as useful or harmful. From the point of view of the one affected a so-called harming spell is in every case furnished with harmful mana.

Whether events, objects, places, times or beings possess mana is not necessarily apparent externally. That can only be concluded from their *effects*. They have to demonstrate that they possess mana.

Events, objects, places, times or beings mostly demonstrate that they possess mana not only by achieving *intended effects in unusual form* with its help, but also *effects not normally expected from them*. This can happen in various ways.

If a spear hits its target more often than others, or skewers larger fish than others, then it must possess mana. In this instance the unusual effect can also be caused by the mana of the one wielding the spear. The proof that it is indeed not the mana of the spear but of the person fishing would be evident if he achieved the same unusual effect with different spears as previously with the one spear.

Not everything that achieves the intended effect or shows itself to be particularly efficient also possesses mana. A tool that is better to work with than others is rather particularly "serviceable" than necessarily equipped with mana. Situations where an object evidently possesses mana are those where there is only a slight possibility of actually achieving an intended effect. The smaller the possibility, the greater the mana that can be present. This means that the proof that a spear possesses mana lies not just in the comparison with other spears, but in the fact that, for example, it hits the same spot several times in succession.

A location that has mana is expected to heal people of diseases and all kinds of afflictions. Herbs used for making medicine are considered to be especially effective if they grew at such a place. Places with these qualities ("places of power") can also be prominent stones, cliffs, springs, waterfalls, rivers, mountains, grottos, burial places and all kinds of shrines or holy places. The mana emanating from such a place can also have dangerous effects and cause birds or planes flying over it to plunge to the ground (Fuhrmann 2001:90).

There are times and periods which are advantageous for people, bringing them good fortune, e.g. in Folk Islam the month of Ramadan, in Christianity the night from Holy Saturday to Easter Sunday. In many societies certain times of the day or year are considered to be dangerous, e.g. Wednesday, when sexual intercourse might be forbidden in order to prevent the conception of a handicapped child (Werner 2001:113).

If someone is not injured after falling from a tree, or just manages to dodge a falling coconut at the last moment, on-looking Micronesians react with the words, "Wow! You must have a lot of mana today!" Europeans would presumably say that the person was *lucky*.

There are people whose bearing makes such an impression on others that it produces an attitude of respect and obedience. The *authority* of such a personality comes from the mana which they (clearly) possess, and which also belongs to their *spoken word*. The more meekly their directions are followed, the greater must be their mana. In this connection the concept includes not only the category of authority but also that of *power* and *charisma*.

Status and mana are mutually contingent. Those who show they have mana enjoy high status. Conversely mana is attributed to those having status, even when the status is only presumed.

The mana of the spoken word of such an authoritative person can, like any other mana, become dangerous. If he pronounces a curse on someone opposing his will, it will bring calamity on the latter and can cause death.

Because of this feature the concept of mana can take on considerable importance in the thinking of Christianized ethnic groups. It is fundamental to regard *prayers* as language events from which one expects extraordinary effectiveness in the sense of mana. The higher the ecclesiastical office of the one who prays, the greater will be the effects; that is the expectation. Hence, in a situation where prayer is required, those called on are always the ones presumed to be of the highest rank. If, by contrast, representatives of a church hierarchy, missionaries or local clergy mention something which is a sin, if only by name, then the person who committed it must fear becoming the victim of a *curse* through the spoken word of the person in authority.

On the other hand the mana of the clergy has mostly a positive effect. It is expected that having a clergyman on board a canoe or in a truck greatly reduces the risk of an accident at sea or on the road, even if the vehicle in question is in a doubtful condition.

Being in the company of people whose mana could signify danger obliges one to observe a number of rules of behaviour. Someone who enjoys special status on account of his authority is *taboo*, which means that respect towards him is demanded, and a breach of that could result in unfortunate consequences.

There are even emotions which possess mana and have corresponding effects. If someone with status harbours feelings of displeasure, hatred, or simply the desire to punish someone, then it is expected that the person on the receiving end of these emotions will sooner or later be overcome by misfortune, illness or death. In some societies the result is that out of fear of such consequences people apologize to those of higher status if they simply think that they might have insulted them in some way, building up a stock of reconciliation, as it were.

Everything that can be said about people and mana also applies to spirits. The higher their mana, the higher their status among those of their kind.

Events for which one can find no explanation, *happenings* which are so unimaginable that they could not occur in the way they do, these are likewise frequently ascribed to the working of mana. Mana can emanate from both people and objects. In many instances a spirit being is involved. Here mana denotes something which in European-Western societies would be described as a *miracle*.

Spirit beings which are able to create something from nothing by acts of the will or of speech, hurl lightning and release floods, can do this because of their mana.

Most animistically oriented ethnic groups know accounts of spirit beings who, with the assistance of mana, brought forth the world and mankind. The physical strength that may have been employed is not associated with mana, and is therefore given another word in the languages concerned.

❑ Suggestion for own investigations: the relevant linguistic forms should be documented and the differences in their meanings investigated.

5.3   Emergence, Acquisition and Loss of Mana

If events, objects, places, times and beings possess mana, then they have to demonstrate it. That is why it is mostly by chance that one discovers it, and also its loss. On the other hand one can intentionally furnish objects and even people with mana, or increase it. This happens mostly through contact with an object or being which already possesses it.

In former times the Maori of New Zealand saw the possibility of acquiring mana through cannibalism. Parts of the body of deceased persons believed to possess mana, usually relatives, were ritually consumed in order to appropriate their mana (Harvey 2000:168).

There is a widespread notion that mana is transferred or originates *within the framework of an action* which has a characteristic structure according to the particular society or culture. The procedure of this action follows rules, mostly quite strict ones. Only if they are carefully adhered to does the *ritual* represented in the action cause the mana to emerge as intended.

Mana as a feature of the personality can hardly emerge in the context of such an action. But the ritual probably produces heightened mana in someone who is taking up an official position, e.g. one with a title ("chief"). In Christian churches with animistic background one expects greater effects from the prayer of a bishop than from a vicar's prayer or the prayers of "ordinary" Christians. This ability is actually not the result of mana being transferred during the blessing as part of the inauguration into the office; it is counted as a bestowal of mana which has accrued during the ritual.

In more recent times a person acquires mana and with it the authority of office by passing an exam. This gives him the title, to which respect and obedience must be accorded, if his mana is not to have a negative effect.

In certain religious groups sexual activity is regarded as a source of mana. By means of this claim the leaders ("gurus") of such groups often succeed in sexually exploiting their female adherents.

Events, objects, places, times and beings may lose or may have lost mana, but it is not possible to recognize this from external observation, any more than the presence of it. It is the *absence of effects* which leads to the conclusion that mana is no longer at work in them. Ageing title holders with fading intellectual capabilities gradually lose their mana, their authority and their status. There are perceptions related to this which appear remarkable to European-Western observers:

In many ethnic groups of New Guinea the men believe that there is a massive loss of mana during heterosexual intercourse, leading eventually to their death. By contrast homosexual intercourse between older and younger men produces an increase of mana, and semen promotes growth in the young.

Among the Luwu of South East Asia there are complex notions summed up in the word *sumangé*. In a strange way it signifies both the dream ego and the agent of extraordinary effects, and in addition something akin to a life force, of which a person has a fairly large supply at the beginning of his existence, but slowly loses in the course of his life. According to the accounts of the author (Errington 1983), people scatter *sumangé* on their travels, discarding it with loss of body parts, fingernail clippings, bodily excretions, giving off warmth, casting shadows, leaving footprints, and even down to the words they speak.

The Bororo of South America have similar notions (Crocker 1985:42) and they are also found in the popular beliefs of antiquity, described in detail by Muth (1954).

5.4   Mana and Magic

From what has been described so far it is evident that there is a close connection between the concept of mana and that of *magic*. In simple terms magic is the teaching of techniques with the help of which one can manipulate the powers which are superior to man and transcend his abilities, whether for one's own use or for harming others. Through exact performance of rituals (correctly spoken formulae, correctly executed procedures of sacrifice etc.) such powers are induced and even forced to do what one desires. The hallmark of magic is the inevitable, automatic aspect (Hirschberg 1988:291). If a ritual for creating or activating mana is carried out in the prescribed way its efficacy cannot fail; this is how it is perceived by those who make use of magic in any kind of way.

Magic can therefore be understood as the opposite of what can be termed "proper religion", i.e. man's commitment to the powers he perceives as being over him, and his subjection to them. Those using magic do not subject themselves to these powers, but *take control* of them.

Magic and its associated notions of mana as the agent of extraordinary effects are not necessarily linked to the participation of spirit beings. They can, together with their mana, be involved in magical phenomena and events, but as a rule the corresponding rituals manage without them. *Hence mana has no intrinsic personal character*. Conceptually therefore, magic and notions of spirit beings are to be kept separate from each other if they are to be described and understood correctly. This is why Fasching, in dealing with this issue, makes a distinction between "magic" and "demonism", the latter giving too strong an impression that it is mainly evil spirits that participate in the practice of magic (2000:198-199). From the animistic perspective this is not at all the case.

Magic is employed in almost all societies for the purpose of coping with certain problems in life, and when reference is made to it in popular scientific writings mention is often made of *magic spells* or *charms*. There is a wide palette available: there are spells for the weather, rain, fertility, love, healing, harm, defence and levitation (to give a boat good buoyancy in the water and stop it sinking). Specialists in these practices are hence called *sorcerers,* a term which is no longer the preferred one in ethnology.

Rituals which are intended to bring about the extraordinary by means of magic can contain *linguistic formulae* ("incantations"). But this does not serve to define them. The magical effect can also be achieved without speech. In many cases it is sufficient to observe the rituals, i.e. the sequence of steps which have been correctly handed down. This sequence can replace the magic formula.

Such mechanisms can also be involved with *amulets* and *talismans*. People use them because they believe they have discovered that they are effective in extraordinary ways and therefore possess a kind of mana. Their possession of mana has been shown to be evident to those using them, or it is assumed that they were rendered capable of extraordinary effects through being part of a ritual or act of consecration.

In ethnology a conceptual difference is maintained between amulets and talismans: amulets are used more for warding off misfortune and keeping evil away. Talismans, by contrast, are claimed to bring luck and other good things. Objects and rituals for preventing misfortune are called *apotropaic* (Greek *apotropein* to turn away).

Often the connection between amulets, make-up and dress is generally so narrow that no clear boundary exists between them (Rahm-Mottl 2002/03). This is particularly true with regard to women's fashions. Mirrors attached to clothes keep away evil spirits (cf. ch. 8.2). A necklace can contain a pearl which is claimed to repel the so-called evil eye (cf. 5.6).

Amulets and objects for decoration can be further embellished with engraved or enclosed linguistic formulae, words and quotes from holy writings such as the Koran (Müller 2001). Sometimes the mana depends on the numbers 3 or 5, which are considered to repel misfortune and can be recognized by the form of the object (triangle, five-pointed star, so-called pentagram etc.).

In a wider sense amulets and talismans feature in the most diverse forms in European-Western cultures. *Votive figures* representing human and animal bodies are erected or buried. A special kind of *cross* is claimed to ease the pain of giving birth. *Stones with holes* aid against diseases of the eye, *animal teeth* symbolise a threatening gesture to ward off evil spirits. *Pomegranates* are symbols of love and fertility, a *ring of elder bushes* planted round the house is claimed to repel ghosts, and *blackthorn shrubs* protect from calamity caused by curses, *weather crosses* from hail and frost (Fasching 2000:213).

Fetishes, which are known predominantly in Africa, and depend for their effectiveness on the same characteristics, are a special case. The following is a brief summary of the analysis made by Thiel, an established expert on the material, in his introduction to the ethnology of religion (1984:62-69).

A fetish is a material object imbued with (in most cases) an impersonal energy or (more rarely) with an ancestral spirit conceived as a personal force. This force can be activated, manipulated and even enhanced through gifts (sacrifices). Amulets, talismans, objects from daily life and people who possess mana cannot as a rule acquire it by having gifts of any kind dedicated to them. However, it is sometimes possible that mana can be imparted to them through the process of sacrifice, if this is part of the ritual during which mana is expected to arise. The sacrifice is then directed to a spirit being which is expected to bestow or increase mana (Thiel 1977 and 1986).

The word fetish comes from the Portuguese "feitiço", meaning "imitated, artificial" and eventually also "magic". It was in fact the Portuguese who, arriving in the 15th century in West and Central Africa, gave accounts of figurines, masks and similar things which were employed at sacrifices and other religious practices. At that time one simply said that Africans venerated such self-made objects, without trying to understand that in reality there were notions of impersonal forces and personally conceived powers behind them.

The number and variety of fetishes are incalculable. It is not possible to know all the variants even in a single ethnic group. Fetishes are employed in very individual ways, and in individual cases the effects expected from them are narrowly limited. There are fetishes against stomach ache, against dangers when felling trees, for safe travel etc. Basically there is no conceivable occasion where a fetish could not have a part to play.

There is also no problem in fitting fetishes into the modern world. African football teams consult experts and have special fetishes made for preventing their opponents from scoring goals, even in international matches. Such fetishes are either buried in their own goal area to prevent goals of their opponents, or in the opposing goal area to weaken their goalkeeper (cf. Kohl 2000). How the problem of changing ends is solved is beyond my knowledge. Presumably the mana of one's own fetish can only have a negative effect on the opponents. At all events the teams sometimes go looking for hidden fetishes before the start of the game, and if one is discovered there is actual conflict, the animistic equivalent to a doping scandal. Of course students in these ethnic groups also take fetishes with them into their final examinations.

Some fetishes bear famous names, comparable to the swords of Germanic and Celtic heroes (Balmung, Excalibur). Celebrated fetishes are known throughout the whole ethnic group and are mostly linked with the persons who used them, each being a kind of priest for a particular fetish. He prepares it and carries out the ritual, in the process of which the fetish acquires its unusual effect, as a rule against payment for both.

Fetishes can look like statuettes, bearing human features. Such a fetish is then usually referred to as an *idol*. One can imagine a powerful ancestral spirit at work behind it, but that is not necessarily so.

Among the mightiest fetishes are the *clan fetishes,* for with their help political power, and also power over natural events such as rain, thunderstorms etc. can be exercised. Clan fetishes are at the centre of rites which mark the transition from one status to another, e.g. at the initiation of boys and girls, or at wedding ceremonies.

At such rites the fetish is commended with something of value or provided with something edible, in ritual terms, of course, by pouring palm wine and chicken's blood over it, scattering flour over it etc., which are reckoned to activate or heighten its mana.

Masks can be a special form of fetish. Of course this does not imply that all masks are fetishes in the ethnological sense. For example Melanesian masks only rarely have this function. However, African masks such as are found in European-Western museums were probably fetishes in their original setting. Many Africans express this view when they visit museums.

Masks can be seen to be fetishes if they are treated ritually in a similar way to fetishes. However, if it becomes apparent that they do not have the desired effect, i.e. no longer produce mana, then the masks are thrown away or no longer valued. Their lack of effectiveness is proof that the mana or spirit thought to be associated with them is no longer present. Actual fetishes are only rarely treated in this way.

By putting such masks on display in museums, European-Western societies turn them into something quite different from what they were in their original culture. The visiting public regard them as works of art. It is not uncommon for ethnologists to describe and understand them as art in correspondingly illustrated books. In their original culture they were quite simply objects for practical everyday use, serving to ensure fertility. Hence they really belonged with the other agricultural implements, albeit with the qualification that they had a strong religious significance.

The Aranda people of Australia and other ethnic groups in this continent have the *churunga* (churinga, tjuringa), which is an object totally different in form, but with a similar function. Churungas are *thunder sticks* or *bullroarers*. They come in many different forms. Many are only a few centimetres long, the biggest up to two metres. Most of them have a hole at one end, with a cord made of hair drawn through it, enabling one to whirl it round one's head. A churunga in action is audible from a considerable distance, particularly after dark, when the noises of the day fall silent. Their humming sound is supposed to represent the voice of mighty spirit beings, and their resonance achieves special effects according to the purpose of the one operating the bullroarer.

Churungas have a special role in magic associated with love, but only in the thinking of men, and for their use. Only adult men own churungas, and they get them humming at night time with the intention of making women compliant to their will. The effect is heightened by making a whole row of churungas hum at the same time. Those who hear such a noise tell of spectacular aural experiences.

The effectiveness is based on a force in the sense of mana, called *djalu*, which is deployed for a great variety of purposes. For example it can set off lightning and storms in order to injure someone. It can repel or banish diseases, and thus achieve effects which are useful.

The construction of such a bullroarer is determined by a complex ritual which must be observed with painstaking precision and proceed without fault. If not, the product will later have no effect, or achieve the opposite of what was intended.

5.5   Mana and Animistic Medicine

The animistic system of thought has a *theory of the origin of diseases, together with their healing*. It has been formed in accordance with the culture and is inseparable from notions of mana and magic. There will be more on this in the following chapters, particularly in ch. 8. At this point I will confine myself to a description of the term medicine. A detailed discussion of the whole complex area of medical treatment in pre-literate societies can be found in **FC** ch. 15.

The systems of animistic medical treatment make use above all of *plants*, but also parts of *animal bodies*. In many ethnic groups types of *earth* and *minerals* are considered to have healing properties.

Medicines in animistic systems are not normally understood to be operative primarily on the basis of their chemical composition. This is secondary or not even considered, because the medicine cannot achieve any healing effect without a corresponding *magic formula* or *production ritual*.

The medicine that a healer obtains by adding various ingredients receives its mana during the process of production. But it receives *mana in its intended purpose* only if each individual action is carried out in the "right" sequence and the accompanying words are spoken without error. "Right" in this sense means: in the traditional way expected and accepted by the members of that society. If the maker commits an error the medicine will be ineffective or will gain destructive, dangerous mana which will induce in the maker the symptoms it is actually supposed to remove.

A healer working according to these perceptions will already have taken special care in collecting the ingredients for his medicine. If he makes a mistake in the process of production he will break off the procedure, burn what he has already developed and start again from scratch, even if he only presumes has made a mistake. If he does not do this, the medicine, furnished with "wrong", i.e. dangerous mana, can accentuate the patient's symptoms that he is trying to remove, and even induce them in himself, make him ill and kill him.

This reveals the *ambivalence* of the term medicine in animistic thinking. It is not only intended to heal, it can also cause death. Hence in the languages of ethnic groups with such an understanding of medicine the word for "medicine" is also the one used for chemicals, aerosols, poisonous substances, pesticides, disinfectants and cleansing agents.

5.6   The Mana of the Evil Eye

Many societies have the notion that the *eye* of a person who is discontented with himself or his fate, is envious or hungry, can cause calamity, disease and death if his *evil glance* falls on something beautiful and desirable, on an object of value, a child or an animal. If an animal is already weakened or ill the evil eye can be fatal. Even the eye of an admirer can be dangerous in this sense. Many societies believe that the mana of the evil eye is able to force tractors to a halt and cause houses to collapse. In addition the evil eye can also be possessed by animals.

It is not possible to perceive outwardly if someone has command of the evil eye. There has to be evidence. The Tuareg people of North Africa believe children acquire it if the mother looks at the face of a dead person while she is pregnant or breastfeeding. This indicates that the condition of ritual impurity could be the cause of a person acquiring the evil eye (Neumann 1983). In many ethnic groups dark-skinned people and the mentally handicapped are reckoned to have it (Streck 1997:142).

One can protect oneself against it by avoiding the presence of such persons so as not to be looked at by them. Protection is also afforded by amulets in the form of a penis or vulva, pearls and certain snail shells in a necklace, or triangular-shaped brooches which are regarded as the stylised form of an eye.

A person's alleged evil eye can also be repelled by holding your hand over your face, a ritualised demeanour widespread in North African cultures. In popular Islamic belief it is known as the "hand of Fatima", among Jews and Christians in the Middle East as the "hand of God" or "hand of Mary" (Rahm-Mottl 2002/03:35). Hence many experts in ancient history consider the representations of hands with spread fingers on cliff faces in the Sahara to be apotropaic.

Related to the evil eye concept is the so-called *evil mouth*. Like the evil eye it can bring about misfortune, but not so much through uttering a curse, where the mana is directly attached to the spoken word, as by the negative effect of praising someone (Neumann 1983:276). This is why the Tuareg are wary of openly speaking positively or admiringly of people, and of the animals and possessions of others. Such talk arouses the suspicion of being envious or not well-disposed towards the owner. Like the evil eye, the evil mouth can even kill, or that is the expectation.

Further titles on the evil eye are those of Bettez Gravel 1995 und Hauschild 1979 and [2]1982.

5.7 The (Folk) Islamic Concept of *Baraka*

reveals clear features of the mana concept, but also includes the meaning "blessing". Mana only has this significance indirectly. In the view of many societies its positive qualities can admittedly produce blessing. However, it is then designated by another word. In order to clarify that *baraka* has an extended meaning some writers dealing with this use the description "power to bless" (e.g. Kriss/Kriss-Heinrich 1960:4).

As regards its grammatical form the word *baraka* behaves in a similar way to mana. In many languages it can be used both as a verb and a noun. Spirits, people, objects, times and places can both *be baraka* and *possess baraka*. In Rif, in the northern part of Morocco, it can also refer to events (Jamous 1981:202).

Baraka can be acquired through contact, through touching, e.g. a holy stone or the gravestone of a saint, by breathing on an object, through saliva, eating together, or simply being present at the same place as a bearer of *baraka*. It can be attached to or permeate people and objects. It grants healing powers to plants such as henna. Although it is basically positive, creative and advantageous, it can also, with the appropriate procedures, be used like mana to make people ill or kill them. It can change things into something else. Hospitality brings about an exchange of *baraka* between guest and host.

Harvest and nourishing food are said to be furnished with it. Butter and olive oil are particularly rich in *baraka*. There it can even increase in and of itself. Newly born children possess heightened *baraka*. It can sometimes also be present in concentrated form in human and animal liver, in horses, camels and sheep. In the act of procreation it can have unusual effects, as evidenced by the birth of twins (Westermarck 1926, 1933). People of status and authority, heads of families, titled people and rulers possess it in heightened measure. With its help one can remove the adverse effects of a curse or the consequences of committing incest.

Baraka is the hallmark of everything holy. Evil spirits fear it and can be expelled by it. The Koran and its texts contain it in abundance. People can, in the real sense of the word, "incorporate" it by writing verses of the Koran on paper and then chewing them and eating them, or dissolving them in water and drinking them. By reciting particular suras one can be protected from toothache or depression. During Ramadan, the month of fasting, there is one night in which *baraka* deploys special effects.

With its help both God and many benign spirits perform miracles. This is also true of holders of religious office such as the marabout, members of orders such as dervishes, hermits, indeed all those who are considered to be holy men and women in Folk Islam. These retain beyond death the *baraka* which characterised them during their lifetime, and that is why their places of burial have sometimes become important places of pilgrimage, where visitors can expect many positive outcomes for their own lives. They are also considered to be places of divine revelation (Neumann 1999:122). At the present time people and weapons involved in jihad can be equipped with *baraka* at such places.

As with mana, there has to be evidence to show that objects and people do or do not possess *baraka*. In the case of objects, frequent use can lead to a lessening of this quality. People can endanger their *baraka* through unauthorized meetings with others. Men must be particularly afraid of losing their *baraka* if they have sexual contact with a woman at the time of her menstruation (Neumann 1983:277). It can result in impotence. In general any kind of demise or lack of success is evidence of loss of *baraka*. This is also presumed to be the case with rulers if epidemics or revolts break out within the area of their jurisdiction. Such events can cause them to be deposed.

An in-depth account of *baraka*, including aspects about it not directly to do with animism, can be found in Chelhod 1955.

5.8   Mana and Witchcraft

Witches are understood to be men and women who are believed by their societies to have the ability to exercise a pernicious influence on their respective societies or on individuals within them, by virtue of the mana, the "power of witchcraft" that they possess. Among the persons held to be capable and guilty of witchcraft, women from the poorer levels of society are usually disproportionately represented. Accusations of active witchcraft are clearly directed at the most disadvantaged and inferior members of a society. This is especially true of Africa (Omyajowo 1983:317). Even today the fear of witches and their activities is very widespread. Roser reports that as recently as 1994 two people in the Central African Republic accused of witchcraft were publicly burnt (2000:92).

But women are not just in greater danger of being labelled witches. They are also significantly more frequently the targets and victims of assaults directed against them by male witches (warlocks). At all events it is particularly women who fear such attacks. This fear is one of the causes of behaviour which European-Western foreigners consider to be sexual promiscuity or even licentiousness. There are occasions when women cannot refuse men without being in danger of the latter using witchcraft to harm them, their children and families. It seems to me that the rapid spread of aids in many parts of Africa is due to the part played by such mechanisms.

Witches and warlocks represent the *epitome of anti-social behaviour* directed against society and its welfare. Their mana is aimed particularly at the success of others, or such is the assumption. In the context of people living together the presence of such notions sometimes develops explosive power, because it is practically impossible for an individual not to join in with the accusations against a witch. Those who dispute the suspicions are liable to be suspected of witchcraft themselves (Roser 2000:100-104).

It is not only women outside the group who are suspected of witchcraft, but also close relatives, mothers and daughters-in-law, women in polygynous marriages, and very old women, whose extreme age can only be explained by the fact that they keep young by consuming the souls of younger women. There are many reasons for being decried as a witch: jealousy of someone, or aggravation, unusual appearance and behaviour, sudden acquisition of wealth etc.

Their presumed malice often causes witches and warlocks to appear as evil spirits, which they are not in reality. More probable is the belief that they engage the assistance of evil spirits when they are planning to do harm. However, they can also influence the "soul" (the dream ego, cf. ch. 11) of a person in such a way as to make it work for them like a slave. It is said of many that they employ whole armies of such "souls". Be that as it may, the key criterion of their activity is their destructive mana.

With its help they can also behave like spirit beings. They are not bound by space and time, make themselves invisible, can move like lightning from one place to another by flying or by riding on objects such as brooms or on creatures such as rats, dogs and goats. They can change themselves into animals and objects, and can cause natural catastrophes, starvation, road accidents and death. There is hardly any social evil, any trivial personal misfortune which cannot be laid at the door of a witch. They make holes in trousers, help thieves to steal, make women barren by turning round the uterus in their bodies, steal men's testicles and cause nightmares. But above all they are cannibals and are after human blood. There is hardly anything that witches and warlocks could not be accused of.

But the most expected and feared evil emanating from them is untimely
death, in childhood, in one's youth, before attaining old age.
They have a lot in common with shamans. It is believed that certain
witches can send out their "soul" (their dream ego) to carry out tasks. During
this period the body of the witch lies in a death-like sleep. In this condition a
man or woman can be identified as a witch, for not even the loudest noise can
wake them up. Their body has remained behind while their "soul" (their
dream ego) is travelling (Frank 1983:211).

Popular notions of witchcraft, including those of popular science, are fond
of combining a large number of elements of animistic and occult origin, and
at the same time they confuse them. However, here also it is essential to bring
precision to the concept if one is to reach a right understanding of these phenomena. Thus the woman who, according to 1. Samuel 28, was approached
by the Old Testament king Saul for advice, and who is sometimes still called
the witch of Endor, was not a witch but a medium (cf. ch. 15).

5.9   Mana and the Concept of the Holy

When mana confers extraordinary effects on events, objects, places, times
and beings, as described in section 5.2, it invests them with the character of
the *holy*. By contrast, events, objects, places, times and beings that do not
possess mana have the character of the *profane*[12].

Everything holy is distinguished by the fact that it is not accessible to everyone all the time, but only when certain conditions have been fulfilled.
These can be met by rituals such as ablutions, to be completed before entering a holy area or a holy period of time, or through wearing prescribed clothing. Muslims enter the mosque without shoes, Jews the synagogue with head-
covering, Christians (men!) without. If these conditions are not fulfilled,
those not ritually so prepared, especially those from animistically oriented
societies, are exposed to danger through the mana belonging to the particular
event, object, place, time or being.

For the European-Western observer the concept of the holy contains a difficulty connected with his language, which impedes his understanding of the
corresponding thought forms of animistically oriented societies. The principle has to be grasped that for members of such societies holy events, objects,
places, times and beings are *taboo*.

---

[12] The term comes from the Latin. There *fanum* (from *fari*=speak and *fatum*=dictum
of fate) originally meant the separated (holy) place where an oracle provided information about the divine will. The area in front was the *profanum*, which in contrast
to the *fanum* was not regarded as holy and could be entered by anyone at any time.

The two adjectives *holy* and *taboo*[13] can best be understood by making the following clear. If you say that events, objects, places, times and beings are *holy*, then you are singling out the *positive* aspects of the holy, leaving the negative ones unnamed. Hence holy actions are those that are *commanded* in connection with the holy. By contrast, if you say that events, objects, places, times and beings are *taboo*, then you are singling out the *negative* aspects of the holy and leaving the positive ones unnamed. Hence actions that are taboo are those that are *forbidden* in connection with the holy. This has consequences for how each particular society thinks of the concept.

In Christian churches that are part of European-Western culture you can find so-called antependiums[14] decorated with the words "Holy, Holy, Holy". By contrast, in the churches of societies not long Christianised and with animistic background or simply with a different language structure, you can find the words "Taboo, Taboo, Taboo" on the antependium. In the former case the positively defined aspects of the concept of the holy are emphasized, in the latter the negatively defined ones.

This can often be a problem when translating the Bible. In many instances "holy" and "taboo" can be used as synonyms[15], if one is sure which aspects the reader is more strongly conscious of when reading them. Sometimes, however, the distinction gives rise to a certain amount of difficulty. If meat is not to be eaten on Fridays, or no work is to be done on Sundays, then those activities are taboo, but not holy.

Holy events from which one expects magic effects include actions which are part of divine worship, blessings, baptism, sacrificial rituals etc. The recital of myths, acts of oration in general, and the Eucharist can also count as holy in this sense.

The number of holy objects is incalculable, ranging from drinking vessels such as the chalice, the garments of the priest such as those the High Priest Aaron had to wear when he wished to enter the holy of holies in the ancient Jewish tabernacle, the mirror in the central room of a Shinto temple, the flutes and drums from a Tambaram house in Melanesia, to the holy scriptures of the so-called high religions.

---

[13] Kohl (1983:60 ff.) has expressed the view that the term taboo, along with others, has become obsolete and even offensive in more recent studies in ethnology and religion. This is probably true with the way Freud, for example, used it. In a textbook such as this, which is dealing with the basic perceptions of pre-literate societies, the term is, in my opinion, indispensable.

[14] Antependium: textile hanging on the front of the altar (altar frontal).

[15] Synonyms are words with the same or similar meaning.

Holy places include sacrificial sites, cemeteries, those which count as the preferred abodes of beings ranked above humans, caves, the vents of volcanoes, regarded as entrances to the underworld and the realm of the dead etc., sacred buildings such as churches, temples, the Kaaba in Mecca. Mountains have a significant role among holy places, e.g. the Fujijama in Japan or the Wutai Shan in China. Some religious studies scholars claim that big ecclesiastical buildings such as Cologne cathedral, the temple architecture of ancient American cultures, the ziggurats of Mesopotamia and the temple compound of Borobudur on Java are to be understood as copies of holy mountains.

Holy times ("times of salvation") in this sense are for example Good Friday and the Saturday night of Easter in Christianity, the fasting month of Ramadan in Islam or the period between the death of an important person and his final burial in animistically oriented societies.

Finally, there are holy beings, which include priests and priestesses, sometimes entrusted with the management of holy places, charismatics, hermits, mediums, shamans, and according to Sterly (1965) also healers in pre-literate societies.

5.10   Mana in Daily Life

Although mana is always something unusual, indeed extraordinary, it is not purely religious, other-worldly, or bound to an other-worldly being. But in the final analysis there is a degree of clear evidence that it has its origins in the beyond.

How remote the concept of mana can be from religious notions can be seen from the following example: Chuuk Islanders describe a passport that is still valid as being invested with mana, similarly a banknote which is part of the national currency, and they invest a cheque with mana when they sign it. This can be observed daily in expressions in local language usage.

5.11   A Brief Definition of the Mana Concept

In summary mana is the agent of extraordinary effects, inherent in events, objects and beings, and able to find expression in terms of authority, charisma, and in rather more rare instances as a life force. Spirits are invested with especially effective mana in proportion to their status, but this is not something exclusively other-worldly or to be attributed to religion.

To conclude, the concept of mana could be described as a typically classic problem of ethnology. In the history of its research two periods can be distinguished. Studies from the period leading up to the publication of the dissertation by Friedrich Rudolf Lehmann (1915) reveal a tendency for speculation, conditioned by a lack of sufficient foundation in terms of initial ethnographic and linguistic data, leading to undue generalisations and lack of balance concerning the mana concept. In his dissertation Lehmann brought together and compared the available reports up to 1915 and published it again in 1922 as an extended edition. His verification that linguistic perspectives play an important role in identifying aspects leading to an understanding of the concept of mana led to a whole row of empirical investigations in the ensuing period. Raymond Firth's essay (1940, 1970) can be taken as exemplary in this respect. Lehmann also worked in depth on the concept of taboo (1930).

Further titles dealing with the mana concept and its setting in particular ethnic groups or regional distribution are: Cunningham 1994, Götz 1995, Greschat 1980, Keesing 1984, Labouvie 1991, Mommensteeg 1990, Lorenz/Bauer 1995, Mandunu 1992, Multhaupt 1989, Schönhuth 1992, Wolf 1994.

5.12   In the Next Chapter

The knowledge of mana, the agent of extraordinary effects pervading the cosmos, is an essential prerequisite for understanding the capabilities and diverse effects which are particularly characteristic of spirit beings as the invisible inhabitants of the world. This is the subject of the next chapter.

The following sources contain more on the theme of this chapter:

Adegbola, E.A.Ade (ed.): Traditional religion in West Africa. Ibadan 1983:317-336.

Bettez Gravel, Pierre: The malevolent eye. An essay on the evil eye, fertility and the concept of mana. New York et al. (Peter Lang) 1995.

Bolz, Peter: Oglala. In: Müller 1983: 422-449.

Chelhod, Joseph: La baraka chez les Arabes ou l'influence bienfaisante du sacré. In: Revue de l'histoire des religions. T.148. Paris 1955:68-88.

Crocker, Jon Christopher: Vital souls. Bororo cosmology, natural symbolism, and shamanism. Tucson, Arizona 1985.

Cunningham, Scott: Mana. Magie und Spiritualität auf Hawaii. Berlin, München, Wien (Scherz, O. W. Barth) 1994.

Errington, Shelly: Embodied Sumangé in Luwu. Journal of Asian Studies XLII, No. 3, 1983:545-570.

Fasching, Gerhard: Phänomene der Wirklichkeit. Okkulte und naturwissenschaftliche Weltbilder. Wien, New York (Springer) 2000.

Feest, Christian F.: Beseelte Welten. Die Religionen der Indianer Nordamerikas. Freiburg, Basel, Wien (Herder) 1998.

Firth, Raymond: The analysis of Mana: an empirical approach. In: Harding/Wallace 1970:316-333.

Frank, Barbara: Ron. In: Müller 1983:204-227.

Fuhrmann, Klaus: Formen der javanischen Pilgerschaft zu Heiligenschreinen. Diss. Freiburg 2001.

Gladigow, Burkhard; Kippenberg, Hans G. (Hrsg.): Neue Ansätze in der Relgions-wissenschaft. München (Koesel) 1983.

Götz, Nicola H.: Obeah – Hexerei in der Karibik – zwischen Macht und Ohnmacht. Frankfurt am Main (Peter Lang) 1995.

Greschat, Hans-Jürgen: Mana und Tapu. Die Religion der Maori auf Neuseeland. Berlin 1980.

Harding, Thomas G.; Wallace Ben J. (eds.): Cultures of the Pacific. New York 1970.

Harvey, Graham (ed.): Indigenous religion. A companion. London, New York 2000.

Harvey, Graham: Art works in Aotearoa. In: Harvey 2000:155-172.

Hauschild, Thomas: Der böse Blick. Ideengeschichtliche und sozialpsychologische Untersuchungen. Hamburg 1979, Berlin [2]1982.

Herrmann, Ferdinand: Symbolik in den Religionen der Naturvölker. Stuttgart 1961.

Hirschberg, Walter (Hrsg.): Neues Wörterbuch der Völkerkunde. Berlin 1988.

Jamous, Raymond: Honneur et baraka. Les structures sociales et traditionnelles dans le Rif. Cambridge et al. 1981.

Keesing, Roger: Rethinking Mana. Journal of Anthropological Research 40.1984:137-156.

Kohl, Karl Heinz: "Fetisch, Tabu, Totem". In: Gladigow/Kippenberg 1983:59-74.

Kohl, Karl Heinz: Beim Fußball helfen die Geister. Spiel, Krieg und Ritual in Ostflores. In: Neumann/Weigel 2000:101-112.

Kriss, Rudolf; Kriss-Heinrich, Hubert: Volksglauben im Bereich des Islam. Band 1: Wallfahrtswesen und Heiligenverehrung. Wiesbaden 1960.

Labouvie, Eva: Zauberei und Hexenwerk. Ländlicher Hexenglaube in der frühen Neuzeit. Frankfurt (Fischer) 1991.

Lehmann, Friedrich Rudolf: Mana. Eine begriffsgeschichtliche Untersuchung auf ethnologischer Grundlage. Dresden 1915.

Lehmann, Friedrich Rudolf: Mana. Der Begriff des "außerordentlich Wirkungsvol-len" bei Südseevölkern. Leipzig 1922.

Lehmann, Friedrich Rudolf: Die polynesischen Tabusitten. Eine ethnosoziologische Untersuchung. Veröffentlichungen des Staatlich-sächsischen Forschungsinstituts für Völkerkunde in Leipzig, Bd. 10. Leipzig 1930.

Linke, Bernd Michael (Hrsg.): Die Welt nach der Welt. Jenseitsmodelle in den Religionen. Frankfurt am Main 1999.

Linke, Bernd Michael (Hrsg.): Schöpfungsmythologie in den Religionen. Frankfurt am Main (Otto Lembeck) 2001.

Lorenz, Sönke; Bauer, Dieter R. (Hrsg.): Hexenverfolgung. Beiträge zur Forschung – unter besonderer Berücksichtigung des südwestdeutschen Raums. Würzburg 1995.

Mandunu, Joseph Kufulu: Das "Kindoki" im Licht der Sündenbocktheologie. Frankfurt am Main 1992.

Mommensteeg, Geert: Allah's words as amulet. Etnofoor 3.1990:63-76.

Müller, Klaus E. (Hrsg.): Menschenbilder früher Gesellschaften: ethnologische Studien zum Verhältnis von Mensch und Natur. Gedächtnisschrift für Hermann Baumann. Frankfurt/Main 1983.

Müller, Klaus E.: Wortzauber. Eine Ethnologie der Eloquenz. Frankfurt/Main 2001.

Multhaupt, Tamara: Hexerei und Antihexerei in Afrika. München 1989.

Muth, Robert: Träger der Lebenskraft. Ausscheidungen des Organismus im Volksglauben der Antike. Wien 1954.

Neumann, Gerhard; Weigel, Sigrid (Hrsg.): Lesbarkeit der Kultur. Literaturwissenschaft zwischen Kulturtechnik und Ethnographie. München (Wilhelm Fink) 2000.

Neumann, Wolfgang: Tuareg. In: Müller 1983:274-292.

Neumann, Wolfgang: Das Jenseits im Diesseits. Die Heiligen im volkstümlichen Islam und die islamische Mystik. In: Linke 1999:117-136.

Neuman, Wolfgang: Schöpfungsmythen nordamerikanischer Indianer. In: Linke 2001:147-172.

Omyajowo, J. Akin: What is witchcraft? In: Adegbola 1983:317-336.

Rahm-Mottl, Ursula: Die magisch-religiöse Bedeutung des Beduinenschmucks im Negev. In: Der Arabische Almanach 2002/03. Zeitschrift für orientalische Kultur. 13. Jahrgang (Berlin, Nov. 2002):33-37.

Roser, Markus: Hexerei und Lebensriten. Zur Inkulturation des christlichen Glaubens unter den Gbaya der Zentralafrikanischen Republik (Erlanger Verlag für Mission und Ökumene) Erlangen 2000.

Schönhuth, Michael: Das Einsetzen der Nacht in die Rechte des Tages. Hexerei im symbolischen Kontext afrikanischer und europäischer Weltbilder. Münster und Hamburg 1992.

Sterly, Joachim: "Heilige Männer" und Medizinmänner in Melanesien. Köln 1965.

Streck, Bernhard: Fröhliche Wissenschaft Ethnologie. Eine Führung. Wuppertal 1997.

Thiel, Josef Franz: Ahnen – Geister – Höchste Wesen. Religionsethnologische Untersuchungen im Zaïre-Kasai-Gebiet. St. Augustin 1977.

Thiel, Josef Franz; (Museum für Völkerkunde Frankfurt): Was sind Fetische? Frankfurt 1986. Werner, Roland: Transkulturelle Heilkunde. Der ganze Mensch. Heilsysteme unter dem Einfluss von Abrahamischen Religionen, Östlichen Religionen und Glaubensbekenntnissen, Paganismus, Neuen Religionen und religiösen Mischformen. Frankfurt am Main 2001.

Westermarck, E. A.: Ritual and belief in Morocco, 2 Bände. London 1926.

Westermarck, E. A.: Pagan survivals in Mohammedan civilization. Amsterdam 1973 (Nachdruck von 1933).

Wolf, Hans-Jürgen: Hexenwahn. Hexen in Geschichte und Gegenwart. Bindlach (Gondrom) 1994.

Chapter 6
Spirit Beings

This chapter explains how people of European-Western and animistic background perceive spirit beings, what attributes they ascribe to them, and how they can be subdivided into three large groups.

6.0   Introduction

The world of animistic perception, as we have got to know it in its basic structure, is a lively place. It is not only populated by material beings, humans and animals, but also by a great variety of beings perceived as immaterial and spirit-like, active in it, shaping it, and from its location within it exercising influence over the material world and affecting human beings.

6.1   Attributes of Spirit Beings

People who think animistically believe that there are many spirit beings that have *always been present*. There is a whole array of others known to have *arisen only in the course of time*. As a rule they are considered to be *imperishable*, hence possessing in principle *everlasting life*, at least in theory. However, there is certainly the possibility that a spirit being can suffer something that can be compared to the death of a living being.

There are spirit beings which accompany a person's life journey. Sometimes they do this in the form of a *guardian angel*, a concept familiar also to European-Western societies. In animistic societies there is a widespread perception that during their physical lifetime each person is accompanied by at least *one spirit being* which assigns itself to them *shortly before or after birth*, and in the most diverse manner. From the European-Western perspective this is something like one's "soul", but from the animistic point of view it is generally a spirit being, equipped with all the attributes of such a one, but *not* regarded *as a "soul" permanently locked inside the body* but as its *spirit double* intermittently or always *living outside the body*, i.e. in its immediate vicinity. There will be more detail on this later, when the animistic concept of man will be further discussed (ch. 11).

Like everything else in the spirit realm spirit beings are *usually invisible*. Mostly they are only heard. But sometimes they can also be seen, mostly only indirectly or partially, for example at night through their faint luminescence or glowing eyes. They are also considered to be visible in dreams, under the influence of drugs or when in a trance.

Common to all is the further quality of *not being bound by space and time*. They can *walk, hover* and *fly* wherever they wish, pass through matter and move from one place to another at any time and at lightning speed, however great the distance may be. Using these attributes they can also penetrate the human body in order to induce (organic and "psychic") diseases, affect the mind, the emotions and the will, and cause people to perform insane actions such as running amok, or influence or "illuminate" the mind, the emotions and the will more positively.

These attributes can be subject to certain restrictions. Chuuk Islanders maintain that a spirit being shut inside a metal container, for example, needs a hole at least the size of a pinprick in order to be able to leave its prison. When spirit beings enter the body of a human being or animal it is claimed that certain openings are preferred, such as the mouth, ears, anus, hollow of the knee, palm of the hand, sole of the foot, armpit, or in the case of children through the fontanelle, where the skin is soft.[16] (Hence, as early as the European Middle Ages it was considered dangerous not to hold the hand in front of the mouth when yawning.) Thus in animistic thinking spirit beings are understood to be *not so totally spirit-like* as would appear to be the case according to (modern) European-Western perceptions. This is also evidenced by the assertion of the South-American Bororo people that when a spirit of the dead enters a human settlement the inhabitants can be aware of it as a gust of wind (Crocker 1985).

The fact that they can squeeze themselves through the smallest of apertures leads to the realization that they can *alter the shape of their bodies in any way they choose*, even *changing into animals and objects*.

Spirit beings have an array of *physical features*. They can *produce sounds, see, hear, smell, taste, and touch*. Their sense organs are mostly far better developed than those of humans. They *sleep, eat* and *drink*, but only for pleasure, for as spirits they are not dependent on regular sleep and taking in nourishment. At times they may also acquire a *body temperature* and *body weight*. Sometimes they develop enormous *physical strength*. They can drag lumps of stone that are too heavy for humans. Spirit beings have *male* or *female* sexual features, in exceptional cases can be *bisexual*, are *interested in sex*, and can *procreate* and *give birth to* children, so called "spirit children".

---

[16] Many writers call these places on the body "gateways of the soul".

Over and above these physical features they are *able to think, to will and to feel*, and consequently have ideas and intentions, can experience happiness and fear, and reveal *qualities of character*. For example, they are described as courageous, cowardly, cunning, generous etc. Apparently there are no human qualities that cannot also be ascribed to spirit beings. All this is indeed evidence of their *personhood*, which also includes being given *names*, at all events the most important of them.

The names of spirit beings indicate their respective *physical characteristics*: "One-eye" or "One-leg", because they lack a part of the body. (There are even spirits with only half a body.) Many names describe characteristic *activities* which they are said to have: Rübezahl ("Turnip-count"), a spirit from the Giant Mountains, is so called because according to one of the many stories about his person he once "made a name for himself" by counting turnips. Thor, the ancient Nordic God of the storm, is regarded as the agent of thunder, and the Chuuk Islanders name one spirit *Nitórótór*, meaning something like "dirty fellow" (Goodenough 2002:110). Many bear the name of the *place* or *region* where they like to reside (rivers, lakes, seas, mountains, cliffs), regarding them as their territory. Others are named according to the *time of day* or *season* when they tend to reveal themselves (e.g. Night Raven).

There are spirit beings who keep creatures such as ants and spiders to work for them. Hence one avoids killing them, because their "masters" could exact revenge (Tauchmann 1983:242).

One of the important characteristics of spirit beings is that they possess *mana*, that quality which enables them to effect the unusual and unexpected.

Spirit beings are not all equipped with the same amount of mana, or mana with the same effectiveness, which means that they have different degrees of *status*. Hence there is a kind of social distinction among them, similar to human society. Some of them enjoy high esteem, one tries to approach them and have dealings with them, others are despised, feared and shunned. This difference in status conceals a fundamental principle of classification with the aid of which spirit beings can be put into three large groups.

6.2   Three Types of Spirits

There is an abundance of terms for spirit beings, e.g. there are spirits of the ancestors, of the mountains, of the bush, of the earth, of the fields, of the house, of the sky; there are unfamiliar spirits, assistant spirits, nature spirits, tormenting spirits, protective spirits, spirits of the underworld, and spirits of the dead. This is not a complete list.

Among these there are many which people neither fear nor particularly esteem. They are *neutral*, so to speak. One accepts that they exist, that they are sometimes active and make themselves noticed. They can startle people by their behaviour, but there is no need to take defensive action.

If these *neutral spirits*, which are *not described in detail* and as a concept represent a somewhat *covert category*, are taken out of the equation, then we are left with either *malevolent* spirits or *benign* spirits. More precisely: *Malevolent spirits have a hostile attitude to human beings and wish them harm; benign spirits display a friendly attitude towards humans.*

With regard to the contrast and difference between them it is important to bear in mind that it has to do with *qualities of character, moods* and *emotions*, i.e. *psychic and moral qualities*. These are essential to the distinction. As has already been mentioned, it is apparent here that spirit beings are credited with intellect, feelings and character, i.e. personhood.

6.3   In the Next Chapter

These two kinds of spirit beings, malevolent and benign, require a detailed description. But before this can be done (in chapters 8 and 9) we must first tackle the issue of the part played by *spiritlike objects* in animistic thinking.

The following sources contain more on the theme of this chapter:

Crocker, Jon Christopher: Vital souls Bororo cosmology, natural symbolism, and shamanism. Tucson, Arizona 1985.

Goodenough, Ward Hunt: Under heaven's brow. Pre-Christian religious tradition in Chuuk. Philadelphia 2002.

Müller, Klaus E. (Hrsg.): Menschenbilder früher Gesellschaften: ethnologische Studien zum Verhältnis von Mensch und Natur. Gedächtnisschrift für Hermann Baumann. Frankfurt/Main 1983.

Tauchmann, Kurt: Kankanaey (u. Lepanto). In: Müller 1983:222-247.

Chapter 7
Spirit Objects

This chapter explains the perceptions of spirit objects held by people of animistic background, the characteristics they ascribe to spirit objects, and how this affects the nature of objects in general and the related concept of the world.

7.0   Introduction

It was mentioned briefly in chapter 4 that spirit objects were unfamiliar or indeed unknown to the European-Western way of thinking, whereas people of animistic background quite simply assume them to be present as a matter of course. Without the conceptual notion of spirit objects they would find the nature of the cosmos completely inexplicable. In fact, a *theory of the nature of the material world* can be quite clearly recognized.

7.1   Characteristics of Spirit Objects

In comparison with perceptions of spirit beings the animistic notions of spirit objects are *very much less differentiated*. When asked e.g. about the source and origin of spirit objects informants could as a rule give no explanation. Their answers were mostly limited to the observation that in their society nobody thought much about it. Only rarely was it stated that they came from the Supreme Being as their creator (e.g. van der Weijden 1981:68).

In principle, as with spirit beings, spirit objects were regarded as *always having been present*.

As with everything in the spirit world, spirit objects are *usually invisible*, unless appearing in dreams, under the influence of drugs, or in a state of trance. In dreams and similar situations people are aware of their own or another's involvement with objects, using a stave, a bowl or a vehicle. These are regarded as spirit-like, and one is aware from the experiences in these situations that spirit objects *look exactly like their material counterparts*.

Presumably it was from experiences of this kind that the Chuuk Islanders developed a theory of the nature of objects. Their theory, with its clear structure, serves as an example in enabling us to understand their concept of man and of the world.

For them all objects in their world possess not only a material form but above and beyond that a second way of existing, which (along with *mettóóch* for thing) they designate with its own word (*ngúún*). This second way of existing, although invisible, is so completely *identical in its form* with the material object to which it belongs that the two could easily be confused. Pictorially a material object and its spirit-like counterpart can be illustrated in the following way:

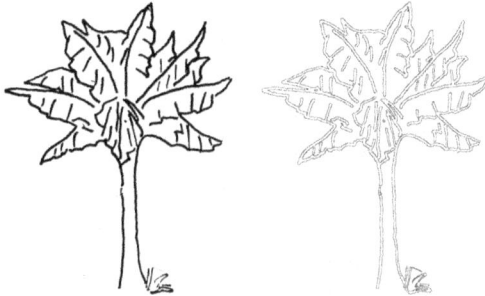

Material object and its spirit-like form

Moreover, a material object and its spirit-like form of existence are not only identical in form, but also in *colour, taste, smell, weight* and other perceivable features. Even the *effects* which they generate count as equivalent, e.g. in the context of medicine or food. A meal in spirit form satisfies a spirit being just as much as its material counterpart satisfies a person. And if it is evident that an object possesses mana, then the same is true of its spirit form.

Just as spirit beings possess eternal life, in a similar way spirit objects also, apart from exceptions, are *imperishable* and *indestructible*. If a material object is damaged, this has no effect on its spirit form. Changes in form are only possible in the kind of way a plant grows, for example. Such a development is paralleled by its spirit counterpart, or, more precisely, the development of the material plant follows the development of its spirit counterpart. *Even when a material object is completely destroyed its spirit form is preserved.*

There are exceptions. Among the few one occasionally comes across in ethnological writings are the notions of the Bororo of Brazil. Crocker (1985:112) records that spirit beings who are offended by the breaking of a hunting taboo punish the man responsible by removing the "spiritual essence" of his hunting weapons and hurling them with such force through the heavens that they glow. This is how the Bororo explain what meteors are. (For the foreign observer this is an indication that in a certain sense animism can equate with "astronomy" or "natural science".)

This also shows that a material object and its spirit counterpart have an independent existence, which even permits them to be *spatially separated*. This feature in particular is to be found in numerous animistic perceptions of the nature of the person and of the structure of the cosmos (cf. below under 7.8). The following must be clearly understood: for the Chuuk Islanders the two prominent features of the *ngúún* of an object are 1. *its spirit nature* (non-physical, non-material) und 2. *its formal identity*, such that its material counterpart appears as its *double*. Hence I refer to this notion of the appearance of objects in immaterial form as the concept of the *spirit double*.

7.2   The Concept of the Spirit Double

The *spirit double* is a *basic concept of animistic thinking*. In 1965, based on Crawley (1909 and 1911), Fischer proposed the term "spiritual double" for his understanding of the "appearance in immaterial form" of people, animals and objects in certain regions of Oceania (1965:255-273). I had adopted this term (1977), but subsequently used "spirit" instead of "spiritual", because the adjective "spiritual" has undergone a change of meaning over the last three decades, i.e. it no longer has the unambiguous meaning of "spirit-like". In his 1999 publication Badenberg still uses Crawley's term "spiritual double", but subsequently (2003), like other more recent authors, he refers to the "spirit double".

Admittedly it must be acknowledged that the Chuuk Islanders' notions of the *spirit double* is a special phenomenon, being regionally and culturally determined and limited to that area (Oceania, Micronesia), and not at all to be expected in the same form elsewhere. There are also only occasional mentions of notions of the nature of objects and subsequent conclusions in the ethnological literature on other regions, so that the universal validity and usefulness of this concept cannot be regarded as firmly established. *However, there are indications everywhere of the presence of the concept of the spirit double, if not in relation to the nature of objects then certainly in connection with the nature of persons.*

This finding suggests that there is a gap in research here of fairly large proportions. Up till now the available basic material is scanty. *I see in this a substantial reason for the fact that animistic systems of thought are still too little understood ethnologically in terms of their cognitive foundations, and can therefore be only imperfectly understood by foreign observers.*

Investigations of ethnic groups in South-East Asia (Mischung 1984, Rousseau 1998) and China (Watson 1982) contain clearer and more frequent references to the presence of these notions than corresponding research on African and American groups. However, more recent studies by African ethnologists show that they are now researching this matter, e.g. Oduyoye 1983. (There is a relevant bibliography in Badenberg 2003/2008: ch. 2.)

7.3 Functions of the Spirit Double of Objects

I mentioned briefly that a material object and its spirit double can be spatially separate. In the thinking of the Chuuk Islanders this condition is the rule. However, the gap or distance between the two is of significance. If it is too big the object in its material form begins to show signs of *impairment*. These impairments are above all noticeable if a spirit double has completely lost touch with its material counterpart, e.g. when various spirit beings have a use for it and take charge of it.

The Islanders become aware that this has happened by the fact that the object in question no longer fulfils its purpose as well as it used to. Axes become blunt more quickly, bowls get broken more easily than those whose spirit double is still present. Meals placed before the deceased as offerings wither or decay more quickly than others, the explanation being that the spirit doubles of the offerings have been consumed by the (spirits of the) deceased. Most striking of all is the declaration that such meals result in no increase of weight in those who eat them, no matter how much is consumed. The *loss of their spirit double* is accompanied by the loss of their *content*, their *nutritional value*.

These examples show that the loss of the spirit double results in at least a limitation of the efficiency of a material object, which must eventually lead to a complete loss of function. By contrast the presence of the spirit double in the immediate vicinity of its material counterpart guarantees the latter's complete efficiency.

❑ Suggestion for own investigations: in order to be sure if this is indeed reflected in a particular system of concepts, *many examples* need to be collected. This means finding as many objects as possible about which informants are convinced that loss of their spirit double affects their efficiency or makes them completely unusable.

7.4 Spirit Double of Objects and the Concept of Sacrifice

In religious studies many kinds of sacrifice are recognized: offerings or sacrifices are associated with prayer requests, thanksgiving, the firstborn, praise; there are human sacrifices, animal sacrifices, burnt offerings, sin offerings etc.

Not all cultures have the concept of sacrifice. Where it does occur it contains in a general sense the aspect of a *gift* or *present* to spirit beings considered to be more powerful than humans. The things sacrificed are those which that society considers to be of value and worth striving for. In the case of so-called *blood sacrifice* it is *animals* or *people*, who are killed. Among the objects assumed to be of use to spirit beings and appropriate as a bloodless offering are especially *ornaments*, occasionally *tools* and *implements*, *toys* in relation to children, but especially *edibles*, including all kinds of *luxury foods* (e.g. alcohol, coffee, tobacco etc.).

Sweet-scented flowers, herbs and *cosmetics*, whose spirit doubles give off the same aromas as their material counterparts, are also very important as gifts.

Conceivably it is imagined that in the case of blood sacrifice one of the various souls (a spirit double?) of the sacrificed animal or person is definitively separated from the body by the act of killing and in this way made available to the spirit being for whom the gift is intended. This notion may be the reason behind the practice of burning the animal or person on an altar. Clear statements concerning it are difficult. It is easier to conceive of such a separation in the case of offerings such as ornaments, tools and food, and also especially with the kind of gift placed in the grave of the deceased at funerals.

7.5   Spirit Double of Objects and Burial Gifts

Up to the time when the Chuuk Islanders began to turn to Christianity they used to bring their deceased relatives not only gifts of food on specially prepared altars but also, for the recently deceased, items such as cigarettes, decorative combs and other ornamental pieces to be placed on the grave, believing that the spirit double of those persons would accept them.

Donations of this kind can indeed be understood as a sacrifice. But objects placed at the grave can also be interpreted as *burial gifts*. They differ from sacrifices in that they are placed in the grave with a somewhat different intention.

Archaeology has shown that already in the very early periods of human history *edible things* in appropriate vessels were among the important burial gifts. The thinking behind this was probably that the dead have a long journey to take before reaching their final destination in the beyond, or must wait until the relatives left behind have carried out the rituals according to which the deceased reach their final status as transcendent beings no longer needing to take in food.

For the same reason the dead are given personal items, weapons, tools, clothing, jewellery, toys etc., in the belief that they, i.e. their spirit doubles, need them for daily "life" and work in the beyond. Sometimes these objects are broken before being placed on the grave, or destroyed by fire, probably with the intention of definitively separating the material and spirit form (Humphrey 1996:196; Müller 1997:64). This may sometimes apply to animals which the deceased owned, to servants, slaves, even to wives, who are killed so they are enabled to follow the deceased into the beyond. (For an ethnography with many relevant details see Hülsewiede 1992).

Bundles of plants in Neanderthal graves may possibly be explained as a sweet-smelling gift for the deceased (Molleson 1981:17).

7.6   Spirit Double or "Soul" of Objects?

Much that is written about animism, especially of the popular scientific kind, usually represents the view that people with an animistic concept of the world regard every thing in nature as "ensouled", i.e. especially objects. This expression (soul!) leads inevitably in almost all cases to the conclusion that objects, (plants, stones!) have the capacity to feel, to will, and even to think, and hence are indeed "alive" in a similar way to animals and humans. At most this is only true *in exceptional cases.* Thus the Nootka people of North America conceive of an underwater world where even the "souls of the trees" are malevolent (Feest 1998:46).

However, as a rule people who think animistically consider spirit doubles of lifeless objects to be no more alive than their material counterparts themselves.

The following statement shows that conceptual clarity is required here, if misunderstanding is to be avoided: "Stones, staves, weapons or clothes have life, for they also appear in dreams" (Schlatter 1999:61). From the perspective of animism they do not have life simply because they have a spirit double visible in dreams. In addition the quote makes a causal connection which is not possible according to animistic understanding.

In my opinion, in order to avoid wrong conclusions it is imperative to avoid the term "soul" and its derivatives ("ensouling") and to replace it with the term "spirit double", not only in investigating and describing the nature of objects but also in researching animistic concepts of man.

Apart from exceptions, the fact that objects and their spirit doubles are not considered by animists to have life does not exclude regarding objects as *locations of spirit beings*, e.g. certain trees or rocks. But their spirit inhabitants are not conceptually identical with the spirit double of the object in question.

7.7   Spirit Double and Visual Representations of
Spirit Beings

Places of sacrifice are not infrequently found in the immediate vicinity of (sculptured, painted) images portraying (symbolically) the particular spirit being or divinity to whom the offering is made. For these also the notion

applies that the (material) image and the spirit double matched to it are separate concepts. It is not only naïve, but a **wrong understanding of animism** to
describe the attitude of people making offerings before such an image as
nothing more than sacrificing to wooden or stone idols. It is recommended to
proceed on the assumption that for people whose religious practices involve
such images the latter are simply the material equivalent of the related spirit
element.

7.8   Spirit Double and the Structure of the Cosmos

If for the Chuuk Islanders, as mentioned, every material object and being,
including humans, possesses a spirit double, then the cosmos as the totality of
all objects and beings has for them a form deviating considerably from the
one perceived in European-Western terms. *Alongside the material world as
the totality of all material objects and beings there exists in parallel to it a
second world as the totality of all associated spirit doubles*.

A pictorial illustration of the structure of their cosmos in terms of *parallel
material and spirit worlds* can be envisaged in the following way:

Viewed like this, such a concept of the world gives the impression of
complete symmetry. In reality there is one area where the two worlds behave
asymmetrically: in the world of material objects (and beings) new objects
(and beings), provided with spirit doubles, are continually coming into existence and passing away. When they perish their spirit doubles still remain,
thus increasing the number that exist. The imbalance between the material
and spirit world thus rests on the simple fact that as a rule there is no material
object or being without a spirit double, but that there exists an incalculable

number of spirit objects and beings which either never had a material counterpart or no longer have one.

7.9   This World and the Beyond

This basic structure of the cosmos is fundamental not only to *a different perception of this world and the beyond*, but also to a different perception of the nature of man. However, this connection cannot be discussed until ch. 11.

7.10   Extent and Validity of the Concept of the Spirit Double of Objects

In 7.2 I mentioned that it is above all in Oceania that the notion of a spirit double of objects can be observed, and that the concept is less apparent or even not recognizable in other cultures. This could be due to the present state of the research, which has no relevant data, because from their European-Western perspective ethnographers were not looking for it or were not alert to it, the concept not being part of their cognitive framework.

The Chuuk Islanders' notion that every material object has its spirit double is in terms of its almost ideal completeness the big exception. Such a concept does indeed present itself as a suitable teaching model for learning about how animists shape their understanding of the world and for using it as a starting point for research in one's own field of work. However, one should by no means expect to find this model everywhere in the same form.

For the present the (rather sporadic) indications of the occurrence of the concept of a spirit double of objects in ethnic groups beyond Oceania allow one only to conclude that at the most those objects (at least) which have a *prominent position* within the culture possess such a double.

7.11   Spirit Double of Rice or "Rice Soul"?

In ethnic groups of South-East Asia, for example, there are notions which possibly correspond to the concept of the spirit double of objects. Among the Sikanese it is a feature of *maize*, whereas pods and beans are expressly excluded (van der Weijden 1981:166). The Batak of North-West Sumatra attribute it to *iron* (van der Weijden 1981:18), but also particularly to *rice*, which in South-East Asia is especially linked with this notion, and occasionally also to the *tools* used for rice cultivation.

In the present state of research it is difficult to say whether the connection really exists. There is a lack of clarity occasioned by the fact that the terms used among the various ethnic groups for the spirit double of rice have been rendered by ethnographers either by "rice soul" or "rice spirit", sometimes with both terms in the same sentence. This often makes it difficult to be precise as to whether an independent spirit being with personal qualities is being described, or whether one is dealing with a genuine spirit double of the rice plant or rice grain in the way outlined at the beginning of this chapter. This distinction is important in as much as there are also personalised rice spirits considered to be protectors of the paddy fields, having their own individual features, and thus not to be understood as being in the form of a spirit double of each separate rice plant.

One indication that "rice soul" or "rice spirit" refers to the concept of the spirit double is possibly reflected in the use of one and the same word for the spirit double of people and animals, as with the Reyang Musi for example, an ethnic group in South-West Sumatra. In his 1996 investigation Psota mentions that the Reyang Musi are acquainted in their culture with plants that possess something for which the same word (*semengat*) is used as for the spirit double of living things. Its presence with the rice plant has to be secured by rituals carried out by specialists (1996:63). Precautions also have to be taken to prevent the spirits of the forest from harvesting the soul of the rice (1996:142). The way this is expressed – the "soul of the rice" could be harvested by spirits of the forest – justifies the assumption that this is indeed to do with the concept of a spirit double of the rice (of the rice plant, the rice grain?) That this could be the case is strengthened by Schneider's statement (1995:110) that the separation of the two leads to the withering and death of the plant, and by Tauchmann's finding (1983:242) that the loss of this element causes disease in the rice.

Faced with these notional presuppositions it would be damaging to harvest or thresh the rice by machine. The grains of rice and their spirit doubles, which can only bring about the nutritional value of the rice by being together, would thus be separated, and the protective rice spirits which determine the nutritional value of the rice would be scared into flight. This could be a reason why in many ethnic groups rice (dry rice) may only be traditionally harvested by hand with a special rice knife.

Van der Weijden 1981 is an important source for information on the existence of so-called "rice souls". She has made a comparative listing of relevant notions in numerous ethnic groups of Indonesia, in which the concept of the spirit double in its strict sense is only occasionally apparent. In most cases "rice spirit" and "rice soul" signify personified beings, often feminine, to whom an offering must be brought, with whom one speaks, who take fright and flee at the sound of whistles and other noises, or who can be called, enticed, angered etc.

Clearer features of a spirit double emerge in van der Weijden's finding that among the Minangkabau on Sumatra each individual rice grain has a soul (*sumangat*), which escapes from the grains and hence can have a detrimental effect on the flavour of the rice (1981:22); similarly among the Ot Danum (1981:64). Certain harvest rituals practised among the Sasak of Lombok likewise lead to the conclusion of a non-personally conceived spirit double, when for example ritual preparations are carried out to enable those "souls" of the rice grains lost during the harvest or in transport or eaten by mice or other pests to gather together in the barn (1981:141).

On Timor as well there is the notion that each individual grain of rice has a "soul" without which it could not grow. Ancestral spirits to whom rice is offered as food only eat its "soul", regarded as the tastiest element in the rice and furnished with the "life energy", and in my opinion this could be an indication that something akin to a spirit double is involved (1981:177).

Indications that more ethnic groups than formerly presumed, in the most varied of regions, are aware of a comparable concept can be found in Descola 1996:235; Hauser-Schäublin 1983:186; Humphrey 1996:57,95-96,196,359; Severi 1993:175; Tauchmann 1983:226; Watson 1982:175; Woodburn 1982:200. However, it should be noted that the examples given are incidental findings and only demonstrate that there is a need for more research.

7.12   Spirit Double of Objects and the Term "Soul Substance"

According to van der Weijden (1981:86) older reports concerning South-East Asian ethnic groups contain indications of notions that rice can atrophy if it loses its "soul substance". It is claimed that there are objects and beings which "scatter" the soul substance, thus likewise losing it. This could indeed have something to do with the concept of the spirit double, but since there is a lack of precise data, including especially the important linguistic analysis, it is difficult to judge. Fischer is also of this opinion (1965:299-313).

In total the number of indications of the presence of a notion of soul substance is so small and the descriptions so strongly distorted by European-Western perceptions of the soul that in my view *soul substance is not a wide-spread concept in animism, but only to be expected in rare and exceptional cases.*

7.13   Need for Research

According to my knowledge of the relevant literature the concept of a spirit double of objects has generally up till now not gained the attention of research that it deserves. Even if it were indeed as rare as presently appears on the basis of the current state of research, its rare presence needs to be demonstrated by a targeted search and its absence securely documented. Such a procedure is termed *falsification*[17].

Ethnographies from other regions than those mentioned thus far, which show or at least indicate that the concept of the spirit double is there present, are those of Okazaki (1985) und Williams (1930).

7.14   In the Next Chapter

Having clarified the aspects of the animistic perceptions of the nature of objects I will return now to the theme of chapter 6 which discussed spirit beings generally. Chapter 8 will deal with the nature of evil spirit beings as understood by people of animistic frame of thought.

The following sources contain more on the theme of this chapter:

Adegbola, E. A. Ade (ed.): Traditional religion in West Africa. Ibadan 1983.

Auffahrt, Christoph; Bernhard, Jutta; Mohr, Hubert (Hrsg.): Metzler Lexikon Religion Bd. 1. Stuttgart und Weimar (Metzler) 1999.

Badenberg, Robert: The Body, Soul and Spirit Concept of the Bemba in Zambia: Fundamental Characteristics of being human of an African Ethnic Group. Bonn 2002. 2nd rev. ed. (edition iwg – mission academics, Bd. 9. Verlag für Kultur und Wissenschaft).

Badenberg, Robert: Sickness and Healing. A Case Study on the Dialectic of Culture and Personality. Nürnberg 2008. 2nd rev. ed. (edition afem – mission academics, Bd. 11. Verlag für Theologie und Religionswissenschaft).

Bloch, Maurice; Parry, Jonathan (eds.): Death and the regeneration of life. Cambridge et al. 1982.

Boyer, Pascal (ed.): Cognitive aspects of religious symbolism. Cambridge 1993.

Crawley, A. Ernest: The idea of the soul. London 1909.

Crawley, A. Ernest: "Doubles". In: Hastings 1911, 4:853-860.

Crocker, Jon Christopher: Vital souls. Bororo cosmology, natural symbolism, and shamanism. Tucson, Arizona 1985.

Descola, Philippe: Leben und Sterben in Amazonien. Bei den Jivaro-Indianern. Stuttgart 1996.

---

[17] Falsification is the rebuttal of a scientific proposition by means of opposing examples. In this instance the proposition is that the concept of a spirit double is more wide-spread than previously assumed. A rebuttal would consist in the fact that a targeted search found no such evidence.

Feest, Christian F.: Beseelte Welten. Die Religionen der Indianer Nordamerikas. Freiburg, Basel, Wien (Herder) 1998.

Fischer, Hans: Studien über Seelenvorstellungen in Ozeanien. München 1965.

Hastings, James (ed.): Encyclopaedia of religion and ethics. Edinburgh 1911.

Hauser-Schäublin, Birgitta: Abelam. In: Müller 1983:178-203.

Hülsewiede, Brigitte: Die Nahua von Tequila. Eine Nachuntersuchung, besonders zu Struktur und Wandel der Familienfeste. Münster und Hamburg 1992.

Humphrey, Caroline with Urgunge Onon: Shamans and elders. Experience, knowledge and power among the Daur Mongols. Oxford 1996.

Humphreys, S. C.; King, H. (eds.): Mortality and immortality: the anthropology and archaeology of death. London 1981.

Käser, Lothar: Der Begriff "Seele" bei den Insulanern von Truk. Diss. Freiburg 1977.

Mischung, Roland: Religion und Wirklichkeitsvorstellungen in einem Karen-Dorf Nordwest-Thailands. Frankfurt am Main1984.

Molleson, Theya: The archaeology and anthropology of death: what the bones tell us. In: Humphreys/King 1981:15-32.

Müller, Klaus E. (Hrsg.): Menschenbilder früher Gesellschaften: ethnologische Studien zum Verhältnis von Mensch und Natur. Gedächtnisschrift für Hermann Baumann. Frankfurt/Main 1983.

Müller, Klaus E.: Der gesprungene Ring: wie man die Seele gewinnt und verliert. Frankfurt am Main 1997.

Oduyoye, Modupe: Man's self and its spiritual double. In: Adegbola 1983:273-288.

Okazaki, A.: Living together with "bad things": the persistence of Gank, notions of mystical agents. In Tomikawa: 1985.

Psota, Thomas: Waldgeister und Reisseelen: die Revitalisierung von Ritualen zur Erhaltung der komplementären Produktion in Südwest-Sumatra. Berlin 1996.

Rousseau, Jérôme: Kayan religion. Ritual and religious reform in Central Borneo. Leiden 1998.

Schlatter, Gerhard: Animismus. In: Auffahrt/Bernhard/Mohr 1999:61.

Schneider, Jürg: From upland to irrigated rice. The development of wet-rice agriculture in Rejang Musi, Southwest Sumatra. Berlin 1995.

Severi, Carlo: Talking about souls: the pragmatic construction of meaning in Cuna ritual language. In: Boyer 1993:165-181.

Tauchmann, Kurt: Kankanaey (u. Lepanto). In: Müller 1983:222-247.

Tomikawa, M. (ed.): Sudan Sahel Studies I. Tokio 1985.

Tomikawa, M. (ed.): Sudan Sahel Studies II. Tokio 1987.

van der Weijden, Gera: Indonesische Reisrituale. Basel 1981.

Watson, James L.: Of flesh and bones: The management of death pollution in Cantonese society. In: Bloch/Parry 1982:155-186.

Williams, F. E.: Orokaiva society. Oxford 1930.

Woodburn, James: Social dimensions of death in four African hunting and gathering societies. In: Bloch/Parry 1982:187-210.

Chapter 8
Malevolent Spirit Beings

This chapter explains the characteristics attributed to malevolent spirit beings by people living in an animistic environment, the effects and influences expected from them, their differences from European-Western perceptions, the commonalities and differences compared with demons in the Bible, and where these spirit beings come from.

8.0   Introduction

Before I begin to describe the characteristics of malevolent spirit beings in detail it is worth recapping briefly some statements from ch. 6.2:

Malevolent spirit beings are those which have a generally hostile attitude to human beings.

It is important to realise that this (simplified) definition has to do with traits of *character, moods and emotions*, i.e. psychic or more precisely *psychic-moral qualities* used to describe this kind of spirit being, which implies the recognition that they possess *intellect, feelings* and character, in other words *personality*.

The terms which indigenous languages have for this kind of spirit being consist as a rule of the general word for "spirit beings", qualified by an adjective such as "evil", "aggressive", "hostile" or simply "bad".

❑ Suggestion for own investigations: find out how this manifests itself in the language where you are located, collecting as many contexts as possible, i.e. phrases used by mother-tongue speakers.

8.1   Physical Characteristics of Malevolent Spirit Beings

These reveal the variety of ways in which malevolent spirit beings are perceived as being active. They are almost always described as being in *animal form* (theriomorphic). Their appearance in *human form* (anthropomorphic) is rarer and only under certain circumstances or with a particular intention.

Many of them are considered to be distinctly rapacious and immoderate, e.g. in a sexual context. They pair off indiscriminately with their own kind, with animals and humans. In this they resemble satyrs, those spirits of the forest and mountains with legs, tails and horns of a goat known to us from

Greek mythology as being the bibulous and lecherous companions of the god Dionysius.

It is apparent that in pre-literate societies malevolent spirit beings are discerned more frequently or in greater numbers than benevolent ones, for you hardly find anyone who would not declare that they had at some time encountered, seen or at least heard the cry or rumble of a malevolent spirit. Children above all are very ready to tell of such experiences.

When malevolent spirit beings are described as being in animal form they reflect those which are feared on account of their aggressive behaviour or appearance. They are endowed with *repulsive features*. Their faces are grimacing and their bodily proportions distorted. They have enormous mouths, limbs which are either far too large or small, claws, a tail, a shaggy hide etc. They have staring eyes, piercing, hypnotic and glowing, especially in the dark. This is why numerous inexplicable *phenomena of light* occurring in nature are viewed as (malevolent) spirit beings, or at least as their eyes, or simply evoked by such spirit beings. This includes insects which emit light signals, creatures which give off marine luminescence, certain kinds of fungi and lichen with phosphorescent qualities, and even meteors, which, however, are not necessarily regarded as malevolent spirit beings. Many ethnic groups consider meteors to be shamans on a "soul journey" or "journey in the beyond" (cf. ch. 14).

It is said of malevolent spirit beings that their *body temperature* is *lower* than that of other living creatures. They feel cold. Their *body odour* is strong and repellent. If a pungent smell of unknown origin is detected somewhere the presence of a malevolent spirit is suspected in the immediate vicinity.

They have no articulate speech and cannot sing, but only *grunt, croak, roar, whistle or squeak*.

They have the acute *hearing* that one associates with animals in the wild. Noise can keep them permanently at bay. In East Asia firecrackers are mainly used. In European-Western societies the smashing of crockery on the eve-of-wedding party fulfils the same purpose. In South German wine-growing villages it was still the custom a few years ago, if a hailstorm threatened, for troops of men to go in among the vines and fire off their guns to drive away the weather spirits. Even church bells were rung for the same purpose.

Malevolent spirit beings do not need to take in *nourishment* in order to "live". If they do it is almost always purely for pleasure and, like animals, they are not particularly selective in their search for food. Many are considered to be cannibals, consuming their own kind. Some of them eat the spirit double ("souls") of people and are able to kill them in this way without directly causing their bodies to be affected. Their urge to eat can be used to keep them at a distance, by throwing them from afar something to eat, not in the sense of a food offering, but in order to appease, divert, and keep them away.

Their *senses of smell* and *taste*, and of course their stomachs, can also tolerate evil-smelling, rotten and decayed material. But they have no appetite for things that are salty, acidy, of sharp or bitter odour. This also enables them to be kept at a distance. Spreading gall or the bitter juice of a certain plant around the area of the front door of the house has a repellent effect on spirit beings with evil intentions. In many areas of the Balkans the strings of onions and garlic hanging from balconies are not just there to be dried. Their pungent odour and taste are claimed to keep away aggressive spirit beings (vampires). A similar notion can be observed in Oceania, where mothers rub orange peel on small children before starting a journey by boat. The nasty tasting juice it contains causes malevolent spirit beings who might want to bite them to lose their appetite. Acrid smoke is similarly effective in driving them away.

Water spirits are widely considered to be *particularly aggressive*. They kill swimmers, anglers and children playing on the bank by pulling them under the water and drowning them. A particular species of these malevolent spirit beings was formerly known to be present in farmyards. Where children were concerned the cesspit was one of the most dangerous places. An effective way of keeping them away from it was to persuade them that the "slurry spirit" would get them if they approached the pit.

Malevolent spirit beings are usually *active at night*, and correspondingly *light sensitive*. During the day they hide in dark places, in hollow tree-trunks, holes in the ground, under stones etc., and only make their appearance as darkness descends.

They do not usually reside in human settlements, but *in the natural world*. Their real home is not the "civilised world" but the wild, "uncultivated" one, the bush outside the village. They make their abode in trees, in the forest, in the desert, in the mountains, in gorges and springs. Many exist exclusively in sandstorms (Neumann 1983:277). In such places people are more vulnerable to their attacks than in their villages. You risk becoming ill, or being blinded if, without having completed a suitable defensive ritual or wearing an appropriate amulet, you stray into their realm unawares. Occasionally, however, they move out from there into human living space. They are drawn particularly to cattle sheds, uninhabited houses and huts, burial places, dark places such as ovens, slaughtering areas, downpipes, sewage channels, toilets, manure heaps and brothels (Fartacek 2002). If you stay there for any length of time you invite danger.

In spite of their spirit nature they are not regarded as so immaterial that they could not leave behind *blue stains*, *scratch marks* on people and *footprints* where the ground is soft, nor is it impossible to impede and block their access to gardens and plantations by surrounding them with a thorn hedge.

8.2   Psychic and Intellectual Characteristics of Malevolent Spirit Beings

At the start of this chapter I mentioned that intellect, feelings and character, i.e. personality, are attributed to malevolent spirit beings. Hence they can also feel *fear*. Apart from the physically determined aversion which they harbour towards acrid smells, noise etc. already mentioned, many of them have a fear of holy scriptures such as the Koran, of symbols such as crosses and horse-shoes, and of substances such as holy water and metal. Hence the latter are particularly suitable as *amulets* (cf. ch. 5.4). They are manufactured from such materials, reveal the forms of relevant symbols or contain words from holy writings. It is believed that they help to keep malevolent spirit beings at a distance, prevent them from penetrating human habitats or drive them out.

It is not just objects made expressly for the purpose that can serve as amulets. They can also be objects of daily use. Among the Tuareg of North Africa anxious mothers lay a knife under the heads of small children when they have to leave the tent (Neumann 1983:277).

Malevolent spirit beings can also be scared by the forms of lions and dragons of dangerous appearance and with bared teeth, or heavily armed figures of guards with wild-looking faces. These are frequently found on both sides of entrances to holy areas and temples.

There is a further characteristic which malevolent spirit beings share with animals. Despite all their dangerousness they are first and foremost *shy of humans*, especially when they encounter large numbers of them.

This leads to two further ways of protecting oneself against a possible attack by malevolent spirit beings. One of them is to shine light or kindle a fire. Powerful pocket torches are considered to be particularly effective for keeping such spirits at a respectful distance. The second possibility is never to leave the house at night, or only when accompanied.

Because of these two characteristics, aversion to light and avoidance of large numbers of people, Christians of animistic background sometimes find two theological themes especially significant: the *biblical metaphor of light* and the importance ascribed to the New Testament concept of *church community*.

In many forms of animism there is a further characteristic of malevolent spirit beings which overlaps with important propositions in the Bible. They are sometimes afraid of the *colour red*. This fact reveals a meaningful connection with the effects of the blood of sacrificial animals, e.g. on doorposts, preserving the Israelites of the Egyptian exile from the attack of the so-called angel of death (Ex. 12), and with the effects of the blood of Jesus (according to numerous references in the New Testament).

As a rule the *intelligence* of malevolent spirit beings is reckoned to be *not particularly high*. In the stories told about them they appear as *idiots*, objects of ridicule. At all events it is supposed to be easy for people to *deceive* or *outwit* them and so protect oneself from them. This can happen in various ways.

When an Asheninca Indian of Peru arrives at a crossroads or a turnoff and wants to meet up later with the person following him he indicates the path he has taken by placing a broken branch as a symbolic barrier across the one he has not chosen. They use the same method to deceive certain malevolent spirit beings trying to follow them out of the forest by placing a branch across the way home that they are actually going to take. This signals to the malevolent spirit that they must take the other direction, which is the wrong one.

Sometimes it is enough to draw a line in the sand with a stick and pronounce a ritual formula as a defence against malevolent spirit beings, to prevent them from crossing this boundary.

In Hongkong you can observe people suddenly and with apparently suicidal intention plunging across to the other side of the road right in front of a bus or heavy truck, without any obvious reason. The explanation is simple. They sense they are being pursued by a malevolent spirit being and hope by this unexpected action to lure it under the wheel of the vehicle.

Malevolent spirit beings are so stupid that they do not recognize themselves, i.e. their own appearance. When they see their grotesque face in the mirror they are startled and run away from themselves. This is why *mirrors* placed over house entrances are a favourite defence against such spirit beings. Many ethnic groups work them into the more visible parts of their clothing, especially that of children.

As an alternative to mirrors hideous masks on the front of a building or the edge of a field fulfil the same purpose. In South India faces with outstretched tongue keep malevolent spirit beings at bay. Asheninca Indians use a red paste to paint special patterns on their faces, with the aim of making themselves unrecognizable and at the same time having a scaring effect.

In China it is believed that malevolent spirit beings can only move in straight lines and are not able to circumvent obstacles in their way. It is thus possible to prevent them from penetrating the house by erecting a wall some distance away across the entrance. Because of their stupidity it is even enough to insert a step of different height into the flight leading up to the entrance in order to overtax their ability to ascend the steps.

Many ethnic groups in South East Asia know about traps for catching malevolent spirit beings (Tschesnow 1985:289).

In many societies a fairly long period of time elapses before children are given a name. The view is that they cannot then be indentified by malevolent spirit beings when family members talk about them or call them. Sometimes they are given temporary names or even code names such as "stinker" or "dickhead" (Müller 1997:40), in order to scare away malevolent spirit beings. For the same reason some people change their names several times in the course of their lives.

Because of their stupidity they are totally unsuitable as helpers in time of need. Hence it is no use turning to them with requests or offerings. Specialists in religious matters, e.g. mediums, have as few dealings with them as ordinary folk, and even shamans generally have nothing to do with them. All you can do is ward them off, keep them away, by putting out something for them to consume. However, as already mentioned under 8.1, this does not happen on an altar, for instance. Often one just tosses something down, at some distance if possible, in order to divert them away from oneself and lure them in the wrong direction.

The *basic emotional mood* of malevolent spirit beings renders them disagreeable. They are considered grumpy, always discontented and quarrelsome.

Their *qualities of character* are also considerably lacking. They are seen to be devious, spiteful, selfish, brutal, destructive and capricious. Most of them have criminal tendencies. They steal like magpies, for example the produce in the fields. Hence damage to crops caused by invisible or scarcely visible pests is sometimes blamed on malevolent spirit beings.

The *mana* at their disposal is *never used positively*, to do good things. The more harmless among them are reckoned to be equipped with little or none at all. The more dangerous a malevolent spirit being is thought to be by the people concerned, the more destructive the mana attributed to it is. Generally speaking, however, their mana is considered to be less effective than that which benevolent spirit beings have at their disposal.

This, together with all the other commonalities they share with animals, lends them a status which puts them on the lowest level of all beings inhabiting the cosmos (cf. ch. 4.5).

8.3   Malevolent Spirit Beings as the Agents of Diseases

Their aggressive behaviour is demonstrated chiefly in the fact that they *bite*. In the course of this, as spirit beings they can penetrate a person's body *unnoticed*, mainly through orifices such as the mouth, nose and ears. Until well into the modern era the reason for holding the hand in front of the mouth when yawning was the belief that this prevented malevolent spirit beings from entering the body. For similar reasons when the Tuareg are travelling in the desert they cover their faces except for a narrow slit for the eyes (Neumann 1983:287). Other places which are endangered are behind the ears, the inside of the hand, the armpits, the back of the knee and folds of the skin (Errington 1983:550). Malevolent spirit beings can bring their bite to bear both outside and inside the body, and at first nothing is felt. The cause of ailments such as stomach ache, gradually becoming worse, with eventual stabbing pains, can be attributed to such bites, as well as swellings of parts of the body that cannot be otherwise explained. It does not even have to be as much as a bite to cause such symptoms. Just the fact of seeing and hearing a malevolent spirit being or a phenomenon caused by it can be enough. When the Asheninca of Peru discover a rainbow, regarded as being caused by malevolent spirit beings, they brace themselves for an attack of diarrhoea.

The notion that malevolent spirit beings are the *agents of diseases* of all kinds is a world-wide concept. It forms the basis of the medical theories of animistic cultures (**FC** ch. 15). The illnesses induced by malevolent spirit beings do not include fractures or arrow wounds, for which the causes are obvious. However, infectious diseases, strokes, lameness, impotence, loss of sight and hearing, gynaecological disorders, etc. among the people of such ethnic groups are put down to the agency of quite specific spirit beings and have to be tackled accordingly.

❑ Suggestion for own investigations: in order to understand how such health problems arise you have to comprehend how the human (and animal) body is perceived. For this you should collect all linguistic terms for the parts of the body, both exterior and interior, together with statements about the functions of the exterior and interior organs. This will provide a description of the ethnic anatomy, ethnic physiology and ethnic psychology of the culture being researched. Also important: collect contexts, not just vocabulary. Examples: Käser 1977, 1989 (part 2) and **FC** ch. 19.

The terms used for being bitten by a malevolent spirit being have an interesting structure. In many languages there are a number of different verbs for "eat" or "consume", and the right one has to be chosen to fit the particular food if you want to be linguistically correct. For example, in a number of languages of South-East Asia and Oceania there is a verb that can only be used for eating raw meat or plant material in whatever form. This verb also means "bite" in the manner of an aggressive dog or an evil spirit. Hence in cultures using language in this way malevolent spirit beings are presented conceptually as a kind of "raw food eater", "carnivore" or both together, a realistic and drastic way of characterising malevolent spirit beings.

❑ Suggestion for own investigations: find out how this is expressed in the language of your location, collecting as many contexts as possible, i.e. phrases used by mother-tongue speakers.

8.4   Malevolent Spirit Beings as the Cause of "Psychic" Conditions

Such spirit beings can also bring their bite to bear on parts of the body considered to be *the seat of the emotions and the intellect*. These are re-garded – although this can vary among ethnic groups – as the heart, kidneys, liver, stomach or simply the interior of the body. Simply as organs of the body they are just as susceptible to the bite of malevolent spirit beings as all other organs. Sometimes, as mentioned under 8.3, accidental contact with them is sufficient, however this is perceived. The difference is that these organs do not react with pain or swellings, but with typical "psychic" symp-toms such as reluctance to work, loss of motivation, depression and moodi-ness. In severe cases such a bite produces a tendency to panic reactions, rage, destructive urges, frenzy, running amok, mental derangement etc. It can even cause abnormalities such as inordinate eating and drinking. Among other types of behaviour triggered by malevolent spirit beings one can include speech disturbances, which according to European-Western understanding have a neuro-physiological cause.

Malevolent spirit beings can also produce such psychic behaviour in ani-mals. When dogs formerly considered to be shy and cowardly suddenly be-come inexplicably aggressive, this is put down to the influence of malevolent spirit beings on the "inside" of the animal.

These are "psychic" conditions which in European-Western societies are described as "occult oppression" and "possession". In this regard the follow-ing should be noted.

People brought up in an animistic environment understand such condi-tions not in terms of the occult or of possession, but as an *illness* not at all or only hardly different from a physical illness in the European-Western sense. It is also wrong to insinuate that they get themselves into such conditions because they deliberately seek contact with the spirit beings that cause them.

For an animist it is unthinkable, indeed suicidal, deliberately to enter into relationships with malevolent spirit beings. Instead one must assume from the outset that psychic conditions which animistically thinking people perceive as an illness in this special sense are regarded in principle as the consequence of inadvertence on the part of the victim or of an imperceptible and unforeseen attack by a malevolent spirit being.

European-Western observers, particularly the church workers among them, find such phenomena particularly striking, and they classify them as possession because they fulfil all the criteria which European-Western perceptions connect with them. However, to apply the term "possession" only to those events that arouse fear does not do complete justice to the reality. *In animistic understanding actual phenomena of possession are something different, being neither a state of illness nor a result of evil spirit activity.* This aspect will be picked up again and discussed in more detail later in connection with the terms "enstasy" and "ecstasy" (chs. 12, 14 and 15).

Nevertheless the unpredictability of malevolent spirit beings and the way they affect people whose lives have been shaped by an animist environment constitute a continual *source of apprehensiveness* and consequently a considerable *loss of quality of life*. If your stay in such a society is only brief, you may not infer very much, but if you live among animistically oriented people for any length of time you become aware of facts which make it very clear to you why those affected express so frequently the need to be *freed from the constraints of such thought structures*.

In any event it is quite clear that *people who think animistically perceive the consequences of contact with malevolent spirit beings differently to observers from European-Western societies*. We must be mindful of that in situations which we perceive as "occult oppression". Only those who comprehend the unfamiliar cognitive framework can assess what kind of help those affected may need: pastoral or medical. One's conduct in this situation can have very strange or inexplicable effects on them if measures aimed at releasing them from the problem are derived without forethought from one's own cognitive framework.

8.5   Exorcism[18]

This is the term which describes the procedures (practised in all religions) used to expel powers felt to be evil, and which have seized possession of a

---

[18] In describing what exorcism is I have adhered closely to Hirschberg's account 1988:142.

person, a place or an object. For this the exorcist employs a ritual in which elements of language (words), gestures (laying on of hands etc.), objects (amulets, a cross etc.) and substances (acrid smoke, gall, holy water etc.) have a part to play.

In Christianity the spirit beings to be exorcised are *commanded* to leave the particular person or place in the name of God or of Jesus (Matthew 8:16; 9:32 ff.) In the exorcism rituals of European-Western folk medicine *linguistic formulas* play an essential part. Warts, for example, are removed by being "addressed". In animistically oriented ethnic societies the exorcist is mostly a shaman, whose task it is to defeat the malevolent spirit beings by combat, or a medium, who, being by function a healer, removes malevolent spirit beings, together with their effects and consequences, by using "medical" remedies (cf. chs. 14 and 15). As a rule their rituals of exorcism contain all those notions according to which malevolent spirit beings can be kept at bay or driven away, as described under 8.1 and 8.2.

Exorcism rituals for driving out malevolent spirit beings are not confined to persons, objects and places. The evil penetrating the larger social environment can also be exorcised, e.g. early modern communities where witches, as the quintessence of evil, were burned, or a settlement of an ethnic group in South America, where in 2002 the following occurred: A man had suffered a heart attack. The appropriate shaman diagnosed this as an attack by a malevolent spirit being, but did not exorcise the patient. Instead, he ordered a pit to be dug, a fire to be lit, and the man to be burned, despite the fact that he still exhibited recognizable signs of life. It was apparent that here the evil threatened not just an individual, but his community.

8.6   Malevolent Spirit Beings and Ethical Norms

In many forms of animism malevolent spirit beings with their ability to influence the seat of the emotions and intellect are held to be the cause of evil thoughts and deeds. In other words, such spirit beings can exercise *influence on the conscience* (the super-ego or ego ideal) of the person. Such notions are at least present in the thought processes of Folk Islam (Karabila 1995, Fartacek 2002), but rather rare in the thinking of animism itself.

8.7   Malevolent Spirit Beings as the Cause of Deformities and Handicaps

In animistic cultures the ugly caricature of the person usually presented by a malevolent spirit being leads to a particular attitude towards children born with *deformities* (birthmarks, missing or extra limbs, cleft lip etc.) or with *rare physical features* (albinism, red hair). Depending on the degree of deformity they may be regarded as not even human, but literally as (materialised) malevolent spirit beings, labelled correspondingly with the term, feared and neglected. Hence they mainly die at a young age, which explains why in such communities one seldom sees adults with noticeable deformities.

The belief that non-European and especially ethnic societies are particularly caring towards disabled people is misplaced. The negative attitude towards the physically and mentally disabled is not only due to the fear of involvement with malevolent spirit beings and the associated danger; it is accentuated by the sense of *shame* felt by *the relatives of the disabled*, who are a threat to the prestige and honour of the group or family etc.

Malevolent spirit beings are blamed for generating deformities and handicaps by biting the unborn, or harming them in some other way. Sometimes such spirits are regarded as the biological fathers of deformed children, by approaching women with *violently sexual intent*. This is why in many societies women take care to sleep on their sides rather than on their backs, and with thighs closed (Crocker 1985:50,163).

According to disclosures in dreams there are malevolent spirit beings with sexual intent which approach certain women disguised as one of their brothers. The consequences are doubly devastating. The women concerned become guilty of incest, which alone can cause the children of such a pregnancy to enter the world disfigured or handicapped.

As well as malevolent spirit beings there is the notion of analogies as the cause of deformities. Pregnant women who eat roast goose risk their child being born with too long a neck, and sometimes pumpkin as food is given a taboo where women are concerned, because it can lead to children developing hydrocephalus (water on the brain).

Parallels to such notions in European-Western folk medicine, to be found well into the modern era, have been recorded by the pathologist Riede (1995).

8.8   Spirits of the Dead as Malevolent Spirit Beings

In certain societies it is assumed that the spirit doubles (the "souls") of people become malevolent spirit beings after their death, wandering around restless and "hungry", because they have endured a so-called "bad" death or for various other reasons can find no ultimate place in the beyond. The Asheninca of Peru believe that when people (apart from shamans) die they leave behind carnivorous-like aggressive spirit beings which threaten the lives even of their own posterity (Käser 1995). This will be looked at in more detail in connection with spirits of the dead (ch. 13).

8.9   Malevolent Spirit Beings and the Demons in the Bible

In the light of the characteristics described so far the notions of malevo-lent spirit beings that animists have are fairly close to what European-Western societies understand as *demons*. However, it would be completely wrong to compare them even approximately with those demonic beings con-nected in pastoral work with the phenomena of possession familiar to Chris-tian psychology and psychiatry. If I understand these correctly, they are per-sonal beings, endowed with intelligence and power, who know how to act consciously and with intent, and are under the command of Satan.

This is often an issue in Bible translation projects. There are certainly conditions attached to using the indigenous terms for malevolent spirit beings to describe the demons mentioned in the Bible if false impressions are not to arise, e.g. in the account of Jesus releasing a possessed man by commanding the spirits tormenting him to seize possession of a nearby herd of pigs (Mark 5). It becomes especially difficult in the mention of the possession of Mary Magdalene, out of whom (in the King James Version) Jesus had cast seven devils (Mark 16:9).

It is indeed unthinkable to take the term for "malevolent spirit being" at face value and use it for the biblical "Satan" if the prevailing notion in that society is that at death all people leave behind a totally malevolent spirit be-ing, as is the case among the Asheninca and many other ethnic groups, above all those of nomadic, hunter-gatherer background. To translate in this way would imply that man is the source of all devils, a theological aberration that no future indigenous theologian could come to terms with.

8.10   So-called Nature Spirits as Special Forms of (Malevolent) Spirit Beings

Not all malevolent spirit beings are considered to be equally malevolent. Some are indeed harmless or are described as neutral. They can be compared to the *goblins, trolls, fairies, giants* and *dwarves* of our own European-Western culture, existing in the natural world around us and playing tricks on people, occasionally scaring them, sometimes also helping them when in need. Among them are countless ones which are environmentally protective. They look after certain plants and animals by keeping disease, pests or ene-mies away. In the rice-growing societies of South-East Asia people refer to "rice maidens" (van der Weijden 1981; Kohl 1998), spirit beings without whose beneficial influence the harvest would turn out poor. These spirits can be dangerous, for example to hunters who are pursuing their protégés, the animals of the forest. Such notions are prevalent in hunter-gatherer societies, which also practise corresponding rituals to ward off attacks by such enraged spirit beings (or the "soul" of the animal itself which has become aggressive), to calm them before or after the hunt by ceremonially pledging to them the bones of the slain animal. An example of such a ritual is the widespread bear ceremony of ethnic groups in the North Eurasian Arctic Circle (Paproth 1976).

Such nature spirits can also be a peril to men whose hunt brings them near their territory and who have not observed a food taboo, e.g. the ban on eating pork. The smell which still lingers on them attracts the spirit beings, which approach them, sometimes even in a sexually attractive form, with the aim of holding them in their domain, or overpowering their "soul" (their dream ego) and so killing them (Strathern 1982:124).

They are also dangerous because they are in the position of exercising control over the forces of nature. They can bring about severe weather, storms, drought, floods, earthquakes, volcanic eruptions, rainbows, eclipses of the moon and sun etc.

Nature spirits usually occupy a *territory*. This does not necessarily have to be in the uncultivated areas already mentioned, which people normally avoid. If there are human settlements or cultivated land in the territory of such a nature spirit, then the latter will care for the welfare of all the living beings and plants that are there, but only under the condition that these behave in ways considered correct by that spirit. Many nature spirits develop preferences and aversions corresponding to certain taboos (things to be shunned or that are forbidden). Menstruating and pregnant women, men who have eaten garlic and whose body odour presents an affront to such a spirit being, must beware of entering its territory. If they do not heed these things, they will feel its displeasure. This is expressed in a similar way to usual malevolent spirit beings, but mostly more violent. For wrongdoings and breaking of taboos occurring in their territory they will take revenge, by setting off natural catastrophes. It is true that people believe that they can mitigate such catastrophes or prevent them in future by means of offerings, but it would be wrong to interpret such behaviour as veneration or simply as a donation on the part of the people affected. The offerings are to appease them, to ward off a threat.

In ethnological writings these spirit beings, considered to be typical but rather harmless, are mostly found in chapters entitled "nature spirits", certainly an appropriate description, bearing in mind that they inhabit the natural environment of man in large numbers and carry on their activities (and mischief) there. However, I have not devoted a special chapter to them, because nature spirits are not to be regarded as consistently harmless or neutral, but rather as difficult to control and hence are perceived as a threat in the same way as malevolent spirit beings. Moreover there is another reason for this decision:

People with an animistic cognitive framework sometimes refer to the distorted figures of political cartoons in European-Western newspapers with the word for malevolent spirit beings, even if they find them laughable. If Chuuk Islanders are asked to classify comically perceived spirit beings as benevolent or malevolent, they opt without much hesitation for the "malevolent" category, because in their culture there is no category of "neutral spirit beings". The allocation is determined by the distorted bodily proportions used to depict people in cartoons.

This conclusion is not without reservations. There are ethnic groups, e.g. the Matsigenka of Peru, where men enter into a kind of married relationship with female nature spirits (fairies) encountered while hunting (Baer 1984). From this perspective they ought to count as benevolent. On the other hand, in their role as wives, these nature spirits exercise considerable coercion over their husbands, leading one to conclude that their basic attitude is malevolent. The American author Ritchie (1996) records an account given to him by a shaman of the South-American Yanomamö about the dramatic tensions which can affect such men.

Among the malevolent spirits are those who achieve a dubious reputation as *bogeymen*, with dangerous sounding names such as night raven or the "black man". Others are notorious as *mischief-makers*, rendering certain places or regions unsafe. There are infamous ones among them particularly feared for providing through their deeds and misdeeds the content for all kinds of stories and tales, which are sometimes widely known.

8.11   Origin

The question of where malevolent spirit beings originally came from or who created them is answered in various ways. In many animistic cultures it is said that they have "always" been there. In others their origin is unknown, apart from those left behind after people have died as described under 8.8 and 8.9. Sometimes their existence is ascribed to a particularly powerful evil spirit being which created them in some manner or fashion.

8.12   In the Next Chapter

This and many other questions are answered in a much more nuanced way with regard to benevolent spirit beings, which are the subject of the next chapter.

The following sources contain more on the theme of this chapter:

Baer, Gerhard: Die Religion der Matsigenka (Ost-Peru). Monographie zu Kultur und Religion eines Indianervolkes des Oberen Amazonas. Basel (Wepf) 1984.

Bloch, Maurice; Parry, Jonathan (eds.): Death and the regeneration of life. Cambridge et al. 1982.

Crocker, Jon Christopher: Vital souls. Bororo cosmology, natural symbolism, and shamanism. Tucson, Arizona 1985.

Errington, Shelly: Embodied Sumangé in Luwu. Journal of Asian Studies XLII, No. 3, 1983:545-570.

Fartacek, Gebhard: Begegnungen mit Djinn. Lokale Konzeptionen über Geister und Dämonen in der syrischen Peripherie. Anthropos 97.2002/2:469-486.

Hirschberg, Walter (Hrsg.): Neues Wörterbuch der Völkerkunde. Berlin 1988.

Käser, Lothar: Der Begriff "Seele" bei den Insulanern von Truk. Diss. Freiburg 1977.

Käser, Lothar: Die Besiedlung Mikronesiens: eine ethnologisch-linguistische Untersuchung. Berlin 1989.

Käser, Lothar: Kognitive Aspekte des Menschenbildes bei den Campa (Asheninka). *asien afrika lateinamerika* 23.1995:29-50.

Karabila, Abdelkhalek: Die Welt der ğinn und der Heiler. Eine volkskundliche Untersuchung in der Provinz Nador (Marokko). Diss. Mainz 1995.

Kohl, Karl-Heinz: Der Tod der Reisjungfrau: Mythen, Kulte und Allianzen in einer ostindonesischen Lokalkultur. Stuttgart 1998.

Müller, Klaus E. (Hrsg.): Menschenbilder früher Gesellschaften: ethnologische Studien zum Verhältnis von Mensch und Natur. Gedächtnisschrift für Hermann Baumann. Frankfurt/Main 1983.

Müller, Klaus E.: Der gesprungene Ring: wie man die Seele gewinnt und verliert. Frankfurt am Main 1997.

Neumann, Wolfgang: Tuareg. In: Müller 1983:274-292.

Paproth, Hans-Joachim: Studien über das Bärenzeremoniell. Uppsala 1976.

Riede, Ursus-Nikolaus: Die Macht des Abnormen als Wurzel der Kultur. Der Beitrag des Leidens zum Menschenbild. Stuttgart, New York (Georg Thieme) 1995.

Ritchie, Mark Andrew: Spirit of the rainforest. A Yanomamö shaman's story. Chicago (Island Lake Press) 1996.

Strathern, Andrew: Witchcraft, greed, cannibalism and death: some related themes from the New Guinea Highlands. In: Bloch/Perry 1982:111-133.

Tschesnow, Jan W.: Historische Ethnographie der Länder Indochinas. Berlin 1985.

van der Weijden, Gera: Indonesische Reisrituale. Basel 1981.

Chapter 9
Benevolent Spirit Beings

This chapter explains the characteristics attributed to benevolent spirit beings by people living in an animistic environment, the effects and influences expected from them, their differences from European-Western perceptions, the commonalities and differences compared with benevolent spirit beings in the Bible, and where these spirit beings come from. One important passage discusses animistic perceptions of the so-called Supreme Being, that benevolent spirit being regarded as the creator of the cosmos.

9.0   Introduction

At the start of this chapter I again refer briefly to what was said in chapter 6 in general terms about animistic perceptions of spirit beings.

In terms of their character and behaviour benevolent spirit beings would appear to be the exact opposite of the malevolent ones described in ch. 8. That is not actually the case in all details. However, as a definition of the term "benevolent spirit beings" a simple reversal of the definition of "malevolent spirit beings" is quite serviceable:

Benevolent spirit beings are those which have a generally friendly attitude to human beings.

This definition also has to do with traits of *character, moods and emotions*, i.e. *psychic-moral qualities* used to describe benevolent spirit beings, which includes the recognition that they likewise possess *intellect, feelings* and *character*, in other words *personality*.

The terms which indigenous languages have for this kind of spirit being consist as a rule of the general word for "spirit beings", qualified by an adjective such as "good", "peaceful", "friendly" etc.

In addition one must take account of the fact that there are ethnic groups which refer to benevolent spirit beings as "human spirits", because they have many of the qualities of (good, normal) people, and because they are assigned to "humans" (as "souls", "dream egos"), or assigned to them during their lifetime.

❑ Suggestion for own investigations: find out how this manifests itself in the language where you are located, collecting as many contexts as possible, i.e. phrases used by mother-tongue speakers.

9.1 Physical Characteristics of Benevolent Spirit Beings

These spirits are generally imagined to have *human form* (anthropomorph). They only appear rarely in animal form (theriomorph), and only under certain conditions or with particular intent (cf. 9.9). The most reliable feature indicating that a spirit being is (almost) certainly benevolent is its complete identity with the external appearance of a human being.

Bodily size and *weight* correspond to those of a person of similar height. In spite of its spirit nature such a spirit being can leave *footprints* in soft ground owing to its weight.

Its bodily weight is yet more apparent when as an ancestral spirit, for example, it is sitting on the shoulders of a medium (possession!) and speaking to its living relatives. If it is a man-size spirit being the crouching or sitting medium may sometimes groan under its weight. Child-size spirit beings are felt to be light, according to what mediums say (cf. ch. 15.6).

Benevolent spirit beings show no signs of disease, physical defects or deformities. They often reflect the *ideal form of beauty* of the respective ethnic group.

Like all spirit beings they are able to exercise impressive *physical strength*. If required they can uproot trees and move lumps of rock around effortlessly. In this regard they are mostly even superior to malevolent spirit beings.

They can *move, run, climb, fly* and *swim* freely, and they like to spend time in *dancing* and similar pleasures. They *breathe* like we do, but can manage for an unlimited period of time without air. When they *sleep*, this is not because they physically need to, but because they consider it to be a pleasant way of passing the time.

Benevolent spirit beings wear *clothing* and *jewellery* and sometimes carry *tools* (of a similar spirit nature to themselves), by which they can be recognized.

They are said to have the same *body temperature* as all living beings. They are considered to be warm-blooded. This could explain why mediums perspire in the course of a long contact (a so-called séance) with the spirit of a deceased person during which the medium and the spirit of the dead are in close contact with each other (cf.ch.15.6).

Their *body odour* is quite the opposite of repellent. They exude a pleasant, partly *beguiling aroma*. If one becomes aware of a pleasant smell of unknown origin somewhere, then the presence of a benevolent spirit being somewhere in the vicinity is suspected.

Benevolent spirit beings can *laugh, weep, speak* clearly and *sing* like ordinary people. Many can speak a foreign language, and there are polyglot geniuses among them who can express themselves in many languages. The evidence for this comes from dreams as well as other sources. However, people who are awake are not addressed directly by them, but rather via a medium (cf. ch. 15).

If there is any doubt about identity then their language ability can certainly differentiate them from malevolent spirit beings, who sometimes appear in human-like form but have no articulate speech. If a spirit being questioned by a medium does not speak or only produces incomprehensible noises then this is proof that it is malevolent and cannot be addressed.

There are ethnic groups who use a *special language* when contacting spirit beings, e.g. the Ngaju on Kalimantan (Borneo), where the mediums have to use the so-called *Basa Sangiang* in all types of rituals in which spirit beings are involved (Kuhnt-Saptodewo 1993:40).

Their *sense organs* are extraordinarily well developed. They can *see* and *hear* much better than both we and animals can, but are just as sensitive to *noise* as their malevolent companions. Loud noises also keep them away permanently. This results in a certain contradiction. If malevolent spirit beings are to be driven away by firecrackers or other noise effects, then it seems that one has to accept that the benevolent ones will also be put to flight. Apparently the intention behind making the noise aimed at driving the spirits away determines largely which kind is repelled. If the noise is made with the clear purpose of chasing off malevolent spirit beings then those are the only ones it affects.

Benevolent spirit beings do not need to take in *nourishment* in order to be able to "live". They do it out of pure pleasure, and in contrast to the malevolent ones are extremely choosy. Many of them are considered to be pronounced gourmets on account of their *sense of smell* and *taste*.

Among the foods of strong taste which they spurn are e.g. fermented breadfruit and salted fish, acidic fruits such as oranges and lemons, and anything bitter. Those who have dealings with benevolent spirit beings or have been specially directed to them for help, e.g. mediums and shamans, must avoid such foods. For them they are taboo.

The spirit beings' senses of smell and taste have a fairly decisive influence on the form of the *food offering* that people bring to them. It is mostly the spirits of deceased relatives, so-called ancestral spirits, to whom such an offering is directed. These accept only mild, tasty and freshly prepared food. Anything salty, sour, with bitter and sharp spices is as a rule not suitable as a food offering. Raw onions on an ancestral altar would be unthinkable and would repel the recipients or even arouse their wrath, with serious consequences.

The fact that spirit beings have a sense of smell is one of their most astonishing physical attributes.
It comes as a surprise to realise that this attribute of benevolent spirit beings is a *worldwide* notion among animistic societies. As will become apparent, it plays an important part not only in sacrificial procedures but also in the related concepts of man, with consequent outworking on behaviour in daily life, at burials, in the practices of mediums and shamans, and numerous other activities.

Bad odours have a repellent effect on benevolent spirit beings, make them angry and drive them away. By contrast pleasant ones attract them, even over great distances, and calm them.

They find human body odour repulsive. Anyone who has dealings with them must pay the most careful attention possible to physical cleanliness. In many cultures no benevolent spirit being would approach a medium who puts no value on personal hygiene.

Among the odours disdained by benevolent spirit beings is that of human genitalia in particular. They avoid menstruating women. This puts such women in danger, because without the presence of benevolent spirit beings they are vulnerable to malevolent ones, which are drawn to bad odours.

This may be the concrete reason for the "impurity" ascribed to women in this condition. It explains the radical measures they take to "separate" themselves as a rule during their period, for example having to live in specially prepared accommodation outside the actual settlement. Otherwise their attraction for malevolent spirit beings would endanger their neighbours.

Benevolent spirit beings are *sexual beings*. In general their sexual interests are directed towards their own kind and not towards people or animals as is the case with malevolent ones. However, there are definitely ethnic groups in which stories of sexual relations between a benevolent spirit being and a man are known, e.g. between a fairy and a hunter who encounter each other in the forest. In many societies it is believed that the union of two benevolent spirit beings produces so-called "spirit children", who may possibly be assigned to the body of a new-born child and accompany it throughout its life as its spirit double (its "soul"). However, female spirit beings do not necessarily become pregnant through sexual intercourse. Their sexual activity is part of their *pleasure-oriented* approach to life.

Benevolent spirit beings are not limited by space or time. They are just as *active by day as at night*, but only *visible in exceptional cases*. They can make themselves visible at any time or simply become visible, like malevolent spirit beings. It is seldom possible for ordinary people to see a benevolent spirit being, at any rate not while they are awake, but at most while dreaming. An exception would be e.g. the hunter and the fairy, as mentioned above. It is mostly mediums and shamans who are assumed to be able to see benevolent spirit beings, not only in dreams and in a trance, but also when awake. Nevertheless it is one of their characteristics to show themselves or make their presence felt more rarely than malevolent spirit beings. When benevolent spirit beings make themselves visible their forms appear so bright that even in daylight they sometimes stand out well against the background. At night there is a greater chance of seeing them, because it is said that their form emits a *pale luminescence* which cannot be perceived in the bright light of day. In another respect they embody that which in European-Western societies is understood as a "shining light". Light is indeed the element in which they live.

9.2   Psychic and Intellectual Characteristics of Benevolent Spirit Beings

Benevolent spirit beings think, decide, have memories and desires, feel joy, love, sadness and anger, i.e. they possess a *seat of the emotions, intellect and character* like we do. They have no fear of light and fire, unlike malevolent spirit beings, who can be driven away by them.

In essence benevolent spirit beings know *no fear*. The fact that they can be driven away by noise is a sign of their disdain of it, not their fear of it. What does command their respect is the presence of benevolent spirit beings who are superior to them, who have more influence, status and power (mana!) than they do, as for example the so-called Supreme Being who made the world and is usually regarded also as the creator of all spirit beings (cf. 9.10). Him they meet with awe and obedience, for otherwise they risk arousing his wrath, which even they must fear.

Their *basic emotional mood* and their *qualities of character* are decidedly positive and render them congenial. They are considered to be even-tempered and serene, polite and approachable, ready to help, brave, prudent and perceptive, self-controlled, conciliatory and honest, industrious and constant. In general terms they adhere strictly to the same ethical code as ourselves.

As a rule the *intelligence* of benevolent spirit beings is *particularly highly* estimated. In stories told about them they appear as clever, wise, quick to understand and with a good memory. In these things they are far superior to the malevolent ones. It is *not possible* for us humans *to deceive them or outsmart them*. Also there is as a rule no magic means ("defensive spell") that could have any effect on benevolent spirit beings. In any case the desire to defend oneself against them would be self-contradictory, for:

On account of their intelligence they are outstandingly suited as helpers in time of need. Hence one can turn to them with requests and offerings. Preferably it is the mediums and shamans, being the experts in their societies with regard to matters of religion, who have dealings with them and deliberately seek to get into contact with them.

With their positive attitude and intelligence benevolent spirit beings are friendly towards man. They are well-disposed towards us and are concerned to let things run in an orderly fashion. This disposition, a feature of their "inner state", i.e. the seat of their emotions, intellect and character, is that which actually enables them to appear as benevolent spirit beings, and it is in this that their essential difference from the malevolent spirit beings is to be seen, whose malevolent intentions are considered to be axiomatic.

In spite of their intelligence and basic positive mood their disposition can occasionally darken. They can become angry enough to give the impression that they are malevolent spirit beings. The reasons why a benevolent spirit being can become aggressive are inappropriate behaviour of other spirit beings, the machinations of their malevolent counterparts, and *wrong actions of people* who do not respect their wishes and demands. That annoys ancestral spirits particularly.

However, their ill-nature is only temporary and can be mitigated by two circumstances. Those who do not go against their wishes but accede to their demands need not fear their wrath. And those who have aroused their wrath can reckon on their willingness to be *reconciled.*

Many spirit beings considered to be benevolent sometimes show themselves to be only hostile, for no apparent reason. It is assumed that they have become malevolent spirit beings. This means that a change of roles, from benevolent to malevolent spirit beings, is possible. As a rule the opposite – those originally malevolent becoming benevolent – cannot happen.

The *mana* that they possess is *generally positive*, having a good effect. The level of mana at their disposal depends on their status within the hierarchy of the spirit world of the ethnic group. On the whole their mana has a higher level of effectiveness than the mana of malevolent spirit beings. This in particular definitely lends them a status which determines their place in the cosmos on a higher level than man.

9.3   Benevolent Spirit Beings as Agents of "Psychic" Conditions

The positive mana which distinguishes benevolent spirit beings is the basis of the effect which they have on the human seat of emotions, intellect and character. When they are present among people, they have a calming effect and so prevent outbreaks of open aggression which would disturb or destroy community cohesion.

However, along with their positive effects benevolent spirit beings can also, like all such beings, penetrate someone's body and unfold their psychic influences there. In order to exercise these positive effects on ordinary people who are neither mediums nor shamans it is as a rule sufficient for them to be in their immediate vicinity. Not even direct physical contact is necessary.

It is worth noting that not only people's emotions and character are positively influenced in this way, but also the intellect, the capabilities of which are enhanced by the presence of benevolent spirit beings to the level of experiences of "illumination". Hence it is expedient for students from societies with an animistic background to do all they can before an examination to ensure the close presence of benevolent spirit beings, by carrying out the appropriate rituals and heeding taboos. For example, this means that they avoid sexual intercourse during the days leading up to the exam. Benevolent spirit beings would feel oppressed by the ensuing body odour. If examination candidates did not heed such taboos, this violation could endanger their performance in the test in a way that would lead one to assume that they had been "abandoned by all good spirits".

9.4   The Abodes of Benevolent Spirit Beings

In contrast to malevolent spirit beings they reside not only in the open in the natural world but have a preference for *people's habitations*, or at least in their immediate vicinity. They are indeed at home in "cultivated regions", not in the wild "uncultivated" ones. Of course they can also betake themselves everywhere where malevolent spirit beings are accustomed to reside.

The realm of the sky (animistically understood) with its numerous layers is a favourite residence of benevolent spirit beings. In the spirit-like landscapes and settlements to be found there they lead a life of joy and happiness, existing in a kind of land of *Cockaigne* or *paradise*, free of adversity, often really living it up. Here they indulge in pleasurable pursuits or deal with all kinds of tasks allocated to them by spirit beings of higher rank. They leave here according to desire or necessity in order to be near to us. They are drawn particularly to places of dancing and celebration. Ancestral spirits are attracted mostly to the vicinity of their living relatives or to places where they themselves spent their human lives.

According to the expectations of people who think in animistic terms a benevolent spirit being has to be really close by if it wishes to help human beings with a problem. When such a situation arises benevolent spirit beings are immediately aware of it, even over very great distances. As a rule, however, they do not get involved from a distance, although they would be able to do so, but move to the locality concerned.

The presence of benevolent spirit beings, e.g. ancestral spirits, in the immediate vicinity of their living relatives can be secured by means of objects with which those spirit beings have some connection, or they can be represented simply in a symbolic way. Thiel (1977:118-119) reports that for this purpose the African Yansi keep so-called "ancestor things" in the village or in the home, e.g. the horn of a roan antelope, filled with soil and snail shells from the grave of that person. There are ancestral pots, baskets, statuettes, masks, wooden artefacts, trees, all with a comparable function.

There are also locations on the earth's surface frequented by benevolent spirit beings and considered to have a spirit nature similar to the spirit inhabitants. Such places are invisible and no one knows their exact position, and so people on the way to the fields or going hunting often enter and traverse them unawares. Benevolent spirit beings indeed have nothing against that. However, they do occasionally feel it to be a disturbance and punish the unknowing intruder. He may get lost, become ill, or meet with some other misfortune.

Among the numerous spirit places frequented by benevolent spirit beings are famous ones where many and powerful spirit beings like to gather. The names of the places and landscapes are rather like the names one gives to local meadows to help in finding the way. For the Chuuk Islanders *Tupwuniyón* ("sunset") is such a place. It is imagined to be "somewhere in the west" and is famous on account of its shining red and yellow hue.

9.5   Spirits of the Dead as Benevolent Spirit Beings (Ancestral Spirits)

Among the benevolent spirit beings the largest group, of which there are countless numbers in most animistic cultures, are the surviving good spirits of the deceased. However, this statement needs to be qualified, for not all animistically oriented societies understand spirits of the dead as a continuation of the personality of the deceased, serving the yet living relatives as ancestral spirits. Indeed, the following should be noted.

The perceptions concerning what kind of spirit being a deceased person finally becomes is decisively dependent on whether the society concerned consists of *settled farmers* or *nomadic* hunter-gatherers and cattle-breeders. The spirits of the dead in agricultural communities usually become benevolent spirit beings, but the spirits of the dead in hunter-gatherer and nomadic communities are usually reckoned to be malevolent and dangerous. *For this reason veneration of ancestors*, apart from exceptions, *is only to be expected in (settled) farming communities, or in those derived from them.*

A benevolent spirit of the dead looks so perfectly like the corresponding deceased person that the latter is recognizable in the former. This is apparent from mediums and shamans, who are able to perceive spirits of the dead when awake, and from dreams in which ordinary people, too, get to see the deceased, and to experience with them what they are doing in the beyond.

Their abilities also permit benevolent spirit beings to adopt other forms. In African ethnic groups ancestors sometimes appear in the guise of snakes or lions, i.e. as creatures considered to be powerful on account of their characteristics. Sometimes they reveal that they are ancestors by behaving differently from what one would expect in such animals. For example, they cannot be driven away by the usual means.

The deceased person can be further recognized by the fact that his spirit is wearing his clothes and decorative items, and carrying his work tools, i.e. the spirit counterparts of those things (cf. ch. 6). Such a notion seems also to have been known in the Old Testament, when Saul, for example, recognises the spirit of the dead prophet Samuel by his clothes (1. Samuel 28:14).

However, physical changes such as the loss of a hand suffered when alive are as a rule not visible on the good spirit of the deceased.

Benevolent spirits of the dead always remain *in close relationship with the area in which the deceased persons previously assigned to them passed their lives*, even if not continuously present. If they stay away from the familiar territory for any considerable length of time they may suffer from homesickness. It is said that they have a longing for their living relatives and acquaintances left behind.

In this connection it is important for each culture to investigate what are the individual sentiments which led that spirit of the dead to behave in this particular way. In ethnic societies the psychic and emotional ties with the people one lives with play an enormously important part. One can therefore assume that they are aware of sentiments which they claim are especially typical of the members of a social group and have indeed actually determined its cohesion and continuance. There is a high probability that these ties are revealed in a clearly understandable expression of the language, describing a sentiment which that ethnic group regards as the highest relational virtue.

Thus among the Chuuk Islanders there is a sentiment which they call *ttong*, an important, if not the most important relational virtue. Family members have mutual emotional ties which result in quite definite mutual expectations. As a rule a relative will do nothing which would hurt other relatives.

He helps them to avoid misfortune, to overcome emergencies, and cares for their welfare and the continuance of the group. The same psychological bonding also exists in the reverse direction between the living members of a social group and the surviving benevolent spirits of its deceased members. They calculate that these spirits behave like living relatives, and all the more so since benevolent spirits of the dead, like all spirit beings, are not limited spatially or temporally and so have considerably extended opportunities at their disposal for looking after the living. They easily find out where to catch most fish or hunt most animals, where a missing boat is drifting on the river or sea and how things are with the crew. As spirit beings they can become aware in good time of the plans of any malevolent spirit beings to inflict disease and other misfortunes on the living. In such instances they have the possibility of asking for the help of powerful spirit beings and thus continually prevent calamity on behalf of the living. They promote fertility in the gardens and ensure that many children are born. In short, their main purpose is the preservation of the group.

This means that benevolent spirits of the dead continue to be members of the social unit to which the deceased belonged and whose personality these spirits of the dead perpetuate. They are not only understood in this way by the living members of the group, but also understand each other in the same way.

People of an animistic cognitive framework do not only have this concept of the group with regard to families and clans, i.e. of the same lineage. Local groupings such as village communities can regard the spirits of deceased fellow inhabitants as "their spirits of the dead". In the same way the inhabitants of several regions in an area feel connected to the good spirits of their deceased fellow human beings. Even the representatives of the various "occupations" or "agencies" such as boat builders, rainmakers, smiths etc. have a group feeling. In many respects their members feel themselves dependent on the benevolent spirits of their deceased "colleagues", who as spirits of the dead continue to be in charge of and concerned with their area of responsibility in the same way as ministers.

However, for people who think animistically the most important relationship between the living and the spirits of the dead continues to be their connectedness with the spirits of the dead of their own families and clan structure. It follows that the integration of benevolent spirits of the deceased into the group of those still living forms an *extension of that group into the beyond*. Thiel, who has made a particular study of these notions among African ethnic groups, calls the concept (1977:109) the "prolongation of this-world's social relationships into the beyond".

Such groups, whether based on relatives or on a locality, do not place importance indiscriminately on all spirits of the dead, but only on the more significant among them. These are the ones who during their human lives possessed special status on account of their knowledge and capabilities. Only these can become *ancestral spirits* in the accepted sense (Roser 2000:48).

❏ Suggestion for own investigations: find out which spirits of the dead, in contrast to spirit beings generally, are given names, and what are the linguistic forms for expressions such as "our ancestors, forbears, tribal spirits" etc.

It would appear that the terms *ancestor cult* and *ancestor veneration*, commonly used in this connection, have crept into the discussion. The African ethnologist Nabofa represents the view (1983:313) that no African "prays to his dead grandfather", but converses with him, putting questions and requests, just as he does with his father still alive. Hence it is not a matter of ancestor veneration or a cult in the sense of "worship". Thiel also (1977:115), one of the best authorities on the various aspects of this practice, comes to the conclusion that ancestor veneration is in principle no different from contact with one's living elders. Young people bring their concerns to older ones. The oldest turn to the (even older) deceased, the only difference in the procedure of making contact being that it is no longer with people but with the spirits of the dead. On the other hand Thiel (1999:209) is right to point out that, if the dealings with ancestral spirits are ritualised and hence can be understood as a sacred activity, then they can be described in terms of worship or a cult. In the event the boundaries between social organisation and the sphere of religion are so vague that one has the impression that they merge seamlessly into each other.

This also becomes apparent during festivals such as All Saints and All Souls. In Mexico Christian families gather at the cemetery on these days to share an exuberant festival in the company of their deceased relatives, with all kinds of good food. In his account of this Thiel (1999:205) perceives, rightly in my view, a kind of ancestor cult. Orthodox Christians in Russia practise something similar at Easter. They believe that their deceased relatives "cross over" to them from the beyond for one day.

Warneck 1909 and Stöhr 1976 have written particularly detailed ethnographic studies on the theme of ancestor veneration and its basis in the concept of man.

9.6   Benevolent Spirits of the Dead and Ethical Norms

Communities of people function on the basis of rules, which have to be adhered to if the group is to continue to function properly as a social entity.

The observance of some rules is necessary for the communal activity of all members of the group, and if one of its members disregards them the functioning of that group, and eventually its very existence, is endangered. A father who does not provide sufficient food for his family puts its welfare and hence its very existence at risk. If it is to be preserved the head of the family and all the other members must keep the rules that are prescribed to them. In order for such rules to guarantee the continuance of those group structures which are important for survival they are anchored so strongly in the people's unconscious that they take on the character of ethical norms, which must direct the behaviour of the group members.

The norms form a yardstick for values. They determine how the group members evaluate their own and each other's behaviour. The good is that which corresponds to the norms and hence maintains the group. Anything contrary to the norm and hence against the continuance of the group is considered bad.

Each person who can be assumed to be rational, i.e. having the ability to act "rightly", knowing what is good and bad in each circumstance. In many instances this recognition is sufficient to cause him or her to behave according to the norms. However, frequently it is not sufficient, namely when the interests of the individual conflict with the interests of the group. In such an event group members tend to act against the norm and hence badly. This constitutes a danger for the solidarity and unity of the community. Therefore in group-oriented and group-dependent societies adherence to the norms can be maintained more purposefully and permanently than is possible through appealing to the conscience and sense of responsibility of the individual.

If ethical norms are under threat animistically oriented societies have at their disposal a characteristic array of notions in which the benevolent spirits of the dead in any social group, i.e. the ancestral spirits, play a central part.

All actions detrimental to the group, theft, murder, deceit, infringement of duty of care etc. are avenged by them. If a member of the community disregards valid norms he arouses the wrath of the ancestral spirits and must reckon on being punished by them accordingly. Every individual member of the group knows this, and is aware of this knowledge as an inhibition against offending the norms. In this way the existence of the benevolent spirits of the dead guarantees the validity of ethical principles in the broadest sense.

All those who infringe the norms put themselves in a condition for which many ethnic groups have a linguistic term meaning something like "guilty" or "sinful". This term comprises everything which puts the benevolent spirits of the dead in an ungracious mood and must arouse their wrath.

❏ Suggestion for own investigations: find the term for "guilty", investigate all its
   derivatives and compounds, collect further all actions and their consequences
   leading to the condition of "being guilty". This should produce a catalogue of
   norms valid for that particular society.

Among the acts which lead to "guilt" are in particular offences against the
ban on incest, i.e. disobeying the rules of sexual distancing from all people
who would otherwise make one incur the guilt of incest. It includes also
crimes such as theft, murder, and indeed every act of unfriendliness towards
members of one's own group. It can even happen that a totally unintended
insult involving a member of the group can incur the sanctions of the benevolent spirits of the dead against the offender, especially if the person insulted
is of higher ranking.

This explains the conspicuous need of the Chuuk Islanders to seek reconciliation with someone of superior status if they are aware that they have
inadvertently offended him. Even the suspicion of having aroused his resentment can trigger the attempt to pacify him.

One can also turn the benevolent spirits of deceased family members
against oneself by not taking account of their personal interests, inclinations
and wishes. For example such a spirit being can ask via a medium that a particular meal be prepared as a "gift" ("offering"). If those so requested do not
take this wish seriously they become "guilty" in the sense described. Their
behaviour does not only violate all the rules concerning treatment of relatives, but must also count as a serious transgression against the demand for
respect towards an older, and therefore superior person. For indeed the benevolent spirits of the dead consider themselves as such, being older than the
living. Moreover as spirit beings they have more influence over the course of
events than the latter, for they possess heightened mana.

The demand to show respect towards one's own benevolent spirits of the
dead is a further indication that they are still regarded as members of the
group, and that they not only represent an extension of the group into the
beyond but also at the same time the invisible apex of the hierarchical group
structure of the living.

People of animistic background generally expect a relative to behave in a
partisan manner for the benefit of the group. This means that unjust treatment
of someone outside the group has to be taken on board and is considered less
serious than unjust treatment of a member of one's own group. If a member
of the group has committed a violation of the norm against a stranger to the
group and is consequently in a difficult position, he can count on the other
members of the group being on his side.

As relatives benevolent spirits of the dead behave in the same way. **Their anger and subsequent punishment is only to be expected if the offence is against one's own group. As a rule norm violations against those outside the group do not have any consequences.** One's own ancestral spirits initiate no proceedings. They even defend the perpetrator against the ancestral spirits of the others who might wish to take revenge on him. However, the person involved does not remain completely free from the fear of reprisals. Indeed it could be that the ancestral spirits of the other group are more powerful than those of his own group. Nevertheless, as a rule norm violations that people commit cannot be avenged by spirits of the dead who do not belong to the group. Overstepping one's authority with regard to another group would bring their own ancestral spirits into the arena. Such instances would create conflict in the beyond.

The fact that in guiding the behaviour of a social group in this way ancestral spirits are exclusively responsible for their own group has far-reaching implications for the way ethics and morality are understood. It is through this that the ethical principles directing the behaviour of the group acquire their actual status. They can only be understood in the context of the group. Morality is not universally valid, unlike in European-Western thought. "Guilt" and "sin" are not defined with reference to a "transcendent" authority, i.e. to a Supreme Being or deity, however conceived. *It is first and foremost the society which lends the ethical norms their credentials and validity.*

9.7   Benevolent Spirits of the Dead as the Instigators of Calamities

If an ancestral spirit is angry, then it is to be expected that a corresponding action will ensue. Whatever he does in his wrath is regarded as punishment for norm violations, whether these are known or unknown. The punishment takes the form of a calamitous event *at some unforeseeable location* in the group.

This means that such a misfortune *does not necessarily affect the person who actually violated the norm* and thus incurred "guilt". In every case of norm violation it is uncertain which member of the group the punishment will target, and at what time. *The consequences of a norm violation have to be born by the group as a whole.* For the individual who did not behave according to the norms this constitutes both a risk and a special responsibility. Hence the knowledge of this risk is a factor exercising considerable pressure on the members of the group to observe the norms.

There is also uncertainty about the time delay between the deed and the punishment. Sometimes several years can elapse before the ancestral spirits decide to impose sanctions concerning a wrong deed. Moreover there is no recognizable connection between the kind of misdemeanour and the kind of resulting calamity.

The disaster that falls upon the group is almost always the illness and death of (one of) their members. The behaviour of a father who endangers the existence of his family through his abuse of alcohol can be the reason why one of his children becomes seriously ill, drowns, or is injured in some other way. Disaster can also take the form of an outbreak of famine because the ancestral spirits have ruined the fields by flooding, withheld the rain or caused a typhoon to destroy the whole structure of the food supply.

For such societies calamity in its various manifestations as a conse-quence of "sin" (as understood by each culture) is in the final analysis always death, or at least a precursor of it.

Whether it is famine, accident, disease, damage to property or any other calamity as the consequence of an individual's violation of the norms, it *always targets the body*, i.e. the destruction of the physical existence of the members of the group, never their spirit doubles ("souls").

Hence punishment for "sins" always concerns one's form of existence in this world. Notions of a "hell" where people must atone after (physical) death for wrongdoings committed during their "visible" life are rare ex-ceptions in animistic concepts of the cosmos.

Such an exception is found among the Karen of South-East Asia, who be-lieve that spirits of deceased evil people arrive at a place in the beyond where they are cooked in boiling oil (Mischung 1979:140).

9.8   Benevolent Spirits of the Dead with Special Status

Not all benevolent spirits of the dead are of real significance for a social group, able to attain the status of ancestral spirits. Some of them become more well-known than all the others. People speak with admiration of them, of *their capabilities and achievements*. The latter are the basis of their posi-tion in the hierarchy of the spirits of the dead. These are men and women who were known for their intelligence, their knowledge, and their predomi-nantly positive disposition, and already of particularly good repute during their lifetime, having conceived and given birth to progeny, lived in good accord with their neighbours, and completed all rites of passage (Thiel 1999:208). They are for the most part deceased people of titular[19] rank

---

[19] In ethnology the use of the term "chieftain" is now "no longer politically correct".

("chieftains"), famous magicians, healers, mediums and shamans. They are all people who in their lifetime possessed special status on account of the features of their personality.

Such spirit beings give proof of their elevated status by showing that they are able to perform unusual things. They can do this because they possess an especially large degree of mana, enabling them to deal with problems which appear hardly or not at all solvable. This means that they are more able than other benevolent spirits of the dead to help the living in situations of need, provide sufficient food and progeny, eradicate disease, bring success to undertakings of all kinds etc. They also know how to cope on their own in all situations. They converse in clear, understandable language, and their pronouncements show that their honesty and uprightness are incorruptible. They do not lie or deceive. If any one of their prophecies (e.g. via a medium) is not accurate, this demonstrates, it is claimed, that the tenure of their status is over and they have become malevolent "lying spirits".

In many ethnic groups honesty and love of truth is ascribed in a special sense to the benevolent spirits of deceased children. Moreover the Chuuk Islanders always hold that such spirits give proof of special status. On the other hand there are societies in which the spirits of deceased children are not credited with any of these qualities and have no status, for the simple reason that they died before they could acquire it.

Spirit beings of high status are coveted counsellors in all of life's situations on account of their enormous knowledge and ability. Living people of rank and leadership inquire of them concerning political decisions and their consequences. Fundamentally there is no issue which could not be put before such a spirit being.

As well as this it is possible for them to impact the body, the seat of the emotions, the mind and character, and influence people's behaviour without them being directly aware of it. If such a spirit being puts the right thoughts into the mind of a healer, he will give a particularly exact diagnosis of a disease. A craftsman receiving such help unawares operates his tool with a surer hand and is in less danger of ruining a valuable piece of work through carelessness.

This exertion of influence, which the living experience unawares, is sometimes linked with the notion that the effective spirit being is close to those particular persons or has bodily contact with them. The Chuuk Islanders say of a person whose particular qualities or achievements stand out, that a benevolent spirit of this kind "is sitting on him, riding him" (*wááni*). In a sense this relates to a notion of "possession", but with the effect being in all respects regarded as positive, for the thinking, feeling and determining of the person involved are thereby "illumined, enlightened".

Even before their death such people also give rise to the expectation that they will become spirit beings of this kind. The outward indication of their status is the name they acquire after their transformation into a spirit of the dead, which they themselves also convey via a medium. Their names signify them as "master" or "mistress" of a region (e.g. *Ratu Kidul*, equivalent to "Mistress of the South Sea", Schlehe 1998), indicate them as a specialist in some sphere of that particular society such as birth and nurture (e.g. *Nikow-upwuupw*, approximating to "birth-originator"), or as a talent in the area of social entertainment (e.g. *Sowupwérûk* "master of the dance").

When it comes to the names they give themselves, or which people give them, the imagination knows almost no bounds. The names of benevolent spirits of the dead endowed with somewhat less status denote those who bear them according to various physical characteristics, e.g. "yellow man"; or in connection with objects which they always carry around with them, e.g. "fish basket", or relating to typical ways of behaving, e.g. "mast climber".

The remaining benevolent spirits of the dead, who are unable to attain this status, retain the names of the people whose personality they are perpetuating. It is true there are also malevolent spirit beings with individual names, but they did not acquire these themselves but received them from the people. If spirits of the dead give themselves new names and announce them via a medium the living are obliged to regard them as endowed with special status.

9.9   So-called Assistant Spirits or Guardian Spirits (of the Shaman)

These form a category of spirit beings which like the nature spirits are difficult to classify and hence are to be regarded as a special case among the benevolent spirit beings. The reason why they are not easy to classify here is because they appear mostly in *animal form* and hence actually fulfil one of the essential formal criteria for malevolent spirit beings.

There is another reason why they are to be regarded as a special case. Spirit beings of this kind are actually only to be found in forms of animism which have no awareness of benevolent spirits of the dead or ancestral spirits. In societies organised in this way the shaman, whether a man or a woman, is known as the intermediary between this materially conceived world and the sphere of spirit objects and beings, the beyond. The complexity of notions linked with this office cannot be presented in detail until ch.14, but the following can be discussed in advance.

As a rule the activities of shamans do not involve spirits of the dead or ancestral spirits but *guardian spirits* and *assistant spirits*. It is believed that they have always been exclusively spirit beings, having never possessed a body as a material counterpart. There are exceptions in many societies, guardian spirits and assistant spirits whose existence is regarded as perpetuating the personality of deceased shamans.

A so-called *guardian spirit* possesses particularly effective mana and is therefore considered to be especially powerful. In any fight against malevolent spirit beings, spirit monsters and demons of all kinds, with which the world of spirit objects and beings teems, and which can endanger a shaman on his journey to the beyond (cf. ch. 14), a guardian spirit is mostly victorious. Hence guardian spirits are to be regarded as the *shaman's bodyguards*.

A so-called *assistant spirit* likewise possesses particularly effective mana, which in his case manifests itself as outstanding knowledge and wealth of influence of all kinds. Assistant spirits are the *shaman's counsellors*.

Guardian spirits and assistant spirits are regarded as benevolent and therefore appear to the shaman in human form. Many among them would win a beauty contest if they could participate in it (Baer1984:155). In spite of their benevolence, however, they can also appear in animal form. This reveals a certain contradiction, since according to ch. 8 the malevolence of a spirit being is expressly manifest in the form of a (mostly aggressive) animal. But since shamanism is characteristic of societies in which hunting or stock breeding is important for securing their existence it is not surprising that here also there can be animal forms in which (benevolently conceived) guardian spirits and assistant spirits are manifest: the bear, the wolf, the eagle and other raptors, the stag, the reindeer and the hare, and also in South America the jaguar. One should not be surprised that this list contains a number of dangerous and hence defensively powerful animal forms. They are ranked as courageous and therefore well able to exercise successfully their protective function as the shaman's bodyguards.

It is also appropriate for such animal forms to serve occasionally as a *means of transport* for the shaman (or for his dream ego on the journey to the beyond; cf. ch. 14). Assistant spirits in the form of great birds bear him through the air, and he employs the reindeer and stag as mounts.

The relationship between the shaman and his guardian spirits and assistant spirits is described as friendly, which presupposes that they must be benevolent spirit beings. One shaman called them "visitors" or "associates". It is they who choose him as their shaman, as will be demonstrated later. The more assistant spirits he has in his service, the greater is his own mana.

Sometimes, however, they can pose a danger to him, e.g. if he does not follow their instructions. It can happen that he has to ask their permission if he wants to marry. In other respects also he is often dependent on their favour. Sometimes they punish him for the smallest mistakes made during a ritual, by confiscating his "soul" (his dream ego) and in this way being able to kill him. He also makes himself guilty of a transgression worthy of death if he passes on knowledge gained from them to unauthorised people (Crocker 1985), or if he dissociates himself from them.

Among the benevolent spirit beings with high status there exists in practically all forms of religion with a basic animistic structure one being whose rank transcends all others. It is the so-called Supreme Being.

9.10   The Supreme Being

In such religions the Supreme Being is almost always a *man, very ancient* and frequently *otiose*[20], i.e. inactive. In many of the stories told about him he is too old even to be able to move. The Supreme Being usually inhabits the topmost level of the sky, far away from mankind, and no longer leaves that sphere. This is in contrast to the period immediately after the creation, during which he still lived among mankind. If he gets involved at all in what is happening in the world it is by directing spirit beings, which are subordinate to himself, as a rule the ancestral spirits of people on earth. These spirits have immediate access to the Supreme Being and can therefore act as intermediaries between himself and mankind.

Among his most outstanding qualities there is one great feat: he has (in most of the stories) *created the world (the cosmos)*, or more precisely those things in the world which belong to all people irrespectively, the sea, the water, fire.

The act of creation itself is an act of the mind, like *thinking, willing, singing* or *speaking*. After creation the Supreme Being lived for a while among mankind, but then withdrew far away into the sky on account of the depravity of mankind, and since then has no longer involved himself in its concerns. This means that although people still venerate him they no longer have much to do with him, bringing no offerings and seldom praying to him. This is indeed in contrast to their behaviour towards spirit beings, which are ranked lower than the Supreme Being.

---

[20] The Latin *otiosus* has a broader range of meaning: idle, active as regards knowledge, peaceful, withdrawn, sedate. The Supreme Being is characterised by the meanings "idle" and "withdrawn".

It can be assumed that in preliterate religions there is as a rule *only one Supreme Being*. However, in the descriptions of the religions of many ethnic groups there is mention of spirit beings said to be "gods", furnished with a great abundance of power. This signifies that such spirit beings are accorded high status in the associated mythology, and that the deeds and impacts that are reported lend them features that one would connect with the Supreme Being or even with the perceptions of God belonging to the so-called high religions (equipped with sacred writings). For the most part they are responsible for particular areas or aspects of the cosmos. There are spirits of the mountains, earth and sea, rain, wind and fire. Spirits of the sun and moon rule over astral phenomena, spirits of winter and summer, day and night are linked conceptually with seasons of the year and times of day. Even war and peace have their corresponding spirit beings. However, they are not Supreme Beings in the narrow sense of the term. If several spirit beings with such features are found within a society closer investigation should be undertaken to ascertain whether this possibly concerns manifestations of various aspects of a single Supreme Being, as is the case among many Indian ethnic groups.

As regards the actual Supreme Being there are according to Thiel (1984:159) four kinds:

1. The *masters*, in very rare cases also the *mistresses of the animals* or *of the forest among hunter-gatherers*;
2. The *creator beings of the planters*, whose activities primarily gave rise to tuberous plants such as taro, yams etc.;
3. The *creator beings of the farmers*, whose characteristics are similar to those of the planters, and
4. The *celestial beings of the cattle-breeders*, personified in the weather, the powers of nature and environmental factors.

One must not always presuppose the notion that the Supreme Being created the world out of nothingness. There are religions with notions that the world simply always existed, but was continually augmented and perfected during a kind of *primeval period*, in the process of which so-called *primordial beings* or *culture heroes* added springs, rivers, mountain ranges and oceans, thus giving the existing world its actual character.

The Supreme Being is considered to be fundamentally *benevolent* and *wise*. However, he can also become very angry. In many religions there are accounts describing how early in the above-mentioned primeval period, when the Supreme Being still lived among mankind, people committed a deed which had dramatic consequences. It has to do with the first violation of a commandment of the Supreme Being as in Genesis 3, but often with the first murder amongst siblings, as in Genesis 4, or simply of a fellow human being,

as described in the so-called Hainuwele myth of the South-East Asian We-
male people (Jensen 1939, 1948, 1992). In his wrath at the action of mankind
the Supreme Being separated himself from them by driving them from his
presence or by blocking their access to his abode by removing the ladder to
the sky, cutting back the rope by which up to that time one could climb up
into the sky, or by moving sky and earth so far from each other that since
then no one can reach the former any longer.

The *names* used in relation to the Supreme Being are interesting. They include for example the *Only One*, the *Merciful*, the *Sublime*, the *Shining One*,
the *Self-Existent One*, the *Unknown*, the *Unfathomable*, the *Ancient*, the *Infi-
nite*, the *Great Spirit*, the *Great Secret*, the *Owner* and *Creator of all things* etc.
Comparison can be made with Isaiah 9:6. The text of the Swiss national anthem
also contains such elements. Islam recognizes up to 200 names of Allah (Molla-
Djafari 2001). This is evidence of the incomprehensibility with which the Supreme Being confronts mankind; he is always omniscient and omnipotent.

It is not unusual for the Supreme Being to be *married*, sometimes to several wives, and to have numerous progeny. If the Supreme Being is married,
he can be personified as rain, and his wife by association as the earth, which
the rain makes fertile. These notions are to be found especially in the religions of arable farmers and cattle-breeders (nomads). Sometimes his progeny
are regarded as *bringers of culture*, having invented aspects of it such as
technologies and implements: for example the weaving loom, singing and
dancing by daughters of the Supreme Being; hunting, fishing and agriculture
by sons. People acquired these things through dream experiences, a love
affair with them, or through theft.

In the *mythology*[21] (cf. **FC**, especially ch. 13), an important source for
such notions, one of the progeny of the Supreme Being sometimes appears as
wayward, the black sheep of the family, as it were. Usually it is one of his
sons. He is a layabout, always has a roving eye for the women and is excel-
lently equipped for the purpose. It is not uncommon for him to possess an

---

[21] This can refer either to the totality of myths characteristic of a particular religion,
or the (scholarly) study of myths. The Greek term mythos means approximately
"legend", "poetic narrative of heroes, spirits, gods". According to Haekel (1971)
myths are stories handed down orally and anchored in the religious life and world
view of a culture. Their function is to take matters which cannot be explained in
simple terms and dress them up as actions that can be related and discussed.
Through such dramatisation the inexplicable becomes meaningful and its presence
substantiated. In addition myths form a significant part of the stock of narratives of
an ethnic group, i.e. they constitute one aspect of its oral literature.

oversized sex organ and corresponding sexual potency. He enjoys staging floods, avalanches, volcanic eruptions and other natural phenomena, and spends his time playing all kinds of tricks on mankind. In ethnology he is called the *Trickster*.

The Supreme Being has many features in common with high gods such as Allah or Yahweh, in particular his function as creator of the world. Nevertheless one cannot simply take the name an ethnic group uses for the Supreme Being and apply it to the God of the Bible. In a number of essential points the Supreme Being is quite different from the God of the Old and New Testaments. He is not a god who sacrifices his son for mankind. Also the Supreme Being does not always have the function of a judge before whom people have to give account for their way of life after they have died.

In the daily lives of people of animistic background the Supreme Being is of practically no significance. As a rule he represents nothing more than the very first cause, a *causa prima*, who created the cosmos and its inhabitants and set everything in motion.

If you want to use an indigenous description (one employed by the members of an ethnic group) for the Supreme Being, you have to examine very carefully the qualities which are associated with that being in the thinking of those people. Hence it is no surprise that in many Bible translations the (Indo-European) terms "God" or "Deus" appear in a form accommodated to the phonology of that language, for example "Kot", "Tios" and similar. Of course these terms must also first be filled out with meaning, a process which can sometimes be quite lengthy. The advantage is that they are not tagged with the aspects associated with the name of the Supreme Being in those religions. Nevertheless one should not expect that the introduction of a foreign term will provide a simple solution to all the related problems.

9.11   Graphic Representations of Benevolent Spirit Beings

Apart from Islam, graphic representations of the numinous[22] play an important part in all religions. They are to be found in paintings, in sculptures, both in abstract and in concrete form. In Christianity these have developed over the centuries into high quality forms of art and style. We have crucifixes, representations of God as judge of the world or of Christ as Pantocrator

---

[22] Numinous is an adjective derived from the Latin noun numen, meaning among other things "deity" or "divine being". For Rudolf Otto, who introduced the term into religious studies and ethnology, it comprehended not only higher beings, deities etc. perceived as personal, but also powers regarded as impersonal, superior to mankind.

from the Early and High Middle Ages, as Creator from the Renaissance (Michelangelo), statues of the saints, altar paintings (the Isenheimer Altar by Matthias Grünewald) etc. Hindu temples contain among other things thousands of sculpted forms of spirit beings as objects of devotion.

In animistically oriented societies there are representations of benevolent spirit beings, frequently *sculpted* with easily or less easily recognisable human features, in wood, stone or metal, e.g. in Africa (the *masks* of the Makonde) and in Polynesia (the Moai of Easter Island), and also as *paintings*, e.g. depictions on the gables of the large assembly houses ("men's houses") in New Guinea and Palau. The so-called "representation of the ancestors" has a particular significant role in this respect, e.g. in the form of *statuettes* etc. Sculptures of spirit beings are occasionally provided with both male and female sexual features, and represent bisexual beings.

9.12   The (Animistically Thinking) Man and His Relationship to Benevolent Spirit Beings

People whose lives are guided by animism and who cultivate a relationship with their deceased relatives normally sense no fear of benevolent spirit beings, provided that they themselves have done everything necessary in order not to arouse their wrath. They expect help from them in all of life's situations. Also they cannot conceive of any problem situation the solution to which would be beyond the responsibility and competence of some spirit being.

In connection with notions of ancestral spirits Thiel (1999:220) points out that in the traditional religions of Central African ethnic groups man's destiny after death is not to spend life with God. *The desire is rather to be with one's ancestors.* Such a notion can also be found in the Old Testament: those who are dying express the wish to be "gathered to their fathers" or to be buried with them (e.g. Genesis 47:30 and 49:29).

There is, however, a good deal of uncertainty as to whether one will receive help at all from the ancestral spirits and benevolent spirit beings. They do not allow themselves to be forced to give it or be controlled in any way. Those who expect anything from them must always reckon on being refused, for sometimes even benevolent spirit beings make decisions which do not coincide with human desires.

The very fact that one seeks contact with so-called benevolent spirit beings and normally has no need to fear them makes it difficult for European-Western observers, imbued with Christianity, to have a right understanding of animists and their ideas about spirit beings. For us, who define contact with the spirits of the deceased as *spiritism*, and reject it, cultivating a relationship with the spirits of the dead, in whatever form, is regarded as incompatible with being a Christian.

In contrast, animistically oriented people cannot fundamentally understand why they, having become Christians, should no longer venerate and seek the counsel of the spirits of their immediate family, being for them the most well-disposed and benevolent spirit beings they could imagine.

The problems this poses for formulating an indigenous theology and for the conduct of the personal lives of such people are serious. They are very often accentuated by the (animistically understood) *naïve equating of ancestral spirits with demons* on the part of European-Western oriented advisers and pastoral workers who have too little understanding of the concept of the world and of man held by those whose cognitive framework is determined by it. Even within the narrow framework of the notions of ancestral spirits each individual animistic concept of the world and of man is so complex that the necessary knowledge cannot be acquired simply on the side or even by living with the people, but only *by one's own thorough research and meticulous establishing of concepts.*

By contrast fewer problems are presented by those spirit beings which appear in the Old and New Testaments as messengers of God or angels. From an animistic perspective they are interpreted without further ado as benevolent spirits who have "already always" existed.

9.13   Origin

The association of the term "human spirits" with that of benevolent spirit beings in the introduction to this chapter certainly refers first and foremost to their external appearance. However, it can also be seen as having a connection with the origin of benevolent spirit beings. There are countless ones said to have never belonged to a living person, e.g. the angels just mentioned, but in many ethnic cultures most benevolent spirit beings are spirits of the dead, left behind by the deceased people to whom they were assigned during their lives.

9.14   In the Next Chapter

As spirits of the dead it follows that these spirit beings have a *life history* which did not begin with the death of the individual whose life journey they have accompanied. The next chapter is concerned with the characteristics of those benevolent spirit beings whose presence participated in a variety of ways in the (material) body of a person throughout his or her life up to the moment when it changes into a (benevolent or malevolent) spirit of the dead. This so-called *spirit double* of human beings is the theme of the next chapter.

The following sources contain more on the theme of this chapter:

Adegbola, E. A. Ade (ed.): Traditional religion in West Africa. Ibadan 1983.

Baer, Gerhard: Die Religion der Matsigenka (Ost-Peru). Monographie zu Kultur und Religion eines Indianervolkes des Oberen Amazonas. Basel (Wepf) 1984.

Crocker, Jon Christopher: Vital souls. Bororo cosmology, natural symbolism, and shamanism. Tucson, Arizona 1985.

Haekel, Josef: Religion. In: Trimborn 1971:72-141.

Jensen, Adolf Ellegard: Hainuwele: Volkserzählungen von der Molukken-Insel Ceram. Frankfurt 1939.

Jensen, Adolf Ellegard: Das religiöse Weltbild einer frühen Kultur. Stuttgart 1948.

Jensen, Adolf Ellegard: Mythos und Kult bei Naturvölkern: Religionswissenschaftliche Betrachtungen. München 1992.

Kuhnt-Saptodewo, Sri: Zum Seelengeleit bei den Ngaju am Kahayan. Auswertung eines Sakraltextes zur Manarung-Zeremonie beim Totenfest. München 1993.

Linke, Bernd Michael (Hrsg.): Die Welt nach der Welt. Jenseitsmodelle in den Religionen. Frankfurt am Main 1999.

Mischung, Roland: Religion und Wirklichkeitsvorstellungen in einem Karen-Dorf Nordwest-Thailands. Wiesbaden 1984.

Molla-Djafari, Hamid: Gott hat die schönsten Namen … Islamische Gottesnamen, ihre Bedeutung, Verwendung und Probleme ihrer Übersetzung. Frankfurt am Main et al. 2001.

Nabofa, M.Y.: Erhi and eschatology. In: Adegbola 1983.297-316.

Ritchie, Mark Andrew: Spirit of the rainforest. A Yanomamö shaman's story. Chicago (Island Lake Press) 1996.

Roser, Markus: Hexerei und Lebensriten. Zur Inkulturation des christlichen Glaubens unter den Gbaya der Zentralafrikanischen Republik. Erlangen 2000.

Schlehe, Judith: Die Meereskönigin des Südens, Ratu Kidul. Geisterpolitik im javanischen Alltag. Berlin 1998.

Stöhr, Waldemar: Die altindonesischen Religionen. Handbuch der Orientalistik. Leiden 1976.

Thiel, Josef Franz: Ahnen – Geister – Höchste Wesen. Religionsethnologische Untersuchungen im Zaïre-Kasai-Gebiet. St. Augustin 1977.

Thiel, Josef Franz: Trauerriten in "Naturreligionen". In: Linke 1999:201-210.

Thiel, Josef Franz: Tod in der Gemeinschaft. Sterben und Trauer bei den Bantu in Zentralafrika. In: Linke 1999:211-223.

Trimborn, Hermann (Hrsg.): Lehrbuch der Völkerkunde. Stuttgart 1971.

Warneck, Johannes: Die Religion der Batak. Ein Paradigma für die animistischen Religionen des Indischen Archipels. Leipzig 1909.

Chapter 10
Man and His (Material) Body

This chapter explains the different ways in which people in pre-literate, ethnic etc. societies perceive the functions of the human (and animal) body, its anatomy and physiology. The chapter deals in particular detail with their understanding of the location of the emotions such as joy, fear and anger, their concept of the will, the mind and character traits, and why the European-Western term "soul" is not appropriate in this context.

10.0   Introduction

The comparative description of the notions of the human body in European-Western and non-European societies (ch. 3.6) produced the conclusion that the term body did not pose any special difficulties of understanding for speakers of Indo-European languages when investigating animistic concepts of man. Nevertheless those working in medicine should be prepared to face a variety of very different notions regarding a number of individual aspects of the *anatomy* and *physiology* of the human and animal body if they want to understand the people correctly, for they talk about their body and its conditions very differently, because their concept of the body is of a different mode.

To give just one example, it has been shown on the basis of certain structures of their language that the Chuuk Islanders have the notion that breath does not pass into the lungs but into the heart. Hence they classify coughing and asthma as diseases of the heart (Käser 1989). This determines how they express their expectations of the doctor, and of his diagnosis and treatment: something for the heart to deal with the cough. If the European-Western doctor is ignorant of this he will not understand why indigenous patients react with mistrust if he does not defer to them.

Knowledge of perceptions of the body are indispensible for understanding animistic concepts of man. This has already been pointed out in ch. 3.1.

Most societies understand the body to be an organism in which all organs are responsible for the purely biological processes, with **the exception of one**, which fulfils a clearly separate task. This organ, sometimes conceived of simply as a location in the body, proves itself to be **primarily the seat of the emotions**. It is the location in the body where joy, fear, anger etc. are sensed.

In addition, and this reflects a vital difference from European-Western notions, this organ also proves to be the *seat of the intellect*. Thus it is at the
same time the location in the body where *thought processes* unfold and
where the *memory* lies. On closer examination it is nearly always apparent
that a person's *qualities of character* are also manifested here.

10.1   The Human Body and the Location of the Emotions, Intellect and Character

When a Chuuk Islander talks about his feelings he occasionally motions
with his hand towards an area of his body in the region of the upper abdo-
men, roughly where the breastbone ends. For him this is the place or the organ where, so he says, anger, fear, joy etc. are located.

*This location in the abdominal cavity functions like a normal organ of
the body, and hence possesses no characteristics of an independent existence in the sense of the European-Western notions of a soul. When the
body dies this organ, like all other parts of the body, ceases to function and
no longer exists.*

There is clear evidence that this concept is not just limited to Chuuk, but
exists worldwide. In societies with a comparable culture it should certainly be
reckoned that the thinking is similar.

❑ Suggestion for own research: the easiest way to discover this location is to ask
where in the body anger, fear, joy etc. make themselves noticed.

The organ of the body where the emotions are located can differ among
societies. It is almost always the larger and particularly noticeable ones which
are involved. Among the Germanic ethnic groups it was the *heart*. There are
ethnic groups which classify depression as "heart disease" (Hülsewiede
1992:428). In the Old Testament, as well as the heart, the *kidneys* are named
in connection with emotions (in the King James version the 'reins': Job
19:27; Psalm 7:9; 16:7; 73:21; Jeremiah 11:20; 17:10; 20:12). Among many
North American Indian groups it is the *liver*, for the Palau Islanders the *larynx*, for others the *midriff* or the *stomach*. In many instances people simply
refer to the *insides* or the *centre* of the body when they mean the seat of the
emotions[23].

---

[23] The relevant literature refers to these locations in the body as "organ soul" or
simply as "body soul". I avoid these labels because they contain the term "soul"
which assumes personhood, which is not appropriate for these locations in the body,
being "organs".

Often this location in the body is not only the seat of emotions such as anger, fear and joy. The Chuuk Islanders also always indicate this location when they are talking about *thoughts, deliberations, memories, talents, knowledge, ability, intentions, expressions of the will* and *features of character*. For the European-Western foreigner these concepts and processes, apart from expressions of the will and features of character, belong to the realm of the mind or the *intellect*, the seat of which is the head. However, for the Islanders these processes and concepts are to be seen as functions and conditions of that location in the body where primarily the emotions are manifested. It follows that for them there is no strict conceptual separation between *intellect* and *emotion, thinking* and *feeling*.

It is apparent that the people of ancient Rome were also aware of these notions. The Latin noun *cor* (usual term for heart) is used in conjunction with *pectus* (usual term for breast) in many contexts, signifying "vessel of the mind, seat of the intellect."

The conceptual *identification of emotion and intellect* in the thinking of the Chuuk Islanders can be demonstrated linguistically. Terms such as anger, fear and joy are organized in so-called *semantic* or *lexical fields*[24]. The data for the Chuukese language shows that words for emotions and for intellectual processes in their respective semantic fields are classified under the same head term (Käser 1977). One should likewise expect that in societies with a comparable culture there will be a semantic field which if investigated would indicate similar classifications.

It is further apparent that there is a pronounced need for research especially in this sphere of *ethno-psychology*[25]. There is a considerable lack of basic material such as research into the structure of the above-mentioned

---

[24] A semantic or lexical field denotes a segment of reality by a set of related words. Example: boots, loafers, slippers etc. are kinds of shoes: anger, joy, grief etc. are kinds of emotions.

[25] The term ethno-psychology is problematic. Hirschberg (1965) equates it with the earlier term folk psychology and with the current terms transcultural psychology or psychological anthropology. It investigates the characteristic effects of a (foreign) culture on the personality development of its members. (Hirschberg 1988 no longer uses the label ethno-psychology). Further literature: Adler 1993, Black 1999, Dittrich/Scharfetter 1987, Dracklé 1996, Hollan/Wellenkamp 1994, Hsu 1972, Iwasaki/Kashima/Leung 1992, Lutz 1980, Morice 1978, van Quekelberghe 1991, Reichmayr 1995. – In the more narrow sense the ethno-psychology of a human grouping is understood as the totality of knowledge by means of which they themselves comprehend and describe their emotional world and the resulting behaviours and mentalities.

semantic fields or lexical fields for emotions and intellectual processes, in the absence of which one can gain no certain knowledge of the "psychology" which indigenous societies possess about themselves and correspondingly apply.

❑ Suggestion for own investigations: collect as many words as possible for emotions, intellectual processes and qualities of character, always in context, find out what they can all mean and then look for the generic term. As a rule of thumb use three questions: 1. What is the word for this particular emotion, intellectual process, quality of character? Result: you get a word. 2. What else does the word mean? Result: you get (ideally) all situations in which that emotion, process, quality of character is involved. 3. What kind of emotion, intellectual process, quality of character are we talking about? Result: you get the generic term (the method is described in detail in **FC** ch. 19).

The notion that the *head* features in this connection is actually seldom encountered. Many ethnic groups are unaware of the functions of the brain in people and animals. This can be ascertained with certainty using the falsification method (cf. ch. 7.13).

❑ Suggestion for own investigations: collect as many linguistic expressions as possible (contexts) in which the word "head" is mentioned in relation to intellectual or emotional concepts, and ask about the functions of the brain. If this draws out no examples or statements, or only a few, this is proof of very little or complete lack of importance of this area of the body among this particular ethnic group.

At this point one is confronted with a problem of terminology which must be solved if confusion of concepts is to be avoided and clarity of argument ensured. For the continuing course of the discussion constant repetition of the phrase "seat of the emotions, intellect and character" is too cumbersome. The term "soul" must also be excluded because from the Western-European context it is too closely bound up with features of being and personhood, which do not apply here. My solution is to propose the acronym *SEIC*, formed from the initial letters (*S*eat of the *E*motions, *I*ntellect and *C*haracter) to represent *the bodily organ or location in the body where emotions and expressions of the will are perceived, where intellectual processes take place and become conscious, and whose qualities become evident, among other things, through traits of character and personality.*

It is almost self-evident that, understood in this way, a person's SEIC is also the organ providing the ethical criteria for evaluating his actions, a benchmark which he needs if he is living in community with others. Whatever word he uses to refer to the SEIC nevertheless signifies the *conscience*, the *super-ego* or the *ideal ego*. It is particularly important for psychologists, psychiatrists and pastoral workers to understand this when they are involved with people who understand their own psychology in this way.

As a rule such a SEIC is possessed by all things that can achieve self-engendered movement, for this points to the conclusion that they have a will of their own: animals, people and spirit beings. *Plants and inanimate things have no SEIC* in this sense. This holds true except for the qualification that there are societies in which a SEIC is attributed to volcanoes, the sea or the wind[26]. On closer observation, however, the "expressions of the will" of these natural phenomena prove to be those of spirit beings controlling the volcanoes, the sea or the wind and activating the power of nature inherent in them.

This SEIC is of special significance as a criterion of the *difference between man and animals*. People are different from animals (and malevolent spirit beings) on account of their greater intelligence, i.e. a quality (of the mind) which they count among the qualities of the SEIC.

In the light of the conditions attached to these concepts it would be of interest to ask how *special aptitudes, above-average intelligence* and *extraordinary qualities of character* are explained.

Among the Asheninca of Peru the heart is regarded as the SEIC. They are not aware of its function as the central organ of the circulation of the blood. Normally animals and humans have only one heart. However, there are people who possess more than one. These are distinguished by their special intellectual qualities, among which is the ability to achieve access to hidden knowledge and make it available to others. They are the shamans (*sheripiari*). A shaman can possess up to four hearts with corresponding intelligence and feats of memory, a phenomenon which must be considered later in another connection (ch.14.3).

The Chuuk Islanders have a quite different explanation of extraordinary talents and qualities of character. Such people are provided with several spirit doubles, furnishing them even as children with an above average effective SEIC, favouring them with a more intensive development of their personality and furthering dispositional features which later lead to rank and reputation. Such people attain titular rank ("chiefs") with authority (mana), become significant healers and mediums, or are reputed to be wise.

---

[26] The Greek philosopher Aristotle (384-322 BC) believed that plants did indeed have a "soul", but without conscious awareness and consequently without desires.

❑ Suggestion for own investigations: ethnological research into these notions is still almost a blank page. In my opinion it is extremely important to have more precise knowledge of the extent of these notions in each society, for this concept is part of the basic knowledge needed for developing indigenous principles of education and teaching practice. Above all one must have an understanding of the concept if European-Western learning theory is to be successfully adapted ("contextualised") in relation to the requirements of indigenous teacher training policies and programmes.

The characteristics of the SEIC consist in total of a large number of separate notions which together, like a mosaic, constitute the spheres of the emotions, the intellect, and the personality.

10.2   Mutability of the SEIC

One of the more important basic notions is the ability of the SEIC to undergo change or to take on the most assorted *dispositions*. Everything that happens around the person, influencing him and perceived by him, brings about in each case different conditions of the SEIC. For example it can render him content, angry, or contemplative.

Spirit beings, both benevolent and malevolent, can also be involved in such changes. A spirit being can influence a person's SEIC either by being in his vicinity or in immediate bodily contact with him.

If the spirit being is *benevolent*, then psychic dispositions such as a *positive mood* and a *lively intellect*, even to the extent of what in European-Western societies is termed *illumination*, are instilled. It almost goes without saying that the *presence of the spirit double* of a person also produces such dispositions in his body.

An important social consequence of this effect of benevolent spirit beings on the SEIC of a society's members is that they *behave according to the norms*.

These phenomena have already been discussed in ch. 9.3. For comparison it would be useful to read that section again, where the facts were considered from a different perspective.

Malevolent spirit beings can achieve devastating effects on the dispositions of the SEIC if the person comes into bodily contact with them, if they penetrate the body and bring their bite to bear. Panic reactions are believed to result. For no apparent reason the person affected begins to *scream*, to *rage*, becomes *aggressive* or *behaves* in other ways ranging from *strange* to *abnormal*. His *intellectual faculties decline* or *fail*, his *basic mood* becomes *negative*. His symptoms reflect that which European-Western societies call

mental derangement. Sometimes he *runs amok*. This is why many indigenous theories start from the belief that in essence "mental illness" is caused
by malevolent spirit beings.

These phenomena also have already been discussed in ch. 8.4, and likewise for comparison it would be useful to read that section again, where the
facts were considered from a different perspective, looking particularly at
what was said about signs of possession.

10.3   Susceptibility of the SEIC to the Animistic Version of "Psychotropic Drugs"

In 8.4 I pointed out that people living in an animistic environment do not
primarily understand such conditions in terms of occultism or possession but
as a *disease*, hardly or not at all different from physical disease in the European-Western sense. Hence it is not unusual for them to be familiar with
"drugs" which can be used to treat such unpleasant conditions of the SEIC.

If the SEIC of a Chuuk Islander has been "darkened" by contact with a malevolent spirit being or by its bite, he must be treated with the "medicine of
illumination" (*sáfeen asaram*). Its brightening effect on the SEIC is based on a
simple *analogy*: it has glowing colours. Fishermen out on the sea at night are
particularly at risk from the spirits of the sea lurking there. So they take "medicine of illumination", even as a preventative measure, in order to be on their
guard accordingly and to be able to react in a "spirit aware" manner.

There is no doubt that observers from European-Western societies attribute the same effectiveness to these drugs as to "psychotropic" ones. However, one should not immediately assume that their effects emanate from the
chemical constituents which they contain.

In the "pharmacology" of animistic societies it is the way *a substance
looks, feels and smells* that determines its usefulness. Plants with leaves and
flowers of *a particular form and colour* count as remedies against diseases
with corresponding symptoms. For example an inflamed growth may be
treated with red fruit of similar size. Sometimes the effectiveness of a drug
depends on the *essential features of the location* where it is found. Indeed, it
is the *analogies* that provide the expectations of corresponding effectiveness.
This is also true of the medicine intended to illumine the SEIC.

Because of its positive effects on the intellectual faculties an appropriate
drug, with the particular features and characteristics pertaining to each culture, is used especially at the start of any undertaking requiring "a clear
head", as might be said in European-Western societies. For people who think
in animistic terms there is hardly a task without a medicine of some use.

Without it the canoe builder is not keen to get started. With its help he increases his concentration and lessens the risk of ruining with a careless blow of the axe the valuable tree trunk from which a canoe should emerge.

Such medicine is also important for all experts in the field of magic practices. A single careless error in the sequence of the rainmaker's ritual can mean the failure of rain and hence a poor harvest. Similarly a healer who did not take the right medicine would, through making a mistake during the healing ceremony, be in danger of acquiring himself the very symptoms of the patient's disease he was supposed to remove.

In many ethnic groups "medicine of illumination" is part of the shaman's or medium's preparation for ensuring successful contact with a spirit of the dead. It can even bring about a change in the SEIC of (benevolent) spirit beings. This is why "medicine of illumination" is sometimes to be found on the altars of ancestral spirits or before their shrines as part of their food offering.

It is always used by ordinary folk when there is a need for cunning, a good memory, quick intellectual grasp, clarity of thought and speech. It is taken before exams, in planning a war campaign, before important decisions, in learning the complex procedures of a ritual by heart. Its beneficial effect on the SEIC heightens determination, endurance and self-control. It is also used before sporting events such as football matches.

However, it cannot remove abnormalities of the SEIC such as mental handicap etc. which are there from birth. People with such characteristics are often not regarded as human beings, but as malevolent spirit beings, or as connected with them (cf. ch. 8.7).

In addition to all this it must always be born in mind that the animistic concept of pharmacology also applies the reverse principle. A person's SEIC can also be "darkened" with a suitable drug, producing the same results as those that accrue through contact of the SEIC with a malevolent spirit being (Mahony 1970:152).

The Chuuk Islanders are familiar with a substance that can instill self-confidence. It is a kind of *cosmetic* to which, in the course of a ritually determined production process, a specially qualified spirit being imparts the ability to prevent stage fright, shyness and feelings of shame in front of a large audience. The application involves anointing the whole body.

The other side of the coin is an animistic medicinal process claimed to demoralize enemies. There are specialists who produce it, and it is expected to target the SEIC of those considered to be hostile. Getting them to take it or at least have physical contact with it can often only be contrived through conspiratorial behaviour and betrayal.

Another widespread notion is the susceptibility of the SEIC to so-called *love magic*. This is also based on a combination of notions understood in terms of animist medicine. The practices connected with this are aimed at producing sexual attraction. The cognitive model on which it is based reveals a complex structure.

A man or a women wishing to be more sexually attractive, to be loved or desired, goes to an expert in understanding how to employ "love medicine". It is produced on the basis of the traditional cosmetic fragrances of the particular ethnic group, though these days they are (preferably) replaced by those from the local supermarket (Eau de Cologne, L'Oreal, Yves Rocher and others). The expert activates them in a ritual magical procedure with the aim of manipulating the SEIC of the person whose love one is seeking to win or receive. In general the cosmetic prepared in this way is applied to the target person without her knowledge. It is applied to her body secretly, or to a place where she sits, or to somewhere on the path she often has to use. The person applying it must be extremely careful so that family members included in the taboo of incest can under no circumstances come into contact with the substance. For this reason the possessor usually stores it in safe locations outside the house.

10.4   The SEIC as the Location where Learning Takes Place

The notions of what is happening when a person is learning is also part of the perspective that a person's SEIC can be altered by influences from outside.

Information about a society's notions of the learning process can be gained relatively easily by investigating how they are represented in the language. In English one conveys that something has been understood by saying that one has "grasped" it or "got" it, which literally implies "taking hold of it, getting one's hands on it". German has a similarly concrete expression in the verb "kapieren" (from Lat. capere, catch). In French the equivalent verb is "apprendre" (from Lat. apprehendere, to take to oneself). The Chuuk Islanders conceive of the learning process as a process of "hooking into" (*kkáyé*). A song learned by heart is fixed in the SEIC like a fish on the hook (*éé*). Learning and practising are regarded as one and the same in this sense. Teaching (*áyééw*) as an activity is likewise linked to notions implying that the material to be learned is "hooked into".

There are indications that in other societies also one would find thought patterns of this kind concealed in the vocabulary and above all in the metaphorical idioms of their languages, and accessible via them.

❑ Suggestion for own investigations: find out how learning, understanding, mastery of a field of knowledge, of an intellectual or manual skill is manifested in the language where you are working, collecting as many contexts as possible, in terms of phrases used by indigenous speakers.

The Chuuk Islanders notice that children learn more easily than adults. Their explanation is that the SEIC of children is "softer" and hence more easily changed than in grown-ups. The learning material is more easily and more deeply "hooked into" a "soft" SEIC. This has immediate connections with notions of the way the SEIC develops.

10.5   The Development of the SEIC

A person's (and an animal's) SEIC is already there at birth, but at that point does not yet possess its final form. In fact it can never actually attain it, because according to current notions it slowly and continually changes from the moment of birth until death.

In animals the stages of development are less differentiated, but they still progress in much the same way as in human beings.

The Chuuk Islanders' understanding of what European-Western societies refer to as "human psychological and mental development" is guided by the notion that the SEIC of a newly born infant is "small, soft and enclosed". The effect of these three features is to limit its efficiency for a fairly long period of time during childhood. In the course of life it becomes "bigger", "opens out" and "becomes harder", reaching optimum efficiency in adulthood and finally, in old age, becoming so hardened that it falls back into a state of decline.

The characteristics of the SEIC, present at birth and subsequently undergoing change, produce the varied *overall impression of the personality* belonging to each individual at *different ages of life*. The enlargement of the SEIC is the main cause of increasing differentiation of the emotions, its hardening determines rather the character and will, and its opening finally the unfolding of intellectual faculties. However, there is no clear-cut separation of the effects of the three processes, since they happen simultaneously and mutually determine and influence each other.

The SEIC of a newborn child is small and soft. Consequently its expressions of will and emotion are reduced to a minimum and there are no distinctive features of character.

A soft SEIC is easily morphed. This quality explains why one can so effortlessly influence a child, make it afraid, and easily console it. This is why it is not all that difficult to bring up and train small children.

As it undergoes its changes the SEIC has a further role as the location where the linguistic abilities of a child develop. In ethnic societies the notion to be expected is that the mother tongue is instilled not so much through the immediate linguistic and social environment of a person but as a direct consequence of the development of the SEIC. If it is assumed that a child does not actually learn its mother tongue by listening and mimicking, then according to this notion it would learn the language of its ethnic group even if no one spoke to it. Its ability to speak develops along with its SEIC. This means that sometimes language is understood as a kind of racial feature.

Once the SEIC has completely opened it has reached its optimum size and hardness, at which stage all features of human personality and abilities are clearly defined. Individual differences are interpreted as being due to variety in the opening, size and hardness of the SEIC as it develops in different people. If at this point in time a person is more than usually even-tempered, this means that his SEIC has attained greater expansion, with greater hardness and opening than in others. Aptitudes already evident earlier in life mature at the same time as the SEIC.

Malformations of the SEIC are revealed as faults in the image of the personality, inadequate intelligence, little knowledge and ability, lack of self-control etc.

Once the SEIC has reached its normal mature condition its development ceases for several years. During adult life it undergoes no significant change.

When a person reaches 40 years old approximately the SEIC begins to change again. It becomes smaller and harder and begins to close. Intellectual abilities begin to decline, especially the memory. Nothing new is learned any more. The smaller one's SEIC becomes, the less even-tempered one gets, and one's emotional stability fades. This is why old people lose their composure and control more quickly than the young. With increasing hardening of the SEIC one's original tenacity and strength of will switches to obstinacy and self-will. At the end of this development, in old age, the SEIC can eventually forfeit all ability to function. The person becomes confused or shows symptoms of Alzheimer's disease.

However, there are a few people who do not succumb to this development. Their SEIC remains open and large and does not harden. They retain their intellectual abilities, good memory and wide knowledge into old age. Their behaviour is evidence of a "radiant" SEIC, imbued with good sense. They are held to be wise people.

It is very probable that the notions of the seat of the emotions, intellect and character as found among the Chuuk Islanders are present in a similar form in other societies. On the other hand they could be quite different. For those working in education, medicine and pastoral care the task of investigating this is not only worthwhile but indeed vital.

❏ Suggestion for own investigations: the surest way of identifying details of the notions of the human SEIC is to study the vocabulary of the languages concerned, including the structures of the respective semantic fields and the use of metaphor. Metaphor means for example compound concepts like "having a broad heart" (European-Western = being generous; African = being stingy). These should be collected and their meanings analysed. In my experience one fruitful source for such linguistic material is particularly the sermons of indigenous pastors.

All these statements about the human SEIC are in principle valid for spirit beings as well. In order to be reminded of the differences it would be worthwhile, for comparison, to read again what was said in ch. 8.2 and 9.2.

10.6   In the Next Chapter

With the death of the body all functions of its SEIC are extinguished. According to the notions of the Chuuk Islanders everything that a person thought, strove for, and felt during his life is of a *purely physical nature* and hence *transient*. The features of one's personality, composed of the numerous dispositions of one's physical SEIC and manifest by it, *have no existence beyond death*.

However, there exists alongside it a SEIC which does perpetuate the features of human personality beyond physical death. This is the SEIC of the spirit double, that being which is perfectly identical in form to the body of each person, assigned to him throughout his life, yet without material substance. This is the theme of the next chapter.

The following sources contain more on the theme of this chapter:

Adler, Matthias: Ethnopsychoanalyse: das Unbewusste in Wissenschaft und Kultur. Stuttgart, New York (Schattauer) 1993.

Black, Peter: Psychological anthropology and its discontents: Science and rhetoric in postwar Micronesia. In: Kiste/Marshall 1999:225-253.

Dittrich, Adolf; Scharfetter, Christian: Ethnopsychiatrie. Psychotherapie mittels außergewöhnlicher Bewusstseinszustände in westlichen und indigenen Kulturen. Stuttgart (Ferdinand Enke) 1987.

Dracklé, Dorle (Hrsg.): Zur kulturellen Konstruktion von Kindheit und Jugend. Berlin 1996.

Fischer, Hans: Studien über Seelenvorstellungen in Ozeanien. München 1965.

Hirschberg, Walter (Hrsg.): Wörterbuch der Völkerkunde. Stuttgart 1965.

Hirschberg, Walter (Hrsg.): Neues Wörterbuch der Völkerkunde. Berlin 1988.

Hollan, Douglas W; Wellenkamp, Jane C.: Contentment and suffering. Culture and experience in Toraja. New York 1994.

Hsu, Francis L.: Psychological anthropology. Cambridge, Mass. 1972.

Hülsewiede, Brigitte: Die Nahua von Tequila. Eine Nachuntersuchung, besonders zu Struktur und Wandel der Familienfeste. Münster und Hamburg 1992.

Iwawaki, Saburo; Kashima, Yoshihisa; Leung, Kwok (eds.): Innovations in cross-cultural psychology. Amsterdam 1992.

Käser, Lothar: Der Begriff "Seele" bei den Insulanern von Truk. Diss. Freiburg 1977.

Käser, Lothar: Die Besiedlung Mikronesiens: eine ethnologisch-linguistische Untersuchung. Berlin 1989.

Kiste, Robert C.; Marshall, Mac (eds.): American anthropology in Micronesia. An assessment. University of Hawaii Press 1999.

Lutz, Catherine: Emotion words and emotional development on Ifaluk Atoll. Ph.D. dissertation, Harvard University 1980.

Mahony, Frank J.: A Trukese theory of medicine. Ph.D. Dissertation Stanford University 1970.

Morice, R.: Psychiatric diagnosis in a transcultural setting: The importance of lexical categories. British Journal of Psychiatry 1978.132:87-95.

van Quekelberghe, Renaud: Klinische Ethnopsychologie. Einführung in die transkulturelle Psychologie, Psychopathologie und Psychotherapie. Heidelberg 1991.

Reichmayr, Johannes: Einführung in die Ethnopsychoanalyse. Geschichte, Theorien, Methoden. Frankfurt am Main 1995.

Chapter 11
Man and His Spirit Double

This chapter explains how the spirit double (or in some cases the spirit doubles) of a person are constituted, the commonalities and differences they reveal in comparison with the spirit double of objects, their characteristics and functions, why one of them is termed the dream ego, where they originate, and what are the conceptual links between a person's dream ego, his shadow image and his mirror image. A brief excursus summarises the history of the concept from pre-history via antiquity to modern times.

11.0   Introduction

In ch. 3.7 I compared the perceptions of the body, soul and spirit of man in European-Western and non-European societies and established that whereas there is not a lot of difference in the thinking of various societies as regards the way the body is understood, the concepts of soul and spirit are usually extremely diverse. It follows that speakers of European-Western (Indo-European) languages must expect to come up against considerable problems of understanding when investigating animistic concepts of man, because the terminology representing the ideas of soul and spirit are conceptually very different in languages with a non-Indo-European structure.

In ch. 6.1 I explained that the Chuuk Islanders start from the notion that each object in their world possesses not just a material form but beyond that a second, spirit-like way of existing, so thoroughly identical with its material counterpart that one could confuse the two. Since each material object appears to have a spirit-like replica I termed the latter its *spirit double*.

I also pointed out that although these notions of a *spirit double* relate to a very particular and limited phenomenon within a geographically restricted (and poorly researched) cultural region (Oceania, Micronesia), and hence should not be expected in the same form elsewhere, *there are nevertheless indications of a similar concept linked to the nature of man in numerous ethnic groups all over the world.*

It is apparent that nowhere is the notion found that man only possesses just one spirit double. This is only true of objects, assuming that a spirit double is indeed ascribed to them. By contrast it is assumed in almost all societies with an animistic cognitive framework that man is accompanied throughout his life by several spirit doubles. The Chuuk Islanders believe that each person possesses at least two, a benevolent one (*ngúnúyééch*) and a malevolent one *(ngúnúngngaw)*. Hence their concept of man consists of three elements:

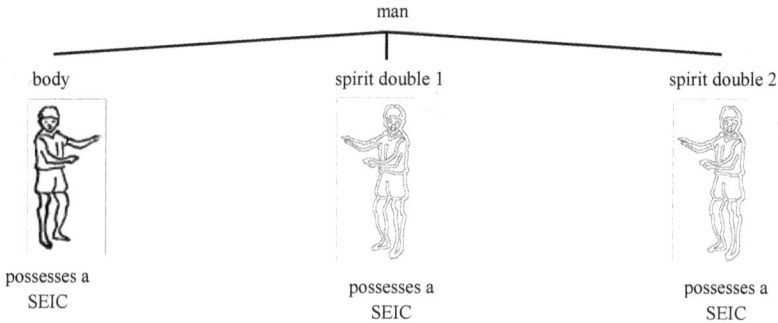

	man	
body	spirit double 1	spirit double 2
possesses a SEIC	possesses a SEIC	possesses a SEIC

As the diagram makes clear, one important aspect of this concept of man is the fact that not only the body but also each of its spirit doubles possesses a seat of the emotions, intellect and character (SEIC), and hence personhood, implying that they are regarded as individual, independent personalities in terms of their thinking, feeling and willing.

There are societies, such as the Karen of South-East Asia, where man possesses more than 30 spirit doubles (*k'la*), as Mischung (1984) has shown in his very precise investigations in North Thailand.

On closer investigation one becomes aware that there is one among them which stands out from the others, both linguistically, and as being more important than the others and characterised in exclusively positive terms. It is called *k'la hkö hti*. The others, according to Mischung, are bad, useless and stupid (1984:123).

This description is true in the same way for the malevolent spirit double of the Chuuk Islanders. It is extremely less important for a person than his benevolent spirit double. Hence in both concepts of man, that of the Karen and of the Chuuk Islanders, there is *a spirit double holding a prominent position*[27]. The others, whether one or many, are of little or occasionally even of no conceptual importance.

If a larger number of animistic concepts of man are compared with regard to how many spirit doubles a person can possess, it is evident that the Karen concept has the most. To have only two accompanying spirit doubles is rather the exception.

---

[27] In this context many writers speak of the *main soul* of a person, e.g. Mischung (1984), Merill (1987).

11.1   A Simple Model as the Starting-point for Understanding Animistic Concepts of Man

With its limitation to only two spirit doubles the Chuuk Islanders' concept of man provides, as it were, a simplified version of the Karen model. This renders it particularly suitable for demonstrating and discussing the individual aspects which constitute an animistic concept of man in general and the concept of a person's spirit double in particular. Hence the following diagram will serve as a guide in further discussion:

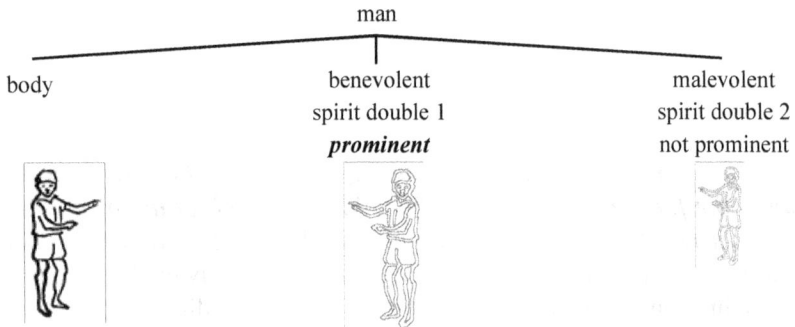

	man	
body	benevolent	malevolent
	spirit double 1	spirit double 2
	prominent	not prominent

11.2   The Prominent Spirit Double of Man as Dream Ego

Among the Karen, the Chuuk Islanders, and societies with evidence of the existence of several spirit doubles belonging to a person, the prominent spirit double is different from the lesser ones *in two essential features*:

First: only the prominent spirit double of a person perpetuates his personality after death, and only this one, as a kind of immortal *second ego*[28] or *self* of the person, can as a rule become an *ancestral spirit*.

As for the fate of the others, there are various solutions. They are either forgotten, vanish into the environment, in the forest, in the mountains, in the

---

[28] This must not be confused with the very specific Central American and occasionally also African (Frank 1983) notion of a person's so-called *alter ego*, also called *tonal* and *nagual*. This refers to a creature that really exists, born at the same time as the person and living with him in a kind of shared destiny. Their two biographies constitute a single life's journey (Tauchmann 1983:226): everything that happens to the creature is experienced by the person and vice versa. Hence animals used for food can never be alter egos. For ordinary people the correct term is tonal, and nagual for people of position: healers, shamans and other titles (Hirschberg 1988:334). For more detail see Neumann 1981 und Werner 2001.

wild, uncultivated regions, thus becoming beings like the nature spirits described in ch. 8.10, or they become malevolent spirit beings, doing harm to people, causing diseases etc.

Secondly: only the prominent spirit double of a person is regarded as *the being whose experiences form the content of dreams.*

These two characteristics, the second ego and the being of dream experiences, neither of which are ascribed to the other spirit doubles of a person, persuade me to follow Fischer's proposal (1965) and refer to it from now on as the *dream ego.* (As to how people with an animistic cognitive framework understand dreams in individual detail, this will not be discussed until ch. 12).

❑ Suggestion for own investigations: the best way to discover the term for the dream ego is to pursue the question of what happens to a person after death. If it is apparent that it is a spirit being perpetuating the personality, then it is fairly certain that one has hit upon the dream ego. One must then ascertain more closely whether there are other spirit beings accompanying the person during his life, and how they differ from the former. At the same time one should never refer to "souls", but use terms appropriate for it in that language. Only so can informants speak about concepts in a way that is free from European-Western features.

If the concept of the dream ego underlies the prominent spirit double of a person, the Karen concept of man (and of many other animistically oriented ethnic groups) reveals the following form:

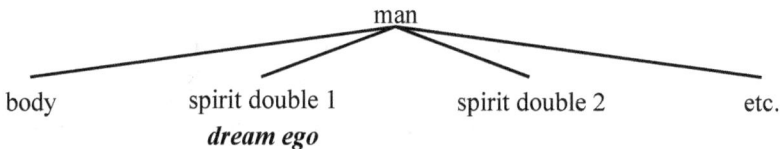

man

body   spirit double 1   spirit double 2   etc.
              dream ego

Correspondingly set out, the Chuuk Islanders' simpler concept of man which I used as a demonstration model, with a total of only two spirit doubles, looks as follows:

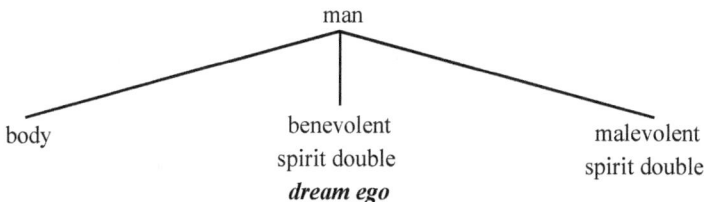

man

body   benevolent   malevolent
              spirit double   spirit double
              dream ego

Since as a rule only the prominent spirit double has significance as a person's dream ego during his life, and the others hardly or not at all, it can be assumed that *man*, understood in animistic terms, consists of *body and dream ego*, both being regarded as independent personalities, each with its own SEIC, separate in the way it thinks, feels and wills:

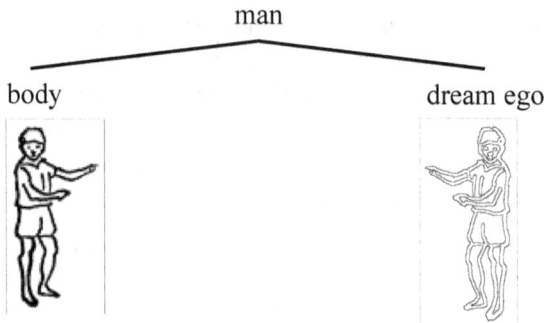

This division of man into *two personalities* led Marilyn Strathern (1988) to speak not of the individual but of the *dividual*. In this she gets to the heart of the matter, although it remains to be seen whether the term itself is really of use.

❑ Suggestion for own investigations: in reality any concept of man expressed in animistic terms consists of such a plethora of details that investigators, particularly if they are beginners, may feel swamped. It is therefore advisable to limit oneself at first to the two most important elements of this concept of man, i.e. the *body* and the *dream ego*, and use these as a graphic model for one's own investigations. One can then leave the other spirit doubles of man on the back burner and bring them back in once body and dream ego have been understood.

Animistic notions of spirit beings are *much more nuanced* than notions of spirit objects. This also holds true for the concept of the dream ego (and for the other spirit doubles of man). The wealth of detail that informants are able to name when questioned systematically about man's dream ego is impressive, far outweighing what they have to say about notions of the spirit double of objects in terms of incisiveness, complexity and significance. However, in their statements about the dream ego it also becomes clear that underlying it are the simpler, less complex characteristics of spirit objects. A person's dream ego is, as it were, a spirit object in a more powerful form.

11.3   Dream Ego, Shadow and Mirror Reflection

One is struck by the fact that in the languages of animistically oriented ethnic groups the terms for the dream ego are also used for *man's mirror reflection* and for the *shadow* he casts. In addition it is sometimes used for a *drawing* or *photo* in which he is depicted. In popular scientific works and also in older ethnographic studies it was concluded that such people were referring to their mirror reflection or shadow etc. as their "soul", or considered soul and shadow to be indentical[29]. This may be true in some individual cases but is not at all the rule. Certainly the linguistic data cannot be interpreted in this simplistic way. This can be shown by looking more closely, for example, at the term "shadow".

The Chuuk Islanders can only refer to the shadow of an object or a person as *ngúún* (spirit double, dream ego) if it reveals its *form*. By contrast the shade one seeks in order to be protected from direct sunlight is called *nnúr*. There is thus a difference in concept between the **shadow** of an object or person and the **shaded area** it creates. The same applies to the reflection in the mirror. Informants who use the same word for image, reflection and shadow were quite able, when asked in more detail, to recognize and discuss the commonalities and differences of these variously perceived phenomena.

Hence the linguistic findings are only correct if qualified with the following statement: *The reason why the term for a person's reflection, shadow and dream ego (including spirit double of objects) is the same is because they reveal two features in common: their non-corporeality and their recognizable form in relation to the objects and beings which cause them. Despite that, they are understood in different ways.*

There is nothing unusual about that. No language can come up with a separate term for every individual aspect without inflating its vocabulary to such an extent that the human memory would be overtaxed. Hence languages behave economically, by classifying the "most varied" of phenomena under a single term, mostly on the basis of a single feature common to all. The English word "key" can mean a metal object for opening locked doors, it can mean a symbol in music notation indicating pitch, and it can represent a book with the rules for deciphering a secret code. The rationale behind the shared linguistic term is the similarity of the way the function of the three types of "key" is understood. The considerable differences between them have no linguistic role. However, it would be ridiculous to try to conclude that the three "keys" are identical or not to be distinguished. The English speaker, in using the language consciously and reflectively in this way, does not experience the limitation to one and the same term as a hindrance in perceiving the differences in the objects thus grouped under the same concept. (Things are somewhat different when speaking without conscious reflection.)

---

[29] Many writers speak of a person's **shadow soul** in this connection.

Unambiguous statements from informants prove that this principle can also be applied to the terms mirror reflection, shadow and dream ego or spirit double. For the Chuuk Islanders people, animals and objects always have a reflection and a shadow, even when their dream ego or spirit double is not (no longer) present, is stolen or lost in some other way. By contrast reflection and shadow can be neither lost or stolen. Even corpses, having no longer a *ngúún* in the sense of a dream ego, cast a *ngúún* as a shadow when light falls on them. It is different with spirit beings, of whatever kind. It is said of them theat they can cast no shadow. But they usually have a reflection (cf. ch. 8.2).

❑ Suggestion for own investigations: Fischer (1965:255) points out that up till now the available ethnographic sources concerning Oceania with regard to reflection, shadow etc. are not precise enough for definitive statements. *That is still true for Oceania, but also for societies outside Oceania.*

When investigating the meanings of words in this context one should also especially find out how events connected with reflections are understood (linguistically). For this purpose one should collect appropriate statements and contexts which emerge from the following questions: how does one say "there is a reflection in the water", "someone is looking at himself in the mirror", or "the sun is reflected in the water"? The answers often provide access to connected but previously unsuspected areas of terminology, and throw up new questions.

In many societies earth is taken from the place where someone's shadow fell and used, with the aid of a ritual ("harming spell") to bring calamity on that person, make him ill, even kill him. (Badenberg 2002:90). Something comparable is expected if one shoots an arrow at a picture of the person. The notion behind such an action may be to drive away or even kill his dream ego, killing his body in the process. As a rule this is not about the assumption that shadow, image and dream ego are identical, but a kind of *analogy* or *parallel*: the expectation is that the concrete act is symbolic of what is intended to happen to the person to whom the act is directed.

11.4   Characteristics and Functions of the Dream Ego

In order to understand this section correctly one must be clear that it is about a description of the *dream ego belonging to a normal, adult person*. A child's dream ego has some different characteristics and functions, although they are not fundamental. It should also be remembered that as a rule only people and animals can have a dream ego (with a SEIC), whereas plants and inanimate objects can only have a spirit double (without a SEIC).

The dream ego of animals is perceived as being much less nuanced than that of man. It appears as if notions relating to man have been carried over to animals. It is above all *larger, more dangerous animals*, or those that are *important* for that particular society which are credited with a dream ego. Among the Naga of Southern Asia it is their domestic animals, tigers and leopards (Woodward 2000:222), for the Karen of South-East Asia it is elephants, water buffalo and animals such as pigs and hens, which are slaughtered on the death of a person so that their dream egos can follow the deceased for his livestock farming in the life beyond (Mischung 1984:144).

One of the most important features of the dream ego (as with the other spirit doubles) is that they are in principle *invisible*. There are, however, certain situations where they can be seen. A human figure encountered in a *dream* is regarded as that person's dream ego. This also applies to animals. (With objects it is their spirit double.)

People with special gifts or with corresponding positions such as mediums and shamans do not only perceive dream egos and spirit doubles in dreams but also in their *trance* (cf. ch. 12). In many societies it is assumed that mediums and shamans can also do this when *awake*.

Experiences of this kind convince people that their dream egos, like the spirit doubles of objects, are *so completely identical* with the bodies they belong to, in all perceivable characteristics and effects, that *the two can be confused*, whether in new-borns or in the elderly[30]. This holds true apart from the qualification that a person's injuries or mutilations are usually not visible in his dream ego, and no malfunctioning organs are to be found on it. Thus the dream ego of a blind person can as a rule still see.

Being physically identical in form includes the clothes that the dream ego is wearing. Such notions appear to have been present in the Old Testament (cf. ch. 9.5).

There are situations where a person's dream ego becomes visible deliberately. In such a case it can also be perceived by non-specialists when they are awake, usually by relatives or by the actual person to whom it has been allocated. Informants mostly describe such events in the following way: the dream ego in question suddenly appears out of nowhere, e.g. in a house with the doors shut, or on a forest path, and then suddenly vanishes into nothing, or makes no reply when spoken to, although it can hear and speak.

In many societies *brief visible appearances* of the dream ego of a living person are believed to indicate that something bad has happened to him at that moment, that death has caught up with him, or that some such event is imminent.

---

[30] Many writers speak in this connection of the *soul-image* of man.

As regards physical characteristics there is no difference between the dream ego and benevolent spirit beings. What was said about them in ch. 9.1 and 2 is also true of the dream ego. There are, however, a few differences which are significant.

A child's dream ego sometimes undergoes the same changes as its body, which is developing into an adult. It continues to grow until it has attained the final size of an adult. Hence a dream ego has a *personal life-history*.

The fact that the body, as it grows, is following the dream ego and not the other way round leads to the conclusion that the spirit-like, in animistic terms the "beyond" form of a person, occupies a more substantial, paramount position, influencing its physical, in animistic terms "this world" form and holding it in dependence. This principle also seems to be valid for the cosmos in general.

Although the dream ego of a new baby has the same form and size as its body, its sense organs and its emotional and intellectual faculties are by contrast already fully developed. This means that *its SEIC*, its own seat of the emotions, intellect and character, *demonstrates all the characteristics of an adult*, which the SEIC of the baby's body can only acquire over the course of many years. This means that the dream ego of a baby can speak and has no need to learn anything.

The Chuuk Islanders see the proof of this in the fact that benevolent spirits of deceased children, who indeed formed their dream egos while they lived, speak via a medium in the manner of adults and give information about things that only grown-ups can.

If the dream ego possessed no such developed SEIC it would not be able to fulfil its duties on behalf of the body. *Its special task consists in maintaining the physical (this-world) existence of the body*. As a benevolent spirit being with a correspondingly equipped SEIC it is able to recognize in good time if the body is threatened with any calamity on the part of malevolent spirit beings. As a rule it is superior to them in intelligence, physical strength and also mana, and can overpower them or drive them away. As a spirit being it knows what will happen beyond the present moment and can if necessary draw on the help of benevolent spirit beings without being tied to time and place.

A dream ego is aware in good time of any intended attack on the person from a dangerous animal. One then expects either that the dream ego will divert the animal or influence it not to become aggressive, or one counts on the dream ego being able to influence the person's SEIC so that he becomes aware of the threatening danger and reaches safety. The dream ego is even able to do this when the body is asleep. It can for example make the person see the danger through a *scene in a dream*, or cause him to wake up. *In such instances the dream ego personifies the functions of the subconscious.* In so doing it appears at the same time as the *personification of man's instinct for self-preservation.*

Because of the qualities of its SEIC a dream ego is in all respects superior to the person it belongs to. It always knows what the body is thinking, feeling and willing. By contrast the person usually remains unaware of what the dream ego is thinking, feeling and willing. This is indeed evidence of its *independence from the person* to whom it is allocated. However, in one very definite respect this independence is limited.

Normally the dream ego is aware of a strong *sense of responsibility for the body*. This sense is accompanied by feelings which safeguard the cohesion of the members of a social group, feelings which also characterise the group's benevolent spirits of the dead. These are *feelings of concern and care* which lead the dream ego to behave towards the body with a sense of solidarity, as if it were a near relative, brother or sister. This results in a fundamental distinction between the concept of a soul in the European-Western sense and the concept of the dream ego.

During a person's lifetime the dream ego is not enclosed in the body, not physically bound to him (like a soul), but leads a separate existence from its material counterpart (like spirit doubles of objects), and usually resides outside the body. However, because of the fundamental attitude of its SEIC the dream ego is provided with ties to the body which are not of a physical nature but emotional, and (in the European-Western sense) psychic.

Although the dream ego is usually only responsible for the one person to whom it belongs, its interest and care can also extend to benefit that person's children. If one of them is in danger the mother's or father's dream ego would try by all means to direct the attention of the child to whatever is threatening it. In such situations the dream ego takes on the role of a *guardian angel* in the manner familiar to European-Western popular Christianity.

Despite its emotional bond with the body the dream ego is a *completely separate person*, leading an existence which is detached from the body and to a large degree independent.[31] It can remove itself from the body at will, frequently and to some distance, *but not as long as it likes* (cf. 11.5), without the person knowing, and without any consequences for him. However, be-

---

[31] Based on this characteristic the dream ego is also given the term *free soul* in ethnological literature.

cause it is emotionally bound to him it usually stays in the vicinity, so that it can see him. It is his constant companion, wary of going any great distance.

Since the presence of the dream ego cannot normally be perceived one seldom knows exactly where it is at any given moment. There are ethnic groups in South and Central America who imagine that a dream ego can sometimes reside *inside the body*. When a person is awake it is to be found in the *heart*. When he is asleep it is located outside the body (Neumann 1981, Käser 1995). In such societies informants say that they know whether or not their dream ego is present. When it is they feel heavier.

❑ Suggestion for own investigations: many ethnographic studies, if they do at all give any information about the nature of the dream ego, give no express informa-tion about where it normally resides, simply assuming that it is in principle "in" the body, only leaving it "in dreams". This is not precise enough and should in each case be carefully examined and the data verified.

As a rule it is not possible for a normal person in the course of his life ei-ther to reciprocate the emotional relationship of his dream ego with himself or actively to influence his dream ego or cause it to behave in particular ways. Exceptions are mediums, shamans, or people with the same gifts, which will be discussed later (chs. 14 und 15).

There are, however, societies such as the Bemba of Africa where a person can *wreck* his dream ego by *behaviour which infringes the norms*, such as abuse of alcohol, immoral way of life etc. Such a person can so weaken and cripple his dream ego that it can no longer fulfil the duties incumbent on it and eventually ends up as a malevolent spirit being, with fatal consequences for the body to which it is assigned. This is why adults are fearful when chil-dren do not behave "decently", and direct their efforts at their children's up-bringing accordingly (Badenberg 2002:81).

So far the discussion has focused on the effects of the dream ego on the body, but there are some further effects which only become evident as re-gards their significance and dramatic impact when one investigates what happens to a person when his dream ego abandons him over a lengthy period of time.

11.5   Absence of the Dream Ego from the Body and Its Consequences

Societies which, like the Asheninca of Peru, believe that the dream ego resides inside the body of the person during the daytime when he is awake, may also hold the perception that he becomes tired and falls asleep if the dream ego leaves the body. During *sleep* as the consequence of the separation of the dream ego from the (inside of the) body the person shows himself to be *no longer fully functional*, for he lacks consciousness. This incomplete state recalls the limited functionality of objects when their spirit double is no longer present, as described in ch. 7.3. One should assume, however, that the notion that sleep is a direct consequence of the separation of the body from the dream ego is only rarely found in animistically oriented societies. In the same way it is not generally accepted that waking up is a result of the return of the dream ego to the body. If such notions exist, they are certainly also involved conceptually in the understanding of trance, as will be shown (ch. 12).

In societies where it is agreed that a person's dream ego normally exists outside the body sleep cannot be triggered by the dream ego separating itself from the body. Sleep is simply a purely physical, "natural" process. Here the absence of the dream ego from the body has quite different conceptual dimensions.

As an independent being a person's dream ego develops its own ideas, intentions and desires, is curious and hungry for experience. Dream egos, just like people, are very much social beings and like to get together with other dream egos for joint enterprises. For this purpose they prefer to move into the different levels of the sky to meet with other benevolent spirit beings or exchange news with the spirits of the dead of their relatives. If there is a celebration in a neighbouring village, with dancing and feasting, it is assumed that not only the people of the region take part but also that a crowd of spirit beings and dream egos strive to get to the event, staying there for days if possible. People who are elderly and immobile not only have to stay at home but have to cope with the fact that their (non-handicapped) dream ego is abandoning them in order to have fun. This puts such people in great danger.

The further the dream ego distances itself from the body, the less able it is to exercise its protective functions, and so the risk of a malevolent spirit being gaining unhindered access to the body is thereby considerably increased. In such circumstances a person can be quite oblivious to the peril he is in, because his dream ego is unable to warn him over a long distance. For the Chuuk Islanders there is a further serious element, for without their dream ego they are left alone with their other (malevolent) spirit double, their *ngúnúngngaw*, which is out to plunge the body into disaster (cf. 11.8).

As a rule one can assume that the dream ego's emotional bond with the body produces such a *feeling of responsibility* and *sense of duty* that it feels compelled to fulfil its proper tasks and remains close by in order to protect it. Also nowhere is the notion found that a dream ego distances itself from the body because of a sense of aversion or after a quarrel.

Some people, however, have to separate themselves for a time from their dream ego because it has a task to fulfil elsewhere. A shaman sends his dream ego on a so-called *soul journey* to his assistant spirits, for example to get their advice on how to treat a patient. Among the Chuuk Islanders the *sowuyótoomey* ("breadfruit sorcerer") sends his dream ego to the island of Éwúr (a spirit concept), in order to fetch the spirit doubles of the breadfruit, who then descend on the trees and produce the real breadfruit. The Germanic tribes held the notion that great heroes were able to send out their dream ego in the form of a predator (werewolf), to fight against an enemy (Augustyn 2002:35)[32].

In such instances the bodies of those affected are in extreme danger, but since, because of their singularity and status, they normally possess *several dream egos*, at least one of them is always able to remain present. There will be more detail on this in the chapters on mediums and shamans (ch. 14 und 15).

One seldom comes across the perception that an ordinary person can decide to send his dream ego to another location. If it does leave him, it does so of its own volition, but frequently also *under duress*.

Normally it is *traumatic physical situations* (also affecting the SEIC) which cause a person's dream ego to retreat to some distance. A sudden scare may make it flee, e.g. at the sight of a malevolent spirit being, or if someone is violently attacked. Mothers make sure their child does not get to look at itself in the mirror too soon. It could be frightened by it. Sometimes the sight of something repulsive is enough. In some ethnic groups it is also a bad thing to wake someone up roughly. The dream ego might feel it is being driven away. Many societies even fear that orgasm presents a danger (Neumann 1981:70).

❑ Suggestion for own investigations: find out how phrases such as "I am frightened (to death)" etc. are expressed in the language.

Accidents in which a person is severely injured can lead to the departure of the dream ego, because it is unable to face looking at the suffering. Even *toothache* can have the same effect. Women giving birth expect their dream ego to leave when *contractions* start. In this condition both she and her child are considered to be particular targets of attacks by malevolent spirit beings. This explains why there are often complex rituals for just this situation, aimed at keeping the dream ego of the woman close by.

---

[32] In the literature on this topic a dream ego with these features is termed a *free soul*. When a dream ego behaves in this way writers term it "excorporising", an imprecise word in most cases, because nothing actually leaves the inside of the body to go into the outside world, but simply distances itself from it.

One particularly bizarre characteristic of many dream egos, as far as European-Western observers are concerned, is their dislike of the smell of beer (Merill 1987). Those who do not wish to risk their dream ego feeling troubled by it, and consequently departing, have to quench their thirst with other drinks.

Sometimes *physical exertion* is enough to lose one's dream ego. Farmers in Thailand are careful not to overwork their buffaloes, otherwise they could lose their dream egos. The same risk applies to the employment of elephants.

With regard to the dream ego of children there is the danger that the child's curiosity for interesting things can lead it to get lost, or it can fail to keep up when the mother is in too much of a hurry and has a baby on her arm. This is why in Africa children are warned about looking in the bush for the place where a rainbow is touching the ground.

It can happen that a person's dream ego is persuaded, or even put under duress by a spirit of the dead or a powerful spirit being, to keep it company, to go with it into the "land of the dead".

Among the Chuuk Islanders the reason why a dream ego is forced to distance itself from the body is because of some *evil deed* committed by that person or by a member of his group, which has to be atoned for. There are instances where a dream ego is itself guilty of such a deed, by behaving in an arbitrary, disobedient or arrogant way towards a superior spirit being, such as an ancestral spirit. This could lead to imprisonment or even the destruction of the dream ego.

Among the Karen of South East Asia children whose *behaviour contravenes the norms* can unsettle their parents' dream egos, who feel that such behaviour is "enough to make them run away" (Mischung 1984).

There are malevolent spirit beings who *steal* the dream egos of living persons or even prefer them as nourishment, a particular kind of cannibalism. Many ethnic groups in Africa believe that the *dream egos of twins* are considerably endangered, because such children, being of striking appearance, excite the interest of malevolent spirit beings. Hence their dream egos must be "consolidated" in a special preventive ritual. *Witchcraft* is particularly feared (cf. ch. 5), for it can be used to carry out a ritual to kill a person's dream ego or force it to leave the body.

In the normal course of events it is perfectly all right for a person's dream ego to leave the body for a while without its absence causing any harm. The European-Western notion that a person dies the moment his soul (his dream ego) departs is completely foreign to animistic societies.

If it stays at a location some distance from the body for a lengthy period – how long that might be is actually not precisely delineated – the person suffers something which in the literature on this topic is termed *soul loss*. Physical symptoms begin to emerge. One sure indication of the absence of the dream ego is a *sense of fatigue* at a time when one does not expect to feel tired, e.g. after waking up from a deep sleep. If the dream ego does not return to the body the person's general condition deteriorates more and more. The fatigue develops into **weakness, illness, apathy, depression** and finally *loss of consciousness*. Symptoms such as **heart attack** and **stroke**, or **coma**, even something less dramatic such as diarrhoea are viewed as indications that a dream ego has been away for a long time. The decline of physical strength can be accompanied by severe **emotional** and **mental disturbance**. The person affected becomes aggressive, enraged and eventually insane. It is true that blame for these conditions can also be put on malevolent spirit beings who in the absence of the dream ego have unhindered access to the body and its SEIC. However, the symptoms also occur solely because of the fact that the person's dream ego is absent.

Hülsewiede (1992:433) reports that in Central America among the Nahua of Tequila the "mental illness" of an adult person is traced back to unrecognised soul loss in childhood, which after such a long time can no longer be remedied.

From the description of these various connected notions it is apparent that the consequences of a long absence of the dream ego from a person's body are in complete accord with the consequences of the separation of objects from their spirit doubles. In both cases the effects are not immediate, but set in after a period of time.

As is the case with objects after the loss of their spirit doubles, so also with people there is a noticeable *limitation of efficiency* following the loss of the dream ego, leading to progressive physical decline. Among the individual organs of the body this affects especially the functions of the SEIC. Only when the dream ego is present can one be said to be complete as a person, meaning first and foremost that the emotional and mental faculties are intact, that consciousness, memory and capacity for thinking, willing and decision-making are present, and that one is also physically fit.

In simple terms, for people with an animistic cognitive framework the presence of the dream ego in the body or in its immediate vicinity is the essential prerequisite for life itself.

This is why those who write about the dream ego speak of a *principle of vitality*[33], applicable also (albeit in a slightly limited form) to animals and

---

[33] Based on this feature the dream ego is often termed *vital soul* or *life soul* in ethnological literature.

objects, e.g. to plants such as rice (Mischung 1984:122). Real life, without restrictions, is only possible when body and dream ego are working together in close proximity.

11.6   Ensuring the Presence of the Dream Ego with the Body

It would indeed seem that people's fears that their dream ego can remove itself from the body and hence endanger it are common throughout the world. Hence societies who are afraid of such a thing take measures to obviate this danger (Müller 1997).

One closes the mouth of yawning children, and also one's own, not only to prevent malevolent spirit beings from entering the body but also to make it impossible for the dream ego to escape, always assuming that it is located there. Cracks in walls are plugged, and one is careful to close windows, above all if a child is sleeping near them. Indeed all automatic measures against the penetration of malevolent spirit beings are also appropriate for preventing a person's dream ego from escaping.

As well as such automatic provisions there is a host of ritual procedures with the same effect. In many South Asian societies a thread tied round the wrist serves as a symbolic restraint to keep both a person's and an animal's dream ego close to the body. For newly born babies there is a proper ceremony for this purpose.

Among the Karen care is taken to maintain one's emotional composure. To lose one's temper is to risk the departure of the dream ego (Mischung 1984).

If it has to be accepted that a person's unfortunate condition has been caused by the absence of his dream ego, and if dreams reveal where it might possibly be residing, then various possibilities are on offer to bring about its return.

It does not require much effort if a medium or a shaman is asked to remind an absent dream ego of its duty or to find out why it has departed. It costs somewhat more if the matter has to be dealt with "medically".

The Chuuk Islanders have a specially tailored ritual for this (amwééngún). From all kinds of ingredients, but above all from the blossom of a particular tree with a pleasant scent, hence especially esteemed by spirit beings, the healer responsible for treating such conditions prepares a special brew, of a shining red colour and giving out an intensively pleasing aroma. With its help the absent dream ego is enticed back, even from a very great distance, for its heightened sense of smell exercises a seductive compulsion.

The shamans of the Matsigenka of Peru retrieve an absent dream ego with the help of a ritual during which the healer lays a tuber on the patient's head and blows on the top, which is supposed to cause the dream ego to re-enter the body (Baer 1987:76)[34]. Comparable notions are also found in Tibet (Stein 1969, Corlin 1988:71). Tauchmann (1983:321) even gives an account of nets which can be used to catch absent dream egos.

11.7   Characteristics and Functions of Lesser Spirit Doubles

In contrast to the concept of the dream ego there is a noticeable lack of information about the person's other, lesser spirit doubles, not only in the ethnographic studies dealing with animistic phenomena but also the statements of members of such societies and cultures. This leads one to conclude that only the dream ego is of significant conceptual importance in the context of the overall concept of man, whereas the other spirit doubles have at most a *peripheral role*.

Among the studies which provide any information at all one should mention the already frequently cited work of Mischung. He it was (1984:123) who observed that for the Karen the 30 lesser *k'la* are *bad*, *useless* and *stupid*, embodying the natural forces which reach into the person, the destructive, uncontrollable aspect of the human principle of vitality, its brutish component, defined and feared by people in the same way as the wild animals. In addition they cause nightmares. Nevertheless they are clearly part of the human life principle, for when they (with their animal appearance and because of their voraciousness) leave the body to which they are assigned, the latter becomes ill and dies, thus experiencing something comparable to the "loss of soul". They can be brought back by putting out nourishment in the form of a food offering consisting of poultry meat, rice and rice liquor. Sometimes it is enough to "call" them.

Sometimes a persons *bones* (and those of an animal) possess spirit doubles in this sense. Together they form a spirit skeleton. Such notions are involved in Siberian shamanism. There are graphic depictions on shamans' ceremonial garments reminiscent of a skeleton. Figures with similar features can be recognised in Palaeolithic cave paintings. According to Baer (1987:72) when a person dies the spirit doubles of his bones come together in a so-called "skeleton soul", which moves around scaring people.

This indicates that a person's lesser spirit doubles are furnished with all those characteristics which are typical of malevolent spirit beings.

---

[34] The author terms this location a "door of the soul".

Among the Chuuk Islanders this is also comprehensively the case with people's lesser spirit doubles (*ngúnúngngaw*). Each living person only has one, even though he should have several dream egos. It is *not pre-existent*, but comes into being together with the body, in which it remains *enclosed* for the person's lifetime. It forms a single unit with the body. No notion of the location where it resides in the body, such as one of its organs, has been ascertained. Since it can never leave the body it is considered to be completely invisible, even to mediums. It is assumed that it does not exactly correspond to the ideal of beauty that the Islanders have of a human being, but that on the whole it provides a rather *grim impression.*

Like all spirit beings it has no material body, only a *shape.* However, it has all the sense organs available, in particular a highly developed *sense of smell*, albeit not ever aspiring to the quality of its counterpart, the dream ego. When the body sleeps, it does likewise. *It cannot speak.* It grows and changes with the body, but only until the point of death. Hence a child's *ngúnúngngaw*, in contrast to its dream ego, remains dwarf-size after the death of the body.

The lesser spirit double does indeed possess the *capability of thought* and *will*, but its SEIC never attains the level of development achieved by the body, let alone the dream ego. Its SEIC perpetually remains "dark". This means that a lesser spirit double never attains rationality. Its qualities of character all remain at a degenerate level. It is continually in a bad mood, full of envy, resentment and negativity. It uses every chance that presents itself to do people harm and eventually destroy their physical existence.

Being unable to leave the body, its capacity for action is very limited, in contrast to the dream ego, whose capacity for action is hardly restricted at all. Its damaging influence is targeted mainly at the body's SEIC, by trying to divert its attention from possible dangers, so that it notices them too late, or not at all, infringes taboos etc.

The influence of the lesser spirit double on a person's SEIC is at its greatest if his dream ego has removed itself from him. In such situations it can cause emotional and mental disturbance, extreme mood changes and raving madness, without any outside help from malevolent spirit beings.

With these characteristics a person's *ngúnúngngaw* appears as his *personified urge for self-destruction.*

❑ Suggestion for own investigations: without the concept of a person's spirit doubles, which do not embody the same type as the dream ego, the concept of man held by any particular culture cannot be fully understood, and as yet hardly any useful findings have been available. In the light of this, one should take more serious account of this aspect of field research than formerly.

11.8   Excursus: a Short History of Notions of the Dream Ego

There are numerous indications that people developed ideas about this quite early in their cultural history. Müller (1997:18) finds evidence in Neanderthal burial practices of an awareness of "something non-corporeal in man" which releases itself from the body in the form of a "body-independent spirit double", as he terms it, and is able to move "both in this world and the beyond, outside of the confines of space and time", like all other spirit beings.

Notions suggesting parallels to the dream ego as a free soul and vital soul are also found in religions with written texts. The notion of a soul which survives the death of a person can be found in the well-known texts of the early Vedic culture of India. It was perceived as an ethereal, shadow-like being, residing in the body, or as a tiny person living in the heart, directing the body from there and leaving it at death (Wachs 1998:235). Indian Jainism, a religion of salvation, understood the soul as a kind of personality double, furnished with immutability and consciousness (Wachs 1998:236).

With regard to the ancient Near East it is difficult to be certain about notions of the soul in particular, and the concept of man in general. There are two fairly large source areas. The popular notions handed down by word of mouth are to be found in the stories of people and ethnic groups living at that time, i.e. in their so-called oral literature, and in the philosophical treatises about them, i.e. in the written evidence of the academic study of them. The latter, being discussions among intellectuals, were of very little significance for the religious conduct of most other people.

According to *Islamic teaching* the soul of a person is an invisible spirit being with the characteristics of a "lookalike" (Bertholet 1930:8), which (in departure from Jewish thought) is not consistently enclosed in the body, can also leave it during sleep, is required, however, to remain in the immediate vicinity of the person in order to enable the body to exist and function properly. This can simply be ensured by the soul "thinking about the body". One can assume that these ideas are yet more prevalent in the popular form of Islam such as is typical for Africa.

According to Jewish and Old Testament teaching the soul in terms of the SEIC (heart, kidneys etc.) is a separate notion from the soul in the sense of a dream ego (Heb. *nefesh, neshamah,* or *rûah*). The fact that in Hebrew there are three different terms for it does not mean that we have here three different meanings. All three contain the semantic element "wind"[35]. Hence Adam received his soul as God "breathed into" him. (K.J.V. in Genesis 2.7). While

---

[35] According to Rothenbühler (1998:18) the original meaning of *nefesh* is "throat".

the body is alive the soul is believed to be locked in, and life is only possible because of its presence. When it leaves the body, the body dies. The concepts *nefesh*, *neshamah* and *rûah* only took over the functions of a SEIC later.

The notion that God "breathed" Adam's soul into him is also evident, in slightly modified form, in early (Indo-European) forms of European-Western thought, in conceptually linking notions of a soul with the breath, tangible in the meanings of the Sanskrit *atman*, the Greek terms *pneuma* and *psyche*, and the Latin words *spiritus*, *animus* and *anima*.

It is clear that all four terms referred primarily to **air**, **wind** or **breath**. It is conceivable that already early in human history the cessation of breathing at the point of death was equated with the final separation of the dream ego from the body, and that the dream ego was eventually identified with the breath.[36] However, in early Indo-European societies this connection is only present as a metaphor, and so apparently is more symbolic in meaning, and of minor importance as a concept in comparison with that other, genuinely animistic array of notions comprehended in the Latin word *animus*[37].

According to Reis (1962), whose analysis of the meaning of words is meticulous and well worth reading, *animus* in Old Latin is a spirit entity assigned to a person's body (*corpus*) but separate from it in the sense that it possesses a being or personal existence of its own. Malaise and unconsciousness are regarded as symptoms of the absence of the *animus* from the body. The presence of the *animus* in the immediate vicinity of the person is necessary for consciousness, a concept which emerges again in the modern use of the familiar expression "presence of mind". Having these features, the *animus* is recognisably equipped with those elements of being which render it identifiable as a spirit double or dream ego.

From the further development of Latin Reis established that the *animus* is capable of emotions, mental activity and expressions of the will. In addition it is where qualities of character are located. These features identify the *animus* as the SEIC. In this connection the following observation is of importance. If someone is occupied with thoughts, with a particular intention, or simply with love towards another person or object, it is imagined that his *animus* is absent from the body and residing with this person or object, and that he is no longer in control of his *animus* but is obliged to tolerate its absence.

---

[36] Because of this notional connection the dream ego is also termed the **breath-soul** in ethnological studies.

[37] People who are asleep are nowhere regarded as beings without breath, although probably as beings without consciousness. It follows that the breath cannot be identified with the concept of the dream ego (Bremmer 1983:23).

In the merging of these characteristics and processes as perceived in the development of the Latin language the original separation of the dream ego and the SEIC seems to be no longer systematically pursued, or is already in a state of dissolution. This delineates a process which has already occurred in other Indo-European societies and languages. The originally separate set of notions surrounding a spirit double or dream ego on the one hand and a SEIC as the seat of the emotions, intellect, and character on the other draw closer conceptually and are bracketed together in as far as they are denoted by a single term, even if not in all cases. Regarding the Lat. *animus* it is noteworthy that already in ancient Rome it no longer indicated just a kind of dream ego ("soul", "spirit") but over and above that, depending on the context, judgment, consciousness, intentions, resolve, inclination, desire, disposition, mood, character, temperament, heart, courage, pride etc. In the case of *anima* one gains the impression that the word retained more positively the meaning of dream ego, for depending on the context it signified the soul (departed), and shadow.

The fact that, alongside the masculine noun, Latin also has this feminine form *anima* complicates the whole matter and makes judgments more difficult. The discovery that it was the feminine form *anima* which gave rise to the corresponding terms in the modern Romance languages (Fr. *âme*, Span. *alma*) is of interest. It would appear that the development of the meanings of the two words into late antiquity resulted in *anima* corresponding rather more to the dream ego, for it is this term which as *âme* and *alma* survives the death of the body and perpetuates its personality. By contrast *animus* seems to have relinquished this meaning which it originally reserved for itself and become more identified with the intellect and consciousness, for in later Latin literature practically nothing more is said about the fate of the *animus* after a person dies.

The progressive bracketing together in the Indo-European languages of originally separate notions of the person's dream ego as an independent personality, and the SEIC, can be observed particularly well in the meanings of the Greek work *psyche*. In Homer's Iliad (23,72) and Odyssey (11,83) *psyche* still signifies exclusively a person's dream ego, a spirit lookalike whose presence close to the person enables the full functionality of his body including mind and emotions, and whose absence results in all those consequences described in 11.6 (especially well presented in Bremmer 1983). Depending on context, a person's SEIC is termed *thymos*, *noos*, *nous* or *menos*. In addition ancient Greek also features the heart, the lungs, the gall bladder or diaphragm as the seat of the emotions. Later, according to Bremmer (1983:14) towards the end of the 5th century B.C., *psyche* (the being which survives the death of the body) was more and more identified with a person's emotional, intellectual capacities, and qualities of character, primarily, one may assume, under the influence of Greek philosophy, which after Homer concerned itself for centuries with the question of the being of man. This provides an immediate parallel to the Latin *animus*, which originally signified the dream ego, but in the course of time was likewise merged with the SEIC.

In the course of this development the Hebrew Old Testament perspective of a concept of man consisting of body and soul merged with the ancient Greek ideas of Aristotle and Plato, of Thomas Aquinas and his pupils in the High Middle Ages, and eventually with the ideas contributed by the Enlightenment and modern psychology. *With their multitude of ideas they all blurred the original bipartite division of body and soul, and in so doing created all the problems which in the present day hamper us in our understanding of animistic concepts of man* (cf. ch. 3).

The tide of interest in clarifying the complexity of these notions that has developed in European thought since ancient times is apparent in turning the pages of Holzhausen 1998. It was the army of thinkers, philosophers and theologians who, with their astute but also highly speculative deliberations, brought about all the difficulties with which European-Western academic study has to struggle when it is called upon to express itself in precise terms concerning the concepts of "soul" and "spirit". This applies particularly to theology and missiology. As yet neither of them has come up with a unified and satisfactory answer to the question of what happens to the soul and spirit after a person dies.

There are theologians (e.g. Schlatter 1987, Schnelle 1991, Hahn 1993) who are of the opinion that Paul with his concept of body, soul and spirit (e.g. in 1.Thess. 5:23) did not actually mean the tripartite division of man derived from the philosophy of his time. They claim that what he said about soul and spirit has to do merely with two different (non-corporeal) aspects of man's personality and existence. Missionaries, Bible translators and lecturers in theology who are teaching and training people with an animistic cognitive framework are not freed by such interpretations from the dilemma they get into through the wording of such Bible verses. They have no option but to proceed on the basis of this wording, which at first glance refers to a tripartite division of man. At all events this is what strikes people with an animistic cognitive framework when they compare it with their own concept of man. It is no wonder that they then pose the question of what happens to soul and spirit when the body dies.

For so-called animists this is a question of elementary significance, but if we Europeans venture to offer an answer we soon realise how unconvincing for animists our statements about the Pauline concept of man, with its body, soul and spirit, really are. They themselves are able to reply with surprising clarity to the question of what happens to a person's dream ego when he dies. (cf. ch. 3.5 and ch. 13).

11.9   Origin of the Dream Ego and the Other Spirit Doubles of Man

Almost everywhere the dream ego is believed to be pre-existent, already present before a person is born. The Chuuk Islanders say that it comes from the places where the spirits of their own deceased relatives or local community tend to reside. These spirits were concerned for the welfare of the dream ego before it was assigned to a person.

Among groups of hunter-gatherers in Australia the dream egos of those not yet born reside like fish in the ponds and pools of their tribal territories. Similar ideas can be found among Germanic ethnic groups. A nearby lake was considered to be the location of the souls of children waiting to be born. This provides a logical connection with the old popular belief that it is the stork that fetches them from there. There is evidently even an original etymological[38] link between the words for "sea" (lake) and "soul" (Hasenfratz 1986). Rocks and springs of water can also be "nuclei of the soul" as Müller (1997:25) calls them.

Ethnic groups in Siberia have the notion that the dream egos of unborn children live like birds in a tree, guarded by an aged goddess who suckles them (Müller 1997). Among the Cuna of Central America it is held that they come from the 4th level of the underworld, where they are looked after by a female spirit being before being released on to the level of the human race, provided with a body and born by mortal mothers (Chapin 1976:59).

Mormon theology also has the notion of the pre-existence of human "souls": spirits wait their turn to be assigned to an unborn child as its soul (Greschat 1980:32).

Regarding their origin there are for the most part only assumptions. Some ethnic groups attribute to the spirits of their dead the ability to beget so-called *spirit children*, who then assign themselves to a baby as its dream ego. In societies which believe in a Supreme Being or God as their creator they come from heaven, in whatever form the latter may be conceived. Müller (1997:23) speaks of *stores of souls in the beyond* in this connection.

The question as to when and how a child receives its dream ego elicits a great variety of answers. Among Australian ethnic groups there is the notion

---

[38] Etymology is the study of the origin of the words of a language and their development from earlier word forms.

that a "spirit child" reveals itself to a man in a dream, chooses him as his begetter, accompanies his sperm into the uterus of its future mother and is born together with the child.

❑ Suggestions for own investigations: statements like this can only be interpreted properly by understanding the environment in which these concepts are embedded: the perceptions of the body as regards conception, pregnancy and birth. These can diverge considerably from those of Europe and the West. The Chuuk Islanders believe that sperm originates in the spinal column, since its content is of similar colour and consistency. Over-frequent sexual intercourse gives men backache, because increased consumption of sperm leads to "drying out" of the marrow of the spine. Up until the menopause the uterus is continually filled with blood, which is regularly renewed every four weeks from the time of the first menstruation. Pregnancy can already occur some time before first menstruation. Evidence: there are girls who already become pregnant before their first period. During menstruation a woman cannot become pregnant because there is no blood in the uterus. When during sexual intercourse sperm and blood mingle in the uterus, a foetus comes into being through a kind of coagulation process. Blood and sperm must be present in roughly equal amounts. Normally the amount of sperm delivered during one act of sexual intercourse is less than the amount of blood contained in the uterus. Hence several acts of intercourse are needed for pregnancy to occur.

According to a number of Jewish sources the *nefesh* enters the body of the embryo on the 40th day after conception, is born with it, and remains in the body of that person as long as he lives.

Sometimes the point at which the unborn child's movements are sensed is regarded as the reception of the dream ego.

The Chuuk Islanders have the notion that at the time of birth the mother's ancestral spirits are nearby to help her and to protect her and her child from malevolent spirit beings, especially if her own dream ego is absent. The child's dream ego accompanies the ancestral spirits, although sometimes it finds its way to the child on its own, since it already knows the body to which it is to be assigned. However, the time of its arrival cannot exactly be determined. It can be delayed. When a new-born baby becomes quiet, no longer crying, one is aware that its dream ego is there and intends to stay with it. Indeed, a new-born baby should not actually cry at all. If it does, this gives grounds for the assumption that a malevolent spirit being has arrived to brood over it because its dream ego was not yet present.

To be aware of this is an elementary requirement for all whose medical work involves gynaecology. A midwife assisting at a birth with no knowledge of these issues will not realise that she needs to explain why she is trying to get the new-born baby to cry and so get it to breathe. She will only recognise that she has to explain her medically correct (in the European-Western sense) behaviour if she is aware of what the (animistic) cognitive framework of the people she is working with obliges them to believe about what she is doing. If she does not explain things appropriately her behaviour can only appear absurd.

Among many African Bantu ethnic groups, e.g. the Yao of Tanzania, children and youth do not yet have a dream ego. The dream egos of the adult relatives take over the protective functions against the dangers from the spirit world. When one of the adults dies his dream ego is as it were free and assigns itself to a young person who still does not have one. Usually it is the dream ego of a near relative who was already particularly involved with that person during his life. To put it quaintly, it is a kind of *animistic recycling*.

Many authors call this process *reincarnation*, e.g. Mischung (1984:124), who speaks of the spirit of a deceased person returning from the "land of the dead" and assigning itself to the body of a living person as his dream ego. I understand reincarnation as an *embodiment*, i.e. from then on the dream ego resides continually within the body, a somewhat rare notion in animistic societies. This is also true of an event which European-Western societies term *rebirth*. Among the Dowayo of West Africa spirits of the dead refuse to enter a woman's body in order to be born anew together with a body (Barley 1981:153). For this reason I prefer not to use the terms reincarnation and rebirth to describe related animistic concepts.

So far the discussion has only focused on the origin of a person's dream ego, not the *origin of the other spirit doubles* which he might possibly possess in addition. Relevant ethnographic studies hardly make any mention of where they might originate. This may be because ethnographers have overlooked the matter till now. It would seem, however, that such societies have indeed not developed any ideas about it. One possible explanation is that spirit doubles, not being dream egos, come into being together with the body. According to Mischung (1984:124) the Karen believe that when a person is born his *k'la* appear out of nothingness. Statements about their later destiny are similarly vague.

11.10   Several Persons with only a Single Dream Ego

This combination is also possible, in very rare cases. Tauchmann (1983:228) records that in the ethnic group which he researched the birth of twins is considered to be a misfortune, because only a single dream ego is responsible for the two identical bodies. This overloads its task. It can only take care of one of the twins. The neglected one has no prospect of a long life. Less rare, however, are:

11.11 Individuals with Several Dream Egos

Normally people only have one dream ego, even if they are accompanied by a fairly large number of further spirit doubles in addition. There are exceptions to this rule. Certain people are said to be equipped with two or more dream egos.

In ch. 10.1 I showed how foreign cultures sometimes understand exceptional intellectual capacities and special qualities of character. Among the Asheninca of Peru such a person has several SEICs at his disposal, in the form of several hearts, and since (according to 11.4) the heart is considered to be the normal abode of the dream ego he also possesses several of the latter. In rare cases intellectual giftedness can originate even in the presence of a single dream ego, if the latter is itself equipped with a SEIC of corresponding nature.

The Chuuk Islanders believe that a person comes into possession of several dream egos in the following way. If, despite observing every precautionary rule and ritual, a child is stillborn, or dies shortly after birth, its dream ego remains close to the mother, for even at this moment it senses a strong emotional attachment to the body which it is lamenting, and to the mother it is trying to comfort. She experiences this in her dreams. Quite often the dream ego stays by her even until she becomes pregnant again. Indeed, a new pregnancy occurs more quickly than usual in this situation. The child she then brings into the world is the same in every detail as the one that died, for of course it has the same dream ego.

It can happen that this original dream ego does not remain the only one that a child born later possesses, but that at birth an additional one is available, already prepared some time ago for this eventuality by the ancestral spirits of the family. This person then possesses throughout his life two dream egos, which have a positive influence on his destiny. However, such an event as described here is not an essential prerequisite for a person to possess two dream egos. The fact that such a person has developed into an outstanding personality can be sufficient to lead to that conclusion.

11.12 The Animistic Concept of Man and "Pastoral Care"

According to the animistic perceptions described in chs. 10 and 11 man consists of a body and a dream ago, both having a SEIC in the sense of a seat of the emotions, intellect and character. This raises the question of how people with an animistic cognitive framework necessarily understand European-

Western concepts such as "psychology" and "psychiatry", and especially the whole matter of "pastoral care". All three are significantly involved, not least in the training of indigenous "pastoral care workers", theologians, social workers and numerous other church helpers.

The basic issue is: "To what part of the nature of man is pastoral care directed?" It cannot be the dream ego, for that is out of the question when it comes to the causes of an individual's "spiritual" problems. For the same reason pastoral care cannot be directed at the SEIC of the dream ego. *The only meaningful solution is to relate pastoral care to the SEIC of the person's body*. It can only be directed there, and only so can the concept of "pastoral care" be correctly integrated as a concept into an animistic cognitive framework. The same applies to the concepts of "psychology" and "psychiatry" etc.

It can be very difficult to find a word in the respective language which conveys these terms in a meaningful way and is of practical use. It is also recommended to avoid reference to the European-Western term "soul", but look for neutral terminology such as "counselling". This helps to avoid misunderstandings. However, unfamiliar terms and borrowings cannot be totally excluded.

11.13 Summary

The concept of the dream ego forms an essential element of the animistic view of man and the world. A whole raft of further concepts such as notions of the structure of the beyond, the nature of spirit beings, the necessity of ancestor veneration etc. rests on it and is derived from it. Above all it provides people brought up in an animistic environment with answers to the question of what will happen to their personal being at the end of their visible, bodily life in this world. Hence the concept of the dream ego gives answers to that which European-Western societies consider as part of the *question of existence,* an issue in which from an animistic perspective the fate of the dream ego after the death of the body plays a vital part.

11.14 In the Next Chapter

Before that topic can be discussed in detail we must make a brief digression to pick up again on one of the characteristics which defines the dream ego, its functions as *a dream-experiencing being* and its role in the events of *ecstasy* and *trance* as special cases of the absence of the dream ego from the body.

The following sources contain more on the theme of this chapter:

Augustyn, Prisca: The semiotics of fate, death, and the soul in Germanic culture. The christianization of Old Saxon. New York et al. (Peter Lang) 2002.

Badenberg, Robert: The Body, Soul and Spirit Concept of the Bemba in Zambia: Fundamental Characteristics of being human of an African Ethnic Group. Bonn 2002. 2nd rev. ed. (edition iwg – mission academics, Bd. 9. Verlag für Kultur und Wissenschaft).

Baer, Gerhard: Peruanische ayahuasca-Sitzungen – Schamanen und Heilbehandlungen. In: Dittrich/Scharfetter 1987:70-80.

Barley, Nigel: The Dowayo dance of death. In: Humphreys/King 1981:149-159.

Bertholet, Alfred: Dynamismus und Personalismus in der Seelenauffassung. Tübingen 1930.

Bremmer, Jan: The early Greek concept of the soul. Princeton University Press 1983.

Cederroth, Sven; Corlin, Claes; Lindström Jan (eds.): On the meaning of death. Essay on mortuitary rituals and eschatological beliefs. Uppsala 1988.

Chapin, Mac: Muu Ikala: Cuna birth ceremony. In: Young/Howe 1972:59-65.

Corlin, Claes: The journey through the Bardo. Notes on the symbolism of Tibetan mortuary rites and the Tibetan Book of the Dead. In: Cederroth/Corlin/Lindström 1988:63-75.

Dittrich, Adolf; Scharfetter, Christian (Hrsg.): Ethnopsychiatrie. Psychotherapie mittels außergewöhnlicher Bewusstseinszustände in westlichen und indigenen Kulturen. Stuttgart (Ferdinand Enke) 1987.

Fischer, Hans: Studien über Seelenvorstellungen in Ozeanien. München 1965.

Frank, Barbara: Ron. In: Müller 1983:204-227.

Greschat, Hans-Jürgen: Mana und Tapu. Die Religion der Maori auf Neuseeland. Berlin 1980.

Hahn, Eberhard: Erster und zweiter Thessalonicherbrief. Edition C: B, Bibelkommentare zum Neuen Testament Bd. 17. Neuhausen-Stuttgart (Hänssler) 1993.

Harvey, Graham (ed.): Indigenous religion. A companion. London, New York 2000.

Hasenfratz, Hans-Peter: Seelenvorstellungen bei den Germanen und ihre Übernahme und Umformung durch die christliche Mission. Zeitschrift für Religions- und Geistesgeschichte (Köln) 38.1986/1.2:19-31. [a]

Hasenfratz, Hans-Peter: Die Seele: Einführung in ein religiöses Grundphänomen. Zürich 1986. [b]

Hirschberg, Walter (Hrsg.): Neues Wörterbuch der Völkerkunde. Berlin 1988.

Holzhausen, Jens (Hrsg.): Psyche – Seele – anima. Festschrift für Karin Alt zum 7. Mai 1998. Stuttgart und Leipzig 1998.

Hülsewiede, Brigitte: Die Nahua von Tequila. Eine Nachuntersuchung, besonders zu Struktur und Wandel der Familienfeste. Münster und Hamburg 1992.

Humphreys, S. C.; King, H. (eds.): Mortality and immortality: the anthropology and archaeology of death. London 1981.

Käser, Lothar: Kognitive Aspekte des Menschenbildes bei den Campa (Asheninka). *asien afrika lateinamerika* 23.1995:29-50.

Merill, William: Rarámuri stereotype of dreams. In: Tedlock 1987:194-219.

Mischung, Roland: Religion und Wirklichkeitsvorstellungen in einem Karen-Dorf Nordwest-Thailands. Frankfurt am Main 1984.

Müller, Klaus E. (Hrsg.): Menschenbilder früher Gesellschaften: ethnologische Studien zum Verhältnis von Mensch und Natur. Gedächtnisschrift für Hermann Baumann. Frankfurt/Main 1983.

Müller, Klaus E.: Der gesprungene Ring: wie man die Seele gewinnt und verliert. Frankfurt am Main 1997.

Neumann, Wolfgang: Der Mensch und sein Doppelgänger. Alter ego-Vorstellungen in Mesoamerika und im Sufismus des Ibn-Arabi. Wiesbaden (Steiner) 1981.

Reis, Horst: Die Vorstellung von den geistig-seelischen Vorgängen und ihrer körperlichen Lokalisation im Altlatein. Eine Untersuchung mit besonderer Rücksicht auf den Gebrauch der bezüglichen Substantive (animus – anima – cor – pectus – mens – ingenium – indoles). 2 Bände. München 1962 (Münchener Studien zur Sprachwissenschaft, herausgegeben von Karl Hoffmann und Helmut Humbach, Beiheft E, 1. und 2. Teil).

Rothenbühler, Heinz: Abraham inkognito. Einführung in das althebräische Denken. Rothenburg (Selbstverlag) ²1998.

Schlatter, Adolf: Die Briefe an die Thessalonicher, Philipper, Timotheus und Titus. Erläuterungen zum Neuen Testament Bd. 8. Stuttgart (Calwer Verlag) 1987.

Schnelle, Udo: Neutestamentliche Anthropologie. Jesus – Paulus – Johannes. Neukirchen-Vluyn 1991.

Stein, R. A.: Tibetan civilization. London 1969.

Strathern, Marilyn: The gender of the gift: problems with women and problems with society in Melanesia. Berkeley (University of California Press) 1988.

Tauchmann, Kurt: Kankanaey (u. Lepanto). In: Müller 1983:222-247.

Tedlock, Barbara (ed.): Dreaming. Anthropological and psychological interpretations. Cambridge et al. 1987.

Wachs, Marianne: Seele oder Nicht-Ich: von der frühvedischen Auseinandersetzung mit Tod und Unsterblichkeit zur Nicht-Ich-Lehre des Theravada-Buddhismus. Frankfurt am Main, Berlin, Bern, New York, Paris, Wien 1998.

Werner, Roland: Transkulturelle Heilkunde. Der ganze Mensch. Heilsysteme unter dem Einfluss von Abrahamischen Religionen, Östlichen Religionen und Glaubensbekenntnissen, Paganismus, Neuen Religionen und religiösen Mischformen. Frankfurt am Main 2001.

Woodward, Mark R.: Gifts for the sky people: Animal sacrifice, head hunting and power among the Naga of Burma and Assam. In: Harvey 2000:219-229.

Young, Philip; Howe, James (eds.): Ritual and symbol in native Central America. University of Oregon Anthropological Papers. No. 9, 1976.

Chapter 12
Animistic Theories of Sleep, Dream and Trance

This chapter explains how people with an animistic concept of the world comprehend the way sleep, dreams, trances, hallucinations and visions arise, how they understand the content of dreams etc. and derive from them strategies for shaping their
lives.

12.0   Introduction

We have seen that in many human societies dreams and their contents are
viewed as experiences of the dream ego. If we are to have a right understanding of the notions connected with this we must consider the phenomenon of
dreams in conjunction with the phenomena of sleep and *trance*.

It is important to bear in mind that in societies where a person is accompanied throughout life by several spirit doubles the one that perpetuates the
personality after death and is described in ch. 11 as the *dream ego* is the one
that experiences dreams.

12.1   Theories of Sleep

In some of these societies sleep is regarded as a purely physical event with
no causal connection to a person's spirit doubles, nor to the presence or absence of his dream ego in particular. However, other societies believe that a
person's dream ego causes the body to sleep by leaving him or distancing
itself from him.

This recalls the notion of *limited efficiency* in relation to objects which
have become detached from their spirit double (ch. 7.3). In the same way the
condition of sleep, in which a person is no longer fully conscious, appears to
constitute a limitation of normal physical capability, and waking up is proof
that after a period of absence the dream ego has returned to the body.

12.2   Dreaming and Sleeping

As with conditions of sleep, dreams are not necessarily caused by the
dream ego leaving the body and going on its travels. People can still dream
when it is close by. This is proved by dream experiences where the action
unfolds in the immediate vicinity of the person sleeping.

People whose concept of dreams is linked with the dream ego regard them as brief extracts from the regular continuum of experience of the dream ego (including if need be that of their other spirit doubles). The conclusion that dreams are indeed related to the experiences of the dream ego is drawn from the fact that when a dream is interrupted it can be picked up again when sleep is resumed.

12.3   Dreaming and Notions of the Beyond

Dreams offer one the chance to share the experience of what is taking place in that part of the world in which one's dream ego moves. In dreams one meets not only the dream egos of one's immediate relatives and acquaintances still alive but also those whose bodies are already dead, i.e. the beings which perpetuate the personalities of the deceased, whether as ancestral spirits or other spirits of the dead.

These encounters take place in locations conceived as part of the spirit world, in villages, towns, countryside with rivers, lakes and mountains, where sometimes the creatures of fables such as giants, dwarves and fairies, and also dangerous looking spirit beings in the form of dragons and predators walk abroad and strike terror.

Hence dreaming is a kind of *window giving the person of this world a glimpse of the beyond* and allowing him to perceive objects and events whose occurrence would be unknown to him apart from dreams. *Dreams are therefore the actual source of knowledge of the two-fold structure of the world in general, of the nature of the spirit double of beings and objects, and of the otherness of the beyond in particular*.

Finally, experiences in dreams provide the proof for two important basic notions of animistic concepts of man and of the world. First: the form and behaviour of the dream ego of a living person are identical to the form and behaviour of the body. Secondly: purely outwardly the dream ego can in no way be distinguished from spirits of the dead, i.e. those spirit beings, also encountered in dreams, which are viewed as the perpetuation of the personality of the dreamer's deceased acquaintances and relatives.

12.4   Basic Characteristics of Animistic Theories of Dreaming

Societies which believe that people are furnished with a dream ego believe that actually there are two beings participating in the dream event, the dream ego experiencing it and the body which is also involved. This means that experiences in dreams reveal the same conceptual double structure as the world in its totality: the experiences of the dream ego and the corresponding experience of the person dreaming are understood to be running concurrently. This is a key aspect of this dream theory.

However, the following limitation should be noted. This is only about the attempt by people with an animistic cognitive framework to provide a *causal explanation of the phenomenon of dreaming*. In the language of ethnic groups holding such a theory of dreaming the dream event can sometimes appear at the same time quite different in nature as a concept. People describing their dreams say "*I* dreamed." A statement such as "My dream ego had the following experience ..." is practically certain never to be found in any everyday conversation in any society or culture. Hence the way dreams are talked about in the language basically implies that the subject dreaming is the person.

It is difficult to say whether the way the language is used in this connection leads to the conclusion that within such a cognitive framework one's personality as a physical being and that of one's dream ego are conceived as being identical. This needs to be clarified in individual test cases. Even so, in ethnology this is why the dream ego is also termed the *ego-soul*.

❑ Suggestion for own investigations: ascertain the words for sleep, trance, dream, hallucination, vision etc. in the language where you are located, collecting as many contexts as you can, i.e. phrases produced spontaneously by indigenous speakers. Suggested questions: How do you say, "I am dreaming, I have had a dream?" Do they have contexts such as "dream holiday", "dream wedding"? Do the terms you find describe the concepts as conditions or events?

It is noteworthy that from the language data the (physical) person's SEIC is only indirectly involved in dreams. At all events its participation is not expressed as such in the language in most animistic societies. In a way which cannot be more closely explained the sleeping person experiences that which his dream ego experiences, but remembers it later when he has woken up. The part played by the seat of the intellect and the emotions is thus limited to remembering the content of a dream, for it is only the memories that are considered to be located in the SEIC, not the dreams themselves. However, in individual cases the matter is more complicated (Badenberg 1999/2002).

That which is true of people also applies, with some qualification, to animals. It is often assumed they also dream, and that the content of their dreams is to be equated with the experiences of their dream ego.

12.5   Dream and Reality

People with an animistic cognitive framework sometimes realise that they often dream when they have gone to sleep with a particular worry or unfulfilled desire on their minds. Such dreams are likewise readily explained by the notion of the existence of another being which is dreaming, i.e. the dream ego, which is aware of the basis of the worry or the unfulfilled desire and experiences empathy with the (physical) person to whom it is assigned. Consequently it strives to get help, to console or at least give hope.

Someone who has fallen asleep when hungry may find while dreaming that his dream ego knows where fish can be caught or where a group is sitting down to a meal to which one can get invited. Someone who is longing to be back home can cause his dream ego to set off towards it and let him travel along. If a woman whose child was stillborn dreams that it is still alive and longing for her, this shows that the child's dream ego feels so sorry for the woman that it is trying to comfort her by such dreams.

In addition dreams are an effective means of drawing a person's attention to dangers threatening him in the immediate or more distant future. In this connection the *function of the dream ego as a personified subconscious* is particularly evident.

If someone has to climb a tree with possibly rotten branches his spirit double may sometimes let him dream of climbing the tree and falling because the branch breaks. Similarly the dream ego of one of his children can make him dream in advance of the dangers the child can or will get into, in order to make him more watchful in his role as father.

Some societies believe that spirit beings with hostile intent send people dreams in order to confuse them or bring calamity on them. Such dreams have scenes where future events or undertakings are presented as being without problems, and dangers are not recognisable as such.

Dreams containing indications and information from the world beyond are not always so clear as to be understood straightaway. They have to be deciphered, because sometimes the dream ego is tactfully trying to go easy on the dreamer when conveying unpleasant facts, or to make pleasant news even more attractive by dressing up the content. It may be assumed that when doing this the dream egos make use of stereotypical or standardised scenes which vary in character from culture to culture. Thus in some societies people conclude from dreams dealing with money that the dreamer will first experience a disappointment. In this connection many ethnic groups show evidence of having a sophisticated array of *dream symbols*.

Dreams of this kind serve as *omens*[39], for they contain encoded messages in the form of instructions directing people's actions.

---

[39] Omens are signs in nature or the environment which are believed to promise good or evil. In ancient Rome an encounter with a black cat appearing from the left was regarded as an evil omen for the observer (cf. **FC**. ch. 13).

The notional connection between dream content (money) and significance (initial experience of disappointment) may cause the foreign observer to react with astonishment and dismissal, recognizing no causal connection between the two elements. The society in question takes the connection for granted and, despite evident inner contradictions in the theory, regards it as quite certain.

❑ Suggestion for own investigations: collect accounts of dreams, asking informants to write them down or record them orally. A large enough collection can be used to compare and filter out commonalities and differences, and so obtain an understanding of characteristic structures and explanations of the content and symbols of dreams which are typical of that culture.

One of the consequences of the theory that dreams are the experience of one of the spirit doubles is that people who think like this consider that the events and messages in dreams are generally part of reality. *One can recognise how strongly dreams are experienced as real by the fact that Christians with this kind of cultural background sometimes believe that breaking the ten commandments in a dream is a sin.*

Dreams in which what happens is thought to be real can be the cause of social tensions. A woman who has dreamt that her husband is having an affair with another woman may challenge him about it, publicly accuse the other woman of seducing him and sometimes try to bring him to court.

In many instances it is imagined that only the dream egos of the persons involved have had sexual contact. This can lead to the woman's dream ego becoming pregnant and bringing a (spirit) child into the world, which will in due course assign itself to a body.

There are dreams in which deceased forebears (ancestral spirits) reveal that as a token of devotion and veneration on the part of the living they are expecting a gift in the form of an offering, or that their living relatives should hold a so-called feast of merit in their name (cf. ch. 13.7) in order to improve their social position in the beyond, increase their status and hence extend their power inside their spirit setting.

When dream experiences are regarded in this way as revelations in the broadest sense, it is not to be wondered at that people talk to others about their dreams much more frequently and naturally.

In these circumstances the contents of dreams are even understood and called upon as directives for political and private decision-making (Badenberg 1999). Such dreams, which could be termed *revelatory dreams*, are familiar to us in both the Old and the New Testament.

Genesis 41-42 describes a dream which announced to the ruling Egyptian Pharaoh that after seven years of plenty ("7 fat cows and 7 full ears of wheat") the country would be hit by an equally long period of drought and food shortage ("7 thin cows and 7 bare ears of wheat"). Joseph, one of Jacob's sons, interprets the dream correctly and is able to take successful measures against famine in good time.

In Matthew 2:12 the "wise men from the east", as they are called, are told by God in a dream not to go back to Herod on their return journey, as previously agreed in verse 8, and in verse 13 an angel warns Joseph and Mary to take their child and flee to Egypt.

Demandt's report (1998) on the extent to which dreams in ancient Rome were considered to be revelations of future events is worth reading.

The notion of revelatory dreams is also firmly established in Islamic or Islamised societies. If North African Tuareg girls want to know about their future they sleep close to prehistoric burial places, expecting that the spirits of the dead will reveal to them in a dream how their future will unfold (Neumann 1983:279).

The notion of *vocational dreams* is widespread. Such dreams function as directives calling the person to take on a particular role in society, e.g. political leadership, prophet, medium, shaman, healer etc.

Many African churches, e.g. in Cameroon, are aware of a special form of directive in the form of the *conversion dream*. People who have this kind of dream are qualified to be members of a Christian church, having been directed by God, as it were, to join (Jędrej/Shaw 1992:17).

In European-Western societies there is evidence even in the most recent past of the notion of dreams as directives from the beyond. Thiel (1999:204) describes how when he was a child deceased people (in Catholic areas) could inform the living in a dream if they were suffering in purgatory. The dream was felt to be a command to pray for them.

According to the dream theories of some ethnic groups all areas of their culture, even craftwork and related knowledge specific to that culture, were originally only present in the beyond, and were gradually made known to the people of this world through dreams. For example, the weavers of the West African Tukolor people claim that the characteristic designs of their products are received from spirit beings with which they are in contact through dreams (Dilley 1992:78). Müller (1983:18) tells of ethnic groups whose designs for bead embroidery and also song lyrics and tunes originate from dreams. People refer to these as *inspirational dreams*, one of the primary sources of new ideas and *innovations* inside cultures (cf. ch. 15.10).

A comparison of the dream theories of the most varied of cultures reveals that many societies hold that the spirit world of the beyond contains all kinds of knowledge urgently required for solving problems in this material world, but which is not readily available.

Since such societies usually have no knowledge of medical care in the European-Western sense one of their most pressing concerns is the whole matter of illness, or more precisely its unknown causes. People want to know why someone has become ill if they are to take measures against the illness. If the suspicion exists that it was caused by the absence of the dream ego, then the best way to discover where it is residing is through a dream.

If dreaming is considered to be the window into the immaterial world of the beyond, then special weight is accorded *to dream experiences as directives for disease diagnosis and therapy in the field of animistic medicine*. This kind of missing knowledge can be acquired by anybody in a dream. Special abilities are not necessary. Often it is one of those affected, a family member or friend of the patient, who is able to explain by means of a dream how the illness was acquired. Such a person may conceive that the patient's dream ego learned that he had become the victim of a harming spell, or that the dream ego itself had come into contact with a malevolent spirit being and been led astray or prevented from returning to the body etc.

Shamans and mediums in their role as healers may also sometimes have recourse to dream experiences in order to diagnose causes of disease and find remedies (cf. chs. 14 and 15).

However, this method of acquiring knowledge contains many uncertain factors. In the course of natural sleep dreams are random events. They cannot simply be brought about when a concrete event, e.g. disease, throws up questions requiring specific answers relevant to this particular case. One would have to wait till someone dreams the "right" dream and then also communicates it. Instead of this what is needed in emergencies is a kind of dream available anywhere and at any time, a dream "to order", as it were. Certainly its content also counts as the experience of a person's dream ego which has removed itself from the body, but the knowledge thereby gained makes itself available, according to this perception, exactly at the time and occasion where it is needed. Dreams of this kind are not experienced in natural sleep, but in a kind which is artificially induced. Such sleep is called *trance*.

12.6   Trance

In many ethnic groups trance is linked to a number of particular notions. *Trance describes the psycho-somatic state of mind of an unconscious person who (as a rule) has deliberately induced this condition*. Conditions of trance are to be found in various forms in most ethnic groups.

The path of finding solutions to problem situations by means of trance usually involves some effort. This means that, unlike with dreams, it is not accessible to just anybody, but requires the engagement of a *specialist*. Trance is reserved for the *shamans* and *mediums*.

Scientific works dealing with these phenomena from the perspective of psychology speak of dissociation[40] or changed states of consciousness. Talk of possession in this connection belongs rather to the sphere of so-called popular scientific publications and media outlets.

The way a trance is initiated or triggered varies greatly. In Central and South America and Northern Eurasia there is widespread use of so-called *psychotic* or *psychedelic drugs* which influence the central nervous system and cause *hallucinations*. During this process the person concerned experiences *changes in the world of his emotions, loss of a sense of time* and of *self-control*, a sense of *oneness* with the world, the past and the future, feelings of *weightlessness* or *levitation, dissolution of boundaries and of the ego*. He has the impression that *objects are dissipating and merging into each other*. Experiences of *synaesthesia* arise, where what is heard gives an impression of colours, or sight is accompanied by sounds, and one's perception of objects and situations is different from that of people in their normal state. One's visionary awareness of the everyday is restructured and elevated (Buchta 1997/98:25-26).

These experiences are also accompanied by spectacular perceptions of *light* and *colour*. Hence shamans and mediums express the conviction that the drugs themselves have disseminated brightness and given them "illumination". They see flashes of lightning, kaleidoscopic shapes, stars, people, animals, fabulous beings, monsters, but also scenery reminiscent of paradise (Baer 1987:75).

Among the Asheninca of Peru the shaman induces such trances by imbibing a bitter tasting drink produced by boiling *tobacco leaves*. Others use a number of *alkaloid-containing plants*, among them especially the so-called *nightshades*. In Central America people are acquainted with *peyote*, a type of cactus which yields *mescaline*. Shamans of Siberia use the *muscarine* of the fly agaric fungus. Sometimes *alcohol* is the agent (Kortt 1991). The pharmaceutical literature on this topic lists about 100 species of plants worldwide which have been used as psychedelics in this way for the last 3,000 years (e.g. Dittrich/Scharfetter 1987).

As a rule shamans and mediums do not use any drugs which can be addictive. This would endanger both themselves and the existence of their group. Also each dose of the above-named psychedelics used for inducing a trance

---

[40] The term is derived from the Lat. *dissociare* "to separate", and refers to the separation of body and dream ego.

must not be so high as to impair their memory, in case after regaining consciousness they are unable to recall what they experienced as different realities (Buchta 1997/98).

In many societies conditions of trance are induced without any chemical means, for example by *auto-suggestion*, or by *rhythmic* and *acoustic stimulation*. Shamans and mediums *dance*, *drum* and *sing* themselves into trance, forcing and over-activating their motor responses. Others use *breathing techniques* such as *hyperventilation*, in order to bring their body into an exceptional condition. An important part is also played by *sensory deprivation*, the withdrawal of normal and balanced impressions on the senses, e.g. by *pain* and *temperature stimulation*. Those concerned subject themselves to barely tolerable heat and cold in baths of water. *Extreme fasting* leads to disruption of body function through dehydration (severe fluid loss) and hypoglycaemia (low glucose level in the blood). A long period of *sleep deprivation* can induce hallucinations. Many shamans and mediums spend weeks in complete *social isolation* in the wild, in the *stillness* and *total darkness* of a cave, in order to attain a state of trance (Jilek 1987). *Mental concentration*, *auto-suggestion* and *self-hypnosis* are also practised.

Drugs and other techniques for inducing conditions of trance can have considerable side effects. The tobacco brew of the Asheninca causes vomiting, other substances lead to diarrhoea and outbreaks of sweating. Long periods of fasting make shamans and mediums look gaunt and even emaciated. Their unhealthy lifestyle leads to all kinds of deficiency illnesses and an early death through physical and psychic strain. Many endure periods of extreme depression.

The fears that can beset experiences during a trance have been described vividly by Baer (1987) following an experiment on himself. The excerpt is quoted in ch. 14.7.

As well as the trance which is willingly induced there is also the *trance which arises involuntarily*. This can be understood as selection for special honour on the part of a spirit being. However, among those who are occasionally surprised by this there are often some who express their unease at thus having to relinquish any control over what happens to them.

For the European-Western observer such a trance, which comes on people like an attack, is a dramatic event. The presumption that they have been possessed by a malevolent, demonic spirit being imposes itself almost inevitably. He should nevertheless bear in mind that although from his perspective they are clearly possessed, such people whether men or women, consider their trance to have been caused by a benevolent spirit being assigned to them in a special way.

12.7   Basic Features of Animistic Theories of Trance

In whatever way the trance is achieved, it is usually based on the notion that people going into a trance artificially bring their bodies to a state of fatigue. This gives the dream ego (or one of several) the opportunity to leave the body. It sets off into the sphere of the spirit objects and beings, or, in more simple terms, it *visits the beyond*, meeting deceased relatives and other spirit beings there who are regarded as guardians and helpers.

The term used by ethnologists for this kind of deliberately induced liberation by trance specialists of their own dream ego so that it can go looking for its assistant spirits is *soul journey* or *journey to the beyond*. It is described in more detail in chapter 14.5.

The hallucination or vision which the shaman or medium experiences throughout the duration of the trance becomes part of his awareness in the same way as dreams do. Either he remembers the experiences of his dream ego after returning from the trance to a state of consciousness, or he describes them during the trance itself in such a way that those present can share the experiences.

It would seem, therefore, that in the thinking of animistically oriented societies this artificially induced condition of unconsciousness called trance does not fundamentally differ from natural sleep. In both cases the person or his or her SEIC experiences simultaneously that which the dream ego experiences. This is evident, for example, among the Asheninca of Peru, where they use the same term for both "sleep" and "trance". In the same way there is only the one term for "dream" and "hallucination" or "vision". The same is true for a number of other South American ethnic groups such as the Aguaruna, Rasta and others (Brown 1987, Homiak 1987, Baer 1987). By contrast Europeans differentiate between a dream as an experience during sleep and a hallucination or a vision as an experience during a trance.

Further confirmation for equating the concepts of dream and trance can be drawn from the discovery that people whose dream ego reaches a state of ecstasy in trance relate their hallucinations in the first person (Bremmer 1983:34).

❑ Suggestion for own investigations: Schnepel (2001:233) points out correctly that dreaming is "a special form of mental perception and imagination which till now has received too little attention". I strongly recommend that his demand be met that research should tackle this "relative neglect of the medium of dream" and investigate more specifically the political and religious significance of dreaming from an ethnological perspective. Schnepel's article also contains a bibliography with numerous new studies on the topic of "dream" in a great variety of societies, regions and religions, including especially in Islam (2001:250-253).

12.8   In the Next Chapter

Following this excursus on the person's dream ego in its special functions as the being that experiences dreaming, trance, hallucination and vision we return to the animistic concept of man as we consider the events which occur after the death of a person and analyse the perceptions with which it is connected and by which it is understood.

The following sources contain more on the theme of this chapter:

Badenberg, Robert: The Body, Soul and Spirit Concept of the Bemba in Zambia: Fundamental Characteristics of being human of an African Ethnic Group. Bonn 2002. 2nd rev. ed. (edition iwg – mission academics, Bd. 9. Verlag für Kultur und Wissenschaft).

Baer, Gerhard: Peruanische ayahuasca-Sitzungen – Schamanen und Heilbehandlungen. In: Dittrich/Scharfetter 1987:70-80.

Bourguignon, Erika (ed.): Religion, altered states of consciousness, and social change. Columbus, Ohio 1973.

Bremmer, Jan: The early Greek concept of the soul. Princeton University Press 1983.

Brown, Michael F.: Ropes of sand: order and imagery in Aguaruna dreams. In: Tedlock 1987:154-170.

Buchta, Brigitte: Aspekte des Schamanismus in der aktuellen Psychosomatik. Magisterarbeit Freiburg im Breisgau WS 1987/1988.

Demandt, Alexander: Die Träume der römischen Kaiser. In: Holzhausen 1998:200-224.

Dilley, Roy M.: Dreams, inspiration and craftwork among Tukolor weavers. In: Jędrej/Shaw 1992:71-85.

Dittrich, Adolf; Scharfetter Christian (Hrsg.): Ethnopsychotherapie. Psychotherapie mittels außergewöhnlicher Bewusstseinszustände in westlichen und indigenen Kulturen. Stuttgart (Ferdinand Enke) 1987.

Fischer, Hans: Über Seelenvorstellungen in Ozeanien. München 1965.

Fischer-Lichte, Erika; Horn, Christian; Umathum Sandra; Warstat, Matthias (Hrsg.): Wahrnehmung und Medialität. Tübingen, Basel 2001.

Holzhausen, Jens (Hrsg.): Psyche – Seele – anima. Festschrift für Karin Alt zum 7. Mai 1998. Stuttgart und Leipzig 1989.

Homiak, John: The mystic revelation of Rasta Far-Eye: visionary communication in a prophetic movement. In: Tedlock 1987:220-245.

Jędrej, M. C.; Shaw, Rosalind (eds.): Dreaming, religion and society in Africa. Leiden, New York, Köln 1992.

Jilek, W. G.: Veränderte Wachbewusstseinszustände in Heiltanzritualen nordamerikanischer Indianer. In: Dittrich/Scharfetter 1987:135-149.

Kortt, Ivan: Die soziale Bindung des sibirischen Schamanen. In: Kuper 1991:27-43.

Kuper, Michael (Hrsg.): Hungrige Geister und rastlose Seelen. Texte zur Schama-nismusforschung. Berlin 1991.

Linke, Bernd Michael (Hrsg.): Die Welt nach der Welt. Jenseitsmodelle in den Reli-gionen. Frankfurt am Main 1999.

Merill, William: Rarámuri stereotype of dreams. In: Tedlock 1987:194-219.

Müller, Klaus E. (Hrsg.): Menschenbilder früher Gesellschaften: ethnologische Studien zum Verhältnis von Mensch und Natur. Gedächtnisschrift für Hermann Baumann. Frankfurt/Main 1983.

Neumann, Wolfgang: Tuareg. In: Müller 1983:274-292.

Schnepel, Burkhard: Ethnologische Betrachtungen zur Wahr-Nehmung und Wahr-Machung von Träumen. In: Fischer-Lichte/Horn/Umathum/Warstat 2001:233-253.

Shaw, Rosalind: Dreaming as accomplishment: Power, the individual and Temne divination. In: Jędrej/Shaw (eds.) 1992:36-54.

Tedlock, Barbara (ed.): Dreaming. Anthropological and psychological interpreta-tions. Cambridge et al. 1987.

Thiel, Josef Franz: Trauerriten in "Naturreligionen". In: Linke 1999:201-210.

Chapter 13
The Death of the Body and the Fate of the Dream Ego

> This chapter explains how the concept of death is understood in societies outside of Europe and the West, how people behave when someone dies, what happens to the spirit doubles and especially to the dream ego of that person, and how this has led to the development of two main types of animism.

13.0   Introduction

In all human societies the phenomenon of death stands out in terms of its importance. People's preoccupation with it is apparent in the plethora of myths explaining when and how death entered the world, whether it was through someone's thoughtless or reckless behaviour or the ineptitude of an animal. Sometimes it was someone's wicked deed or disobedience towards a high-ranking spirit being which occasioned the latter to punish the perpetrator by making him the very first person in human history to die.

The finiteness of physical life, of which people in any society are always aware, becomes dramatically apparent when a relative dies. A gap is left, which has to be filled, e.g. on the death of someone holding office, for which a successor has to be appointed. Ownership of property has to be clarified and responsibilities newly defined. And, of course, there are people who were emotionally so close to the deceased that they are hard hit and need care in order to come to terms with what has happened.

However, the life of the deceased is not finally at an end, but only the physical aspect. It is clear that there is no human society without the perception that *following physical death one's personality continues to exist in some form or other*. One's "visible" life, conducted and concluded alongside one or more spirit beings (dream ego, spirit double etc.) goes on "invisibly" under completely different circumstances.

A person's departure from the society of the living, as a transition between two forms of existence, is experienced by the relatives as a significant and important transformative event, overlaid culturally and hence ritually to a greater extent than almost any other episode in an individual's life journey.

At the same time the theme of death is surrounded by many taboos. If the subject cannot be avoided, terms are used which remove the drama from the event, or soften it. The deceased has "gone home, departed (Engl. passed away), disappeared (Fr. disparu)".

Many societies understand the concept of death differently from those of Europe and the West. Among the Chuuk Islanders the term *má* refers not only to living beings whose heart and breathing has stopped, but also to those who have lost consciousness through a blow on the head, where it is evident that following this type of "death" they will continue to live. In addition *má* describes plants with drooping leaves, engines which have seized up, batteries which have run out, light bulbs which have blown, arms and legs which are lame or can no longer feel, an impotent penis, etc., i.e. anything which has lost its normal movement or efficiency.

In almost all societies the arrival of death means that physical life has finally reached its end. There are a small number which contain the notion of the so-called "living corpse" which still perceives what is going on around it but no longer responds. This may explain the trouble taken to preserve the body of the deceased, to embalm it and mummify it.

❏ Suggestion for own investigations: find out the words used for sleep, death, dying, unconsciousness, coma, impotence, etc. and collect all the situations where these words occur, also investigating the more vulgar terms (snuff it, kick the bucket), for these also throw significant light on the concept of death in whatever language or society.

13.1   Types and Causes of Death

Normal death, in the European-Western sense of "natural death", occurring through increasing age and the consequent decline of the body, is a universal concept. Nothing can halt this process, not even a dream ego which never leaves the body and takes care that no malevolent spirit being can come near it and harm it.

If someone dies before reaching the age at which he would have died a normal death, there is the suspicion that a malevolent spirit being has brought about his *abnormal* death, because it is *untimely*. In such instances the search is on for what has caused it. One presumes, perhaps, that an ancestral spirit had to punish the untimely deceased for some evil deed, or that his dream ego had left him for too long etc. A fortune-teller is consulted, who as a diviner employs certain procedures[41]. Or it is discovered that his early death was due to the breaking of a taboo, or the infringement in some other way of

---

[41] Divination refers to ritual procedures to help discover what is hidden. It may involve laying out cards, looking at coffee grounds or the entrails of animal sacrifices, casting stones, bones and feathers, in order to find out what is concealed or what the future may have in store (discussed in detail in **FC** ch. 13).

one of the prevailing ethical norms, either by him or one of his surviving relatives, thus making him guilty of a sin as understood by that culture. One particularly dramatic and consequential explanation of untimely death asserts that the deceased had become a victim of an attack by a witch (a "death spell"). An immediate search is then begun for the guilty person, which can lead to serious tensions in that group and society (cf. ch. 5.8).

Very similar to abnormal and untimely death is the so-called *bad death* (Sell 1955). This is suffered by all those who lose their lives *through violence*, in an *unexpected, uncontrolled* way, or by being *in the wrong place*. This includes a broad range of events: killed by a wild animal, by a falling tree, bolt of lightning, murder and suicide, execution, starvation, thirst, drowning and suffocation, beaten to death or the victim of an assault, infection by diseases such as leprosy, by non-fulfilment of religions duties and by licentious behaviour. Even women who die in childbirth or childless die a bad death. Sometimes it is sufficient to die away from home. In the event of the latter one tries to bring the deceased back to his home territory as quickly as possible in order to mitigate the consequences of the bad death.

Many societies regard a bad death as a serious personal failure. Someone who dies in this way has not fulfilled the conditions which characterize a *good death*. He has cut short his life cycle prematurely and has thus not lived a fulfilled life as the Creator intended, has not ordered his house, taken proper leave of his relatives, nor uttered the prescribed "final words". Middleton has described this whole aspect in detail among the Lugbara of Africa (1982:142-143).

The consequences of this understanding of a bad death are serious. The deceased is not properly buried, but left lying, or buried just anywhere. His dream ego can never attain the status of an ancestral spirit, can find no admittance to the "land of the dead" – if such a concept exists in that society; it has to remain in one of its remote and desert regions until its allotted lifespan has expired (Hülsewiede 1992:203), or it moves restlessly through the world as a "hungry spirit" (Kuper 1991), to be placated by the living, who put out or throw down something for it to eat and drink in an out-of-the-way spot. Many assume that they move about for ever in and around where the accident occurred, to scare people, torment them or even drag them to a similar bad death. Many become malevolent spirit beings or vampires who must be avoided (Mischung 1979).

In the Shinto religion of Japan it is thought that the dream egos of those who have died a bad death are particularly restless, aggressive, and a danger to the living if they are not placated by gifts of food and drink (Murray 1988).

In some societies it is believed that a bad death can result in consequences brought about by events that occur after the actual time of death. Mistakes made during the traditional burial ritual can cause the dream ego to become an aggressive spirit of the dead, posing a threat to those left behind (Watson 1982:183). In ancient Greece the surviving dream ego of the deceased was not admitted to the "realm of the blessed" before his body had been properly buried. Creon, the king of Thebes, wanted to punish Polynices for fighting against the city of his fathers by not allowing his sister Antigone to cover him with earth, according to the myth.

Animals can also suffer a bad death. According to Lauby (2000) the Yakut of Siberia believe that the surviving dream ego of a bear that had not been ritually killed lives on as its spirit and can cause diseases and storms. Among the Sami of Lapland hunters crawl into their tent backwards, to avoid being attacked from the rear by a potential angry bear in spirit form that is following them. After the hunt a hunter can also deceive a bear on his way home by symbolically barricading the path with sticks laid across it or drawing circles in the snow to confuse it.

Among the ethnic groups of northern Eurasia there is also the notion that in spite of observance of all the hunting rituals the spirit of a dead bear goes through a phase of emotional instability lasting a few days, or until its bones have been given back to the Lord of the animals in a further ritual. If the latter is correctly celebrated the spirit of the dead animal is emotionally stabilised and returns happily to the Lord of the animals, reporting that his corpse has been treated with care and respect. The Lord of the animals then regenerates the bear by providing its bones with another body. Similar thinking lies behind the behaviour of North American Indians who take strict care that their dogs are not allowed to eat the bones of beavers that have been killed. They have to be laid to rest in water, otherwise the surviving spirits of the dead animals complain about bad treatment, and the Lord of the animals no longer lets them return to the world of men.

13.2 Conceptual Difference between the Living and the Dead

The fact of death requires all societies symbolically to either isolate the deceased from the living or completely *banish* them. In many cultures they may continue to remain members of the group, but with *altered status*. In others they are completely removed.

It is mainly in societies characterized by a *settled way of life*, with ownership and utilisation of the land through related and neighbouring groups, that the deceased are only isolated. Such is particularly the case with (earlier) planters and arable farmers. By contrast complete banishment of a deceased person occurs in societies which do not practise a settled existence, own and use no family land-holding, but regard a fairly large territory as their living space, as was the case among (earlier) hunter-gatherers and nomads. The total

13.3   Banishment of the Deceased

results from the assumption that after physical death the dream ego immediately becomes a *malevolent spirit being*, threatening to force the living into sharing its fate.

Where this notion is held, the banishment can already begin before the person dies. In order to avoid having to tolerate such an aggressive spirit of the dead in their immediate vicinity the Asheninca of Peru sometimes carry a dying person into the forest and abandon him there to his fate. Similar behaviour has been observed among the African Hadza (Woodburn 1982:192). If death takes place in the house, the deceased must be removed as quickly as possible, not by the front door, but via a hole broken through the wall, which is then immediately filled in, to prevent his dream ego, now surviving as an aggressive spirit of the dead, from finding its way back inside.

Banishment of the deceased proceeds further by not burying him on one's own land, in as far as one owns any, but away in the bush, in the forest, in the desert, i.e. in uncultivated ground normally avoided by people. False route markings (cf. ch. 8.2) are intended to confuse the surviving dream ego and prevent it from finding its way back to the house.

The possibility of deceiving the deceased's surviving dream ego is a first indication that from now on one attributes to it only *the limited intellectual ability of a malevolent spirit being*, from whom no help is expected and who therefore does not merit becoming an ancestral spirit.

The dramatic nature of such banishment is demonstrated particularly by the abandonment or burning of the house by those left, in order to erect another some distance away. Sometimes the personal possessions of the deceased, together with the tools he used, are also destroyed. All this signifies that any relationship with him is regarded as terminated.

Overall the events associated with the death of a person in a society with such a procedure of banishment show that the issues to do with death require *little in the way of special arrangements or rituals*, but rather make death appear onerous, and dealing with it similar to waste disposal. The place of burial is not marked with a stone or similar monument. In such societies death is not particularly visible.

Dealing with a body in this way applies also not only to deaths in non-sedentary societies but to all who have died a bad death (cf. 13.1). By contrast, in societies characterised by a settled lifestyle the

13.4   Isolation of the Deceased

by the bereaved family members is carried out very differently. Here the process consists of a sequence of mostly ritualised events spread over various lengths of time in different societies, and the events immediately following the death of a person have clearly different features.

A death in such a society has a particular effect on the whole family lineage, reveals the solidarity of their relationship and brings together practically all the members at the place where it happened. Apart from weddings there is hardly any other event where the extended family meets together in such a comprehensive way and can get to know each other.

A period of activity then begins, its unfolding determined by *rituals* of *death* or *mourning*, which are in part arranged so lavishly that, at least in the case of secondary burials (cf. 13.5), several bereavements are involved, in order to save costs. In the case of children, who as a rule are not yet regarded as full members of society, the outlay is kept to a minimum.

Death rituals are extraordinarily complex and are subdivided into a great number of sections. In essence the task consists of structuring the period leading up to the burial through various activities, thereby helping the bereaved family to come to terms with the crisis that the death has caused. Above all, however, they contain a series of acts aimed at warding off presumed threats to the bereaved through any uncontrolled, aggressive behaviour on the part of the dream ego which has been disturbed by the death of the body. The rituals surrounding the death are to incorporate the dream ego into the community of previously deceased persons and so restore its "normal" behaviour (Crocker 1985:53).

When a death occurs one also expects to encounter heightened activity and machinations on the part of evil spirit beings, and it is believed that these formalised rituals can prevent them from causing trouble. The mourners must observe certain rules governing food and clothing, must not cut their hair, shave, take part in festivals, or they must spend a period of time in reclusion from the community, e.g. the widow. In some societies the bereaved have to leave the house they shared with the deceased until the period of mourning is over.

Sometimes the rituals include the destruction of objects from the personal possessions of the deceased, e.g. tools, weapons, clothes and jewellery. There may be various reasons for this. The bereaved may not wish to be continually reminded of him, or the spirit doubles of these objects are to be available for him after death.

The *name of the deceased* is no longer to be mentioned, if he has to be spoken about. However, any infringement of this custom is only rarely regarded as the breaking of a taboo with serious consequences, but rather as an act of impiety or tactlessness towards the bereaved. There are nevertheless societies where mentioning the name of a deceased person disturbs his surviving dream ego. Avoiding any mention of the name of an important person who has died can lead to replacing a word used frequently in everyday speech with another if the former even partly sounds like the name of that person. This is why following the death of the titled person *Ráyisom* in one of the Chuuk villages in Micronesia the word for rice is no longer *ráyis* but *paraas* (that which patters).

In many ethnic groups there exists the notion that dangerous influences can emanate from a *corpse* or the *presence of a dead person*, affecting the immediate surroundings. It is believed that the corpse emits a malign breath, with the result that visits to the home of a deceased person are not permitted to last very long. Children are instructed to take a deep breath and hold it when they go past a house in which someone has died. Expectant women are warned of the damaging effects of a corpse, and farmers keep animals in calf at a safe distance. The corpses of those who have committed suicide are held to be particularly dangerous in this respect. Elderly people are sometimes reluctant to visit hospitals, believing the air to be detrimental because of the frequent deaths there. Water used to wash dead bodies must be disposed of carefully, and their bed linen burnt outside the village (Watson 1982:168). Incense or other aromatic substances serve as counter measures.

The various rituals connected with death seldom have any rational basis. Not regarding them as taboos is equally risky, for they have a determining influence on the future destiny of the dream ego.

Besides carrying out the ritual duties the most urgent activities the relatives are busy with consist in the preparations for the burial. These must ensue quite rapidly especially in regions with a tropical climate. By contrast in polar surroundings or high up in the mountains it is often necessary to place the body temporarily in a snow grave until the ground has thawed sufficiently for it to be buried in earth. Until a few decades ago such instances occurred also in high-lying villages in Switzerland and Austria.

13.5   Forms of Burial

Burials can take so many forms that a complete compilation and description here would be impossible. There are burials involving earth, trees, fire, water, boats, urns, and so-called sky burials[42]. Burial in the earth can take place in a "cemetery" outside or inside a settlement, in the family land of the deceased or even in the latter's house. Among the Hadza of Africa, who live as hunter-gatherers, bodies are buried in old termite mounds, thus avoiding the strenuous work of digging in hard ground (Woodburn 1982:189).

Sedentary planters and tillers of the soil generally prefer to keep their dead as close by as possible. There is evidence for this as early as the start of the Neolithic period, where it was usual to bury the dead together at certain locations, an early form of graveyard burial (Müller 1997:64). Today also such societies bury them on their own property, even inside their own home-steads. Before Christianisation the Chuuk Islanders buried important members of the family in the floor of the house[43]. There are ethnic groups which have burial places underneath where they sleep.

The body of the deceased is treated in a great variety of ways, often ritu-ally washed, perfumed and laid out in ceremonial dress. If there is no chance of making or procuring a coffin the body is wrapped in cloths or mats for burial.

The various types of burial, together with all the effort and expense in-volved, are often determined by the social position of the deceased. An aged title-holder is buried with pomp, but a child who has undergone none of the rituals of the cycle of life is buried under the simplest of conditions.

The burial itself usually takes place while observing very nuanced and strict rules. The bereaved relatives and guests taking part in the ritual are expected to behave in a particular way. In Europe it is normal to hide one's emotions. A widow who does not weep is regarded as strong and composed. In other societies outbreaks of emotion by the women in the family are ex-pected, and are part of the most important elements of the ceremonial pro-ceedings. In general terms *lamentation* is their task.

An important distinction has to be made between *primary* and *secondary burial*. Primary burials take place immediately or only a few days after a person's death and are by comparison not particularly elaborate. Secondary burials are usually instigated one to two years afterwards, sometimes consid-erably later. In China the Cantonese first bury the body in a coffin, and then, not until about 7 years later, in an urn (Watson 1982:155). This involves exhuming the remains, cleaning the remaining bones and finally burying

[42] In many parts of Asia corpses are placed on tower-like constructions and left for the vultures to eat. The usual term "sky burial" strikes a rather macabre note.

[43] For a detailed description of how in New Guinea originally animistic burial prac-tices became mingled with Christian ones see Fischer (2002).

them, mostly at very great expense. See Topley 1952 and Potter 1970 for further details.

Secondary burials are actually a very old cultural phenomenon. An excavation site in Greece reveals that they were already a normal practice 25,000 years ago (Jacobsen/Cullen 1981:86).

Where secondary burials take place they demarcate the final departure of the deceased from society, his *social death* (Middleton 1982:141-142). It means the extinguishing of any social identity still left after the death of the body and its transition into a new one. During his lifetime the person was part of a network with others in a range of relationships and obligations, which now become newly defined.

Wherever they occur, both types of burial are nearly always closely connected with the on-going destiny of the dream ego, as will be shown in 13.7-9.

13.6   The Dream Ego between the Death of the Body and Burial

In 13.1 it was mentioned briefly that following a bad death a person's dream ego can find no rest and rapidly develops all the signs of a malevolent spirit being.

It is striking to observe that in almost all societies a person's dream ego, no matter how that person dies, enters into an *unstable condition*[44] immediately afterwards. How long it lasts can vary: among the (Muslim!) Sasak on Lombok a full 1000 days (Cederroth 1988:42ff.), according to the teachings of the Shinto religion of Japan 49 days, calculated from the time of death (Murray 1988:1949). This condition of instability only ends when a *chain of events* is concluded in the course of which the former dream ego changes into a *spirit of the dead*. These events either grant it a completely new status or, as with the African Bemba, succeed in assigning it anew to another person as his dream ego (Badenberg 1999/2002). The range of different rituals governing the period immediately after the death of the body are to help the dream ego to overcome and put an end to this condition of *emotional instability* (Pfeffer 1991:61; Karabila 1995:18).

The condition of instability reveals itself in a variety of forms. The deceased's dream ego wanders around aimlessly, it "spooks around". The Tuareg of North Africa believe that it is frequently present at the grave in a noisy fashion, interfering with the sleep of those within earshot (Neumann 1983).

---

[44] Many authors use the term "liminal state" to describe this instability (Århem 1988:288).

The Chuuk Islanders assume that the unstable emotional state of the dream ego is brought about by the stressful event of the death of the body, which also leads the dream ego to mourn. If it has actually caused the death of the body by too long an absence, it now reproaches itself bitterly. It observes the preparation for the burial, sleeps on the mat of the deceased and in order to comfort the bereaved appears to them in their dreams. The latter serve as convincing proof that the dream ego is present among them.

Meanwhile more and more relatives and acquaintances bring their funeral gifts *(owun ménúmá)*, which are intended for the dream ego and are understood as the first actual offering *(ósór)* to the future spirit of the dead that it will shortly become. Before Christianisation such gifts were laid in the coffin, but today they are handed to the bereaved.

Such presents are also clearly intended to draw the dream ego out of its gloomy mood, to comfort it, give it **emotional stability** and so prevent it from totally losing its composure and becoming a scarcely controllable threat. In other societies it is calmed by continually singing about the deceased until the burial, a special form of lament (Watson 1982:172). The dream ego is further to be helped by a detail in the behaviour of the bereaved when laying out the grave.

The deceased's dream ego is, as is believed, emotionally still so linked with the body and devoted to it that it lets itself be buried with it. Before the soil is trodden firm and the grave covered with fresh cement a stick is placed on the coffin and later pulled out. In this way a hole is left, allowing the dream ego to leave the grave and get back in again. Without this "hole for the soul", or if the burial is made too deep, this would not be possible[45]. Sometimes several bamboo tubes can be found at the head end of the grave, enabling food and drink to reach the deceased, sometimes also tobacco smoke, e.g. among the Dayak and Tenggerese of South East Asia (Tschesnow 1985:238).

The notion of an opening for spirit beings to pass through is also widespread in European-Western societies. In the bedrooms of old farmhouses in remote Alpine valleys slides can be found in the walls, to be opened when someone dies in order to make it easier for the soul to reach the outside. For the same reason, in many parts of South Germany, a window is opened immediately after the last breath is drawn. And the so-called "Holy Ghost hole" in the roof vaults of baroque churches was necessary because until well into the modern period it was believed that the Spirit of God needed an aperture in order to descend on the church congregation.

---

[45] Fischer (2002:130) offers another explanation. Writing about a graveyard in New Guinea, he suggests that the hole in the grave is to make it possible for the widow to see her dead husband.

The Chuuk Islanders believe that during the period of its emotional instability the deceased's dream ego returns several times from the grave to the house of the bereaved. As it does it can even be seen. Relatives have declared that they lay await at night watching, and saw the dream ego like a faintly illuminated form, brushing specks of soil from its clothes, straightening its hair and handling the presents – or rather the spirit doubles of those presents – that they had laid on its grave.

However, during these night watches at the grave the relatives have to exercise caution. The malevolent spirit double that people possess together with their dream ego, and which was unable to leave the body during its lifetime, is now loose, audibly moving around in the vicinity as a malevolent spirit. It makes twigs crack, grunts, whistles, and makes its glowing eyes glitter in the dark.

A deceased's dream ego remains close to the dead body for up to five days. Its emotional bond to it is so strong that it would stay with it forever if it could. But the more the body decomposes, the less often it returns to it in the grave, and the shorter the time it stays there with it. The reason for this is its developed sense of smell that all kinds of spirits possess, as detailed in ch. 6.1, 8.1 und 9.1. *The dream ego can no longer tolerate the odour of corruption* and eventually no longer returns to the grave. At this point in time its *final separation* from the body begins, and this happens fundamentally *against its will*.

❑ Suggestion for own investigations: the physical aspect of the sense of smell which characterises the dream ego seems to be world-wide, but has till now hardly been looked at in research. This gap can be filled by paying attention to the rituals to do with death and the behaviour of the bereaved, and collecting and examining the associated language phenomena.

The dream ego's keen desire to remain with the body of the deceased can also be used, however, to keep it nearby as a future spirit of the dead or ancestral spirit, particularly if the deceased was a significant personality, whose abilities and knowledge might continue to be kept available for the family or local community. All that is necessary is to keep the body preserved and odourless through suitable methods such as embalming and mummifying. If this is not possible, it is sufficient to retain the skull or larynx and store them in a worthy place in order to keep the dream ego close by as a future ancestral spirit or at least persuade it to return from time to time from its post-mortal abode.

It appears that in many African societies the dream ego, during the period of its emotional instability, has to be virtually tamed and coerced by means of the rituals to change into a responsible ancestral spirit whose presence will be a blessing and not a curse to those left behind. This process bears many special features.

13.7   Metamorphosis of the Dream Ego into a Spirit of the Dead

One must begin by realising that not all the possible spirit doubles that a person can possess become benevolent spirits of the dead, but as a rule only the one with special conceptual significance, the dream ego, i.e. the one whose experiences are regarded as the content of dreams. The additional spirit doubles which a person can possess generally become malevolent spirits of the dead, or at least completely unimportant ones, residing from now on, like all other malevolent spirit beings, outside the living space where the relatives of the local community of the deceased continue their existence, but where they can return to from time to time.

In societies where at the moment of death the dream ego instantly and for ever becomes a malevolent spirit of the dead no continuity in the relationship between it and the bereaved emerges. It is to be avoided, because it is to be feared as the source of all kinds of evil and – particularly important – because it can provide no help to its group in times of crisis owing to its lack of intelligence. Among the Krahó of South America dream egos become quite shameless as spirits of the dead and in all respects unsocial. Outwardly also they offer also an unpleasant sight. They consist only of skin and bones, avoid the light, and are blown to and fro by the wind (Carneiro da Cunha 1981:167,173). From this state of affairs one can gain some fundamental understanding of what actually happens when a dream ego changes into a spirit of the dead.

Malevolence and lack of intelligence are features of the SEIC, the seat of the emotions and the intellect, possessed both by humans and spirit beings. *Consequently the metamorphosis into a spirit of the dead occurs first and foremost at this location, the SEIC, at the root of the dream ego's personality, as it were. It has to do with an emotional separation between it and the body.*

❏ Suggestion for own investigations: this fact, together with the great variety of notions connected with it in the numerous animistically oriented societies still in existence today, have up till now hardly been analysed by research, despite the fact that they belong very much to the most elementary conceptual structures of animistic forms of thought.

The moment of metamorphosis of the dream ego into a spirit of the dead, as understood above, is also fundamentally registered in the language. For example, among the Asheninca of Peru the dream ego is no longer called *ishire*, but *peiari*.

In societies where the dream ego becomes exclusively a malevolent spirit of the dead it experiences no period of instability which would at some time come to an end; the period begins at the point of death and theoretically lasts for ever. By contrast the situation is entirely different in societies where the dream ego becomes a benevolent spirit of the dead.

Here also the dream ego's SEIC undergoes a fundamental change. *However, the process itself is complex and lasts a fairly long time*. In this connection there is in the relevant ethnological literature a *gap in the research* of considerable proportions. In no ethnographical study known to me have I been able to find any account of how people with an animistic cognitive framework conceive of the change in the seat of the emotions, intellect and character of the dream ego of a recently deceased person. I will therefore report in detail on the process as described to me by my informant *Wupwiini*. Of course his perceptions are only valid for Chuuk. One should therefore be aware that the process may be presented completely differently in other societies.

Soon after the burial the bereaved carefully spread fine sand or ash on the grave and the immediately surrounding area. The assumption is that the dream ego of the deceased will leave the imprint of a foot or a hand behind, to indicate that the moment of its change into a spirit of the dead has come, which also has as its goal its emotional separation from the body and also from the latter's family. This separation occurs as the result of an action which people are not privy to, because it only takes place in spirit surroundings, in the presence of spirit beings. The knowledge one has of it comes from dreams and accounts of mediums whose dream egos can occasionally participate in such events.

It is of some significance that, as already mentioned, the final separation of the dream ego from the body happens against its will. Hence many dream egos are reluctant to go through with it, not wanting to become spirits of the dead. The powerful spirit of an important person who died previously, or an ancestral spirit of such a person, must as one of its "superiors" vehemently command it to be obedient. Occasionally it must even use force. With the help of other spirit beings the wayward dream ego is dragged to a location where its metamorphosis is to take place. This place is an uninhabited island or the calm water of a coral reef. There, for several hours, the dream ego is "washed" by its accompanying spirits, and in the process continually asked about the names of its immediate relatives. As time goes on it gets muddled, and gaps appear in its memory. The process of washing (*wutumas*) continues

until the dream ego is unable to recall a single name. At this point the ancestral spirits who are present shout: "It (the dream ego) no longer has the SEIC
of a person, but the SEIC of a spirit being!"

This description shows fairly conclusively that here also the metamorphosis of the dream ego into a spirit of the dead involves primarily the seat of the
emotions and intellect. The change is also clear from the language used.
From this moment the dream ego *ngúnúyééch* is called *énú*. It should be
mentioned in addition that the terms spirit of the dead or ancestral spirit are
both to be understood as generic, i.e. *énú* refers not only to spirits of the dead
but to all conceivable spirit beings.

The fact that the new spirit of the dead has forgotten the names of its relatives requires further interpretation. For the Chuuk Islanders forgetting
someone's name signifies the dissolution of any emotional bond with the
bearer of the name. If the new spirit of the dead no longer remembers the
name of its relatives, then this is proof that its emotional bond with them has
changed, has loosened. It definitely still knows them, but has become somewhat distant from them, and does not empathise personally so strongly that it
is drawn into their fate. Mischung (1979:139) comments, concerning the
Karen of South East Asia, that their spirit of the dead no longer loves them.

The dissolution of the strong emotional bond with the group that the
dream ego experiences in the course of its metamorphosis into a spirit of the
dead has considerable consequences. Its new status places it on a level above
them, and so it may expect them to behave with respect. Its authority is also
extended as regards ethical matters, for *as a spirit of the dead it can punish
them for infringements against the norms ("sins")*, especially when it has
attained the elevated status of an ancestral spirit. This was not yet possible
while it was still a dream ego (cf. ch. 9.7). In addition it has acquired at this
juncture a further important credential.

*From now on the living members of its family or local group can make
contact with it through a so-called medium, obtain its advice and meet its
wishes.*

At this point in time the boundary is reached where, according to Christian or European-Western thinking, the *occult sphere* of animistic forms of
religion begins. Contact with spirits of the deceased, now termed *spiritism*,
had already been forbidden to the Israelites in the Old Testament period
(Deuteronomy 18:10-12; Isaiah 8:19), a ruling adopted by Christianity. The
difficulties this causes Christians from an animistic background and cognitive
framework have already been discussed in detail in ch. 9.12.

If the process of a dream ego's metamorphosis into a spirit of the dead is
analysed and stripped of each particular local colouring revealed by different

cultures, it can be seen that it involves a kind of *de-individualisation of the dream ego*. Its personality is removed (Middleton 1982:151).

The changes the new spirit of the dead has undergone concern exclusively its SEIC, not its external appearance. In most societies with an animistic cognitive framework it continues to live on just as it did during the lifetime of the body as a dream ego.

Sometimes, by means of accompanying measures, the bereaved can support, improve, and even optimise this process of change into a benevolent spirit of the dead that a dream ego, destabilised and unsettled by the death of the body, has to make. This involves holding the ritual around the death or mourning in a particular way. The assumption is that the more expensive and lavish the ritual turns out to be, the more rapidly and easily the metamorphosis is achieved. In this sense the events surrounding a person's death can take on the forms of a *feast of merit*. In the field of ethnology this refers to social events of a festive nature hosted by individuals and their kinship groups with the aim of gaining *prestige*. This involves the preparation of enormous amounts of food, consumed by numerous invited guests. In the course of feasts of merit such as the *Potlatch* among Indian ethnic groups on the North West coast of America one even destroys large numbers of valuable objects. It is a way of demonstrating how wealthy one is. Such a festival indeed brings about the economic ruin of the group hosting it, sometimes for a long period of time, but their fame is on everyone's lips.

The prestige that is attained by the hosting group can also be acquired by a spirit of the dead if such a feast of merit is given in its name and honour. First, it raises its status to that of an ancestral spirit and can further enhance this, even years later. But above all the attention paid to the dream ego by its relatives, which is apparent in the feast of merit, helps it to cope with the unstable emotional phase which it got into immediately after the death of the body, and the greater the full powers it attains as an ancestral spirit, the more lavish the arrangements of the feast of merit (Tauchmann 1983:232).

Feasts of merit often coincide with the so-called *secondary burial*, which involves exhuming the now skeletal body, cleaning the bones which remain and finally burying them. In such cases the secondary burial marks the end of the dream ego's period of instability. Several years can elapse before it reaches this stage, the reason being the expense involved in such an event, for the bereaved need time to amass the finances required for the costly rituals.

During the feasts of merit and secondary burials which mark the conclusion of the rituals of death and mourning many societies erect *memorial stones* containing *figures representing the deceased*, and these can take on enormous proportions, e.g. among the Batak of Sumatra.

This normally brings to an end the unstable emotional phase, and the newly emerged benevolent spirit of the dead can take account of its new tasks. However, in many societies yet another difficult undertaking awaits it, and it can only master this if it has re-attained its emotional stability which it temporarily lost.

13.8   The Path to the Realm of the Dead

In societies where such a notion exists it is held that the newly emerged spirit of the dead must by all means first travel to the place where it will finally reside before it can find permanent rest or even begin to fulfil its new tasks. This location can have *various names* (realm of the dead, land of the dead, Elysium in ancient Greece, Hel and Valhalla among the Germanic tribes, "the other village" in African ethnic groups etc.). Many terms are reminiscent of European-Western topographical names.

The realm of the dead can be *very far away*. Being situated somewhere in the cosmos as understood in animistic terms, the spirit of the dead must therefore undertake a *journey* in order to reach it.

The motif of the journey is known all over the world (Corlin 1988) and is mostly described as being tedious, in contrast to the popular assumption that spirit beings can move like lightning from one place to another. It is strenuous, because sometimes there is a steep mountain to climb, and it harbours many dangers. Monsters lie in wait for the spirit of the dead as it journeys, and it has to subdue or placate them. Raging rivers, landslides and lava flows block its way, which leads through inhospitable regions in which it will suffer hunger and thirst. In short, the undertaking proves to be a test, which can reach its climax at the entrance to the realm of the dead, where it has to pay an entry fee or a ferryman, e.g. Charon in ancient Greek and Roman mythology, who brings the new arrival across the river to his destination. For the same purpose, among the Garo of South East Asia, the dead must be buried with earrings, for bribing sentries (Burling 1988:32). Many societies have the notion of a bridge in the form of an enormous, sharply-ground sword which the spirit of the dead has to cross, and not all of them manage it. If the journey is finally unsuccessful, this may be because the rituals of death and mourning were not completed, or the feast of merit had not met all the required conditions (Hülsewiede 1992:288).

In quite a number of ethnic groups the route of the journey is conceived as being so complicated and difficult that the spirits of the dead have to be assisted by a *psychopomp* (soul escort) in order to reach their destination. Normally they find their way to the realm of the dead on their own. However, sometimes they lose their way, are detained by a spirit being or led astray. In such instances the dream ego of a shaman has to step in to track down those spirits who are in trouble on their journey, release them and put them back on the right road. (More detail on this role of the shaman in ch. 14.)

In Christianity, too, the notion exists that a psychopomp leads the souls of the deceased over into the after-life. As a rule the angels take on this task (Luke 16:22). Graphic illustrations of this can be found in the superbly presented book by Vorgrimler/Bernauer/Sternberg 2001.

It is also possible that the new arrivals in the realm of the dead are **weighed** (cf. Daniel 5:25-28), in connection with the notion of an assessment of their achievements during their lives. This assumption was prevalent among the ancient cultures from the Mediterranean to the Far East (Wagner 1989:369). It is not in actual fact an animistic notion, for in those societies a person's dream ego is not called to account, as a spirit of the dead, for the way of life of the person to whom it was assigned. As a rule animistic concepts of the world have **no notions of a hell**. It is fundamental that punishment for wrongdoing is carried out on the (earthly!) body of the person, in the form of illness, calamity etc., as set out in ch. 9.7. This illustrates clearly the **focus of animistic forms of religion on this world**, in contrast to the **focus of Christianity on the world beyond**.

In most societies the realm of the dead is conceived as a spirit-like location somewhere in the cosmos, a place where benevolent spirits of the dead especially enjoy living, because here they are in the company of the former deceased from their kinship group or local community. However, they are not in any sense imprisoned there, but can journey at any time to the place of their former visible existence if this should ever become necessary.

Once all the rituals have been completed, and the spirit of the dead has successfully arrived at its final abode, the person who once lived in bodily form in this world, and at the same time as a dream ego in a transcendent form, lives now only as a spirit of the dead in the world beyond.

13.9   Comparative Profiles of the Life of the Body and of the Dream Ego

If the Chuuk Islanders' perceptions of the development of the person with regard to his body and his dream ego are compared, the following picture emerges.

The life of the dream ego is divided into **three phases**. During the first phase, before the birth of the body, the dream ego has the form of a breast-feeding baby and lives with the benevolent spirits of the dead of his kinship group or local community. With the birth of the body to which it is assigned the second phase of its existence begins, during which the body develops in parallel with it into the form of a mature human being. The death of the body does not (necessarily) interrupt the further development of the physical aspects of the dream ego. The independence of its personality remains intact. This is evident in the language, for it is still referred to with the same term *ngúún*. After a few days, however, it undergoes a metamorphosis, which even now does not affect its outward appearance, but exclusively its SEIC. From then on the dream ego has become a spirit of the dead and the term used is *énú*.

The existence of the person's other (lesser, malevolent) spirit double is divided into only **two phases**. It comes into being together with the body and remains firmly bound to it until the death of the latter. With the death of the body this first phase of its existence is ended. It is released and has thus become a malevolent spirit of the dead.

The same expectations are valid for animals, which are likewise furnished with both a dream ego and a malevolent spirit double. The Islanders believe that in the beyond there are animals which are not malevolent spirit beings. It is assumed that a dog which has been a faithful companion of his master in his visible life will also be assigned to him in the beyond. This means that the animal's dream ego will also lead a post mortem existence as a spirit of the dead.

❑ Suggestion for own investigations: this range of concepts also suffers from an extensive lack of reliable fundamental data. However, in searching for such data one may assume that these concepts are broadly less nuanced than they are in the case of human beings. For example, the Chuuk Islanders cannot conceive of the SEIC of an animal's dream ego turning into the SEIC of a spirit of the dead through a *wutumas* ritual etc.

13.10 Summary

A short summary of the content of this chapter reveals the following important facts:

1. A person's spirit double lives on after death and, at least in theory, for ever, i.e. its life-story does not end with death, in contrast to the life of the body.

2. Of the various spirit doubles a person possesses only his dream ego can become a benevolent spirit of the dead. The latter perpetuates his personality after the death of his body. Among the benevolent spirits of the dead certain particularly important ones attain the status of ancestral spirits.

3. The metamorphosis of a dream ego into a spirit of the dead is understood to be fundamentally a change in its SEIC, i.e. its seat of the emotions, intellect and character. This way of coming into being results in a basic change of attitude on the part of the spirit of the dead towards the living members of its kinship group or local community. The emotional distancing which characterizes a dream ego after its metamorphosis into a (benevolent) spirit of the dead releases it from the pressure to have to behave with unconditional group solidarity, and grants it, as an ancestral spirit, the moral and ethical authority which enables it to constrain those left behind to conduct themselves according to the norms.

4. The metamorphosis of a dream ego into a benevolent spirit of the dead is not universal. In societies with a nomadic, hunter-gatherer background it usually becomes malevolent at the point of death. The desire to get in touch with it is considered to be perilous. Hence it is to be feared and avoided, and thus cannot attain the status of an ancestral spirit.

In such societies the thought of death and the time thereafter is uniquely connected with and burdened by a sense of fear.

5. In societies with a settled agricultural background the dream ego, after a period of emotional instability, is as a rule benevolent, perpetuating the personality of its human counterpart and being regarded as a continuing member of the kinship group or local community, to whom one can turn. The more important among them attain the status of an ancestral spirit with the ability to bring help to the living in times of crisis.

In such societies a positive hope for (eternal) life is mostly more clearly evident.

With reference to the differences described in 4 and 5, and as already indicated in the introductory chapter, two main types of animism can be recognized and established. There is:

Animism *without* veneration of ancestors
and
Animism *with* veneration of ancestors

13.11   In the Next Chapter

This simplified statement is not without its problems, for in real situations the two types of animism do not occur with such clear separation. But it also has a decisive advantage. Integrated into each form of animism there is *a characteristic procedure employed by a specialist with the purpose of making contact, as an intermediary, with spirit beings*. In forms of animism without ancestral veneration this specialist is *the shaman*; in forms of animism with ancestral veneration it is *the medium*. Ultimately this statement is also too simple for a full appreciation and description of the various nuances found in reality, and it is best used only as a rule of thumb.

The following sources contain more on the theme of this chapter:

Århem, Kaj: Into the realm of the sacred: an interpretation of Khasi funeral ritual. In: Cederroth/Corlin/Lindström 1988:257-288.

Badenberg, Robert: The Body, Soul and Spirit Concept of the Bemba in Zambia: Fundamental Characteristics of being human of an African Ethnic Group. Bonn 2002. 2nd rev. ed. (edition iwg – mission academics, Bd. 9. Verlag für Kultur und Wissenschaft).

Bloch, Maurice; Parry, Jonathan (eds.): Death and the regeneration of life. Cambridge et al. 1982.

Burling, Robbins: Garo beliefs in the afterlife. In: Cederroth/Corlin/Lindström 1988:31-38.

Carneiro da Cunha, Manuela: Eschatology among the Krahó: reflection upon society, free field of fabulation. In: Humphreys/King 1981:161-174).

Cederroth, Sven; Corlin, Claes; Lindström Jan (eds.): On the meaning of death. Essays on mortuitary rituals and eschatological beliefs. Uppsala 1988.

Cederroth, Sven: Pouring water and eating food. On the symbolism of death in a Sasak community on Lombok. In: Cederroth/Corlin/Lindström 1988:39-61.

Corlin, Claes: The journey through the Bardo. Notes on the symbolism of Tibetan mortuary rites and the Tibetan Book of the Dead. In: Cederroth/Corlin/Lindström 1988:63-75.

Crocker, Jon Christopher: Vital souls. Bororo cosmology, natural symbolism, and shamanism. Tucson, Arizona 1985.

Fischer Hans: Gräber, Kreuze und Inschriften. Ein Friedhof in Neuguinea. Berlin (Reimer) 2002.

Hasenfratz, Hans-Peter: Die toten Lebenden: eine religionsphaenomenologische Studie zum sozialen Tod in archaischen Gesellschaften. Leiden (Brill) 1982.

Holzhausen, Jens (Hrsg.): Psyche – Seele – anima. Festschrift für Karin Alt zum 7. Mai 1998. Stuttgart und Leipzig 1998.

Hülsewiede, Brigitte: Die Nahua von Tequila. Eine Nachuntersuchung – besonders zu Struktur und Wandel der Familienfeste. Münster und Hamburg 1992.

Humphreys, S. C.; King, H. (eds.): Mortality and immortality: the anthropology and archaeology of death. London 1981.

Jacobsen, T. W.; Cullen, Tracey: A consideration of mortuary practices in Neolithic Greece burials from Franchti Cave. In Humphreys/King 1981:79-101.

Karabila, Abdelkhalek: Die Welt der ğinn und der Heiler. Eine volkskundliche Untersuchung in der Provinz Nador (Marokko). Diss. Mainz 1995.

Kuper, Michael (Hrsg.): Hungrige Geister und rastlose Seelen. Texte zur Schamanismusforschung. Berlin 1991.

Lauby, Heiko: Tötung und Regeneration – Zum Verständnis archaischer Weltbilder. Beispiele aus der jägerischen Glaubenswelt. Magisterarbeit Albert-Ludwigs-Universität Freiburg 2000.

Laubscher, Matthias (Hrsg.): Beiträge zur Ethnologie Mittel- und Südindiens. München 1991.

Middleton, John: Lugbara death. In: Bloch/Parry 1982:134-154.

Mischung, Roland: Religion und Wirklichkeitsvorstellungen in einem Karen-Dorf Nordwest-Thailands. Diss. Frankfurt am Main 1979.

Müller, Klaus E. (Hrsg.): Menschenbilder früher Gesellschaften. Frankfurt 1983.

Müller, Klaus E.: Der gesprungene Ring: wie man die Seele gewinnt und verliert. Frankfurt am Main 1997.

Murray Thomas, R. (ed.): Oriental theories of human development. Scriptural and popular beliefs from Hinduism, Buddhism, Confucianism, Shinto, and Islam. New York et al. (Peter Lang) 1988.

Neumann, Wolfgang: Tuareg. In: Müller 1983:274-292.

Pfeffer, Georg: Seelentausch bei den Gadaba. In: Laubscher 1991:51-92.

Potter, Jack M.: Wind, water bones and souls: the religious world of the Cantonese peasant. Journal of Oriental Studies (Hong Kong) 8.1970:139-153.

Sell, Joachim: Der schlimme Tod bei den Völkern Indonesiens. S'Gravenhage 1955.

Tauchmann, Kurt: Kankanaey (u. Lepanto). In: Müller, Klaus E.1983:222-247.

Thiel, Josef, Franz: Tod in der Gemeinschaft. Sterben und Trauer bei den Bantu in Zentralafrika. In: Linke 1999:211-223.

Topley, Marjorie: Chinese rites for the repose of the soul, with special reference to Cantonese custom. Journal for the Malayan Branch of the Royal Asiatic Society 25.1952:149-160.

Tschesnow, Jan W.: Historische Ethnographie der Länder Indochinas. Berlin 1985.

Vorgrimler, Herbert; Bernauer, Ursula; Sternberg, Thomas: Engel. Erfahrungen göttlicher Nähe. Freiburg, Basel, Wien (Herder) 2001.

Wagner, Fritz: "Gezählt, gewogen und zu leicht befunden" (Daniel 5,25-28). Bemerkungen zum Motiv der Seelenwägung. In: Holzhausen 1998:369-384.

Watson, James L.: Of flesh and bones: The management of death pollution in Cantonese society. In: Bloch/Parry 1982:155-186.

Woodburn, James: Social dimensions of death in four African hunting and gathering societies. In: Bloch/Parry 1982:187-210.

Chapter 14
Contacts between the Living and Spirit Beings (1):
The Work of the Shaman

> This chapter explains what things in the animistic concept of man and of the world are important for the work of the shamans (both men and women), what they are used for, what a journey into the beyond is, how a shamanistic séance is conducted, how one becomes a shaman, and what neo-shamanism is.

14.0   Introduction

In the previous chapters where mention was made of the beyond it was shown that this sphere (conceived as spirit-like) and its inhabitants are in a number of ways *superior* to their material counterparts in this world. This is fundamentally evident by the fact that material objects and beings can only be fully functional when their spirit counterparts are present or nearby. It is apparent that in its totality a world beyond conceived in this way corresponds more to the ideal of perfection than this world does.

At every stage in their lives the *imperfection of this world* impinges itself painfully on the awareness of its inhabitants. Of the abundance of mana in the beyond and its amazing effects people can literally only dream. Is it therefore to be wondered at if they attempt to avail themselves of this wealth of mana, power and knowledge which is apparently limitlessly available to the spirit beings?

14.1   Causes of the Need for Contacts

Societies which are structured more simply, i.e. pre-literate ones without complex technology and science, are dependent in a particular way on the natural environment in which they live. Their members are far more powerless in the face of the ups and downs of existence, the violent forces of nature, the failure of rain, above all diseases and death, than people in more complex societies. For people who have to cope with life in the context of such dependency the vulnerability of all their undertakings constitutes a fundamental *threat to their existence*. The sense of insecurity this gives rise to produces in them a heightened *need for safeguards* against the failure of any venture. They have to look for solutions to hitherto unknown problem situations, e.g. in the case of an unfamiliar illness. For the people living in this visible world it is about security in the face of an uncertain fate. This feeling of existential threat is based essentially on the *imperfection and fragmentary nature of all human knowledge*.

However, in the view of people of an animistic cognitive framework, the knowledge they lack is available. The benevolent spirit beings in the beyond preside over it in an ideal way. Located there are the mightiest and most capable spirit beings, furnished with inexhaustible mana, great abundance of power, and immeasurable knowledge. Living there also is the Supreme Being himself, together with a vast host of guardian spirits and other assistant spirits having unhindered access to this mana, this power, and this knowledge, none of which is either present or attainable in the realm of material things.

Among them are spirit beings which are particularly well-disposed towards human beings, i.e. their ancestral spirits and other spirits of the dead which had served the deceased family members during their lives as dream egos. One is therefore justified in assuming that they are more ready and willing than other spirit beings to grant their living kin access to this knowledge which they now likewise command after their metamorphosis into spirits of the dead, for they still belong to their kinship group or local community and must therefore show solidarity with them. However, one is still faced with the problem of how to actually get at their knowledge.

14.2 Procedures for Acquisition of Knowledge Available in the Beyond

Animistically oriented societies are familiar with *two methods* of getting hold of the knowledge they lack, but which is available in the beyond. The first one is the *dream*. Since the contents are conceived as being the experiences of the dream ego, the dream is the accessible source of understanding and knowledge for all persons *individually*. In dreams one obtains answers from one's own dream ego to unsolved questions, as described in ch. 12. In dreams each person can make contact with spirit beings through his dream ego and expect them to be able and willing to help him, whether they are his ancestral spirits or his other assistant spirits.

In ch. 12 it was pointed out that dreams are perceived as a kind of window into the beyond, enabling people in this world to have a glimpse "across the divide", including access to the knowledge available there, knowledge which can be used to develop problem-solving procedures which can be applied in this world.

One fundamental difficulty consists in the fact that dreams, while giving access to knowledge which is lacking, cannot actually be made use of when a situation of need arises. Sleeping and dreaming cannot be called upon at will and at any time. Consequently the acquisition of understanding and knowledge with the help of dreams is somewhat coincidental. Much more secure is the second method, the *trance*.

There is a basic commonality, but also a fundamental difference between a trance and a dream: as in a dream, so also in a trance the events experienced are understood as the experiences of the dream ego. The difference: the trance is not accessible to all people individually, but only to a *specialist*, who functions as a go-between. The latter is essential because a condition of trance can only be attained with the help of procedures, whose manifold attendant circumstances, rules, means, thought forms, contents and goals have to be studied. In addition these procedures are so strongly overlaid with rituals that the layman runs the danger of inadvertently deviating from the ritual and making mistakes. This must not be allowed to happen if contact with a spirit being is to succeed.

Not all societies of this kind lay claim to benevolent spirits of the dead or ancestral spirits who can be approached or asked for help, but only those whose cognitive framework corresponds to an animistic concept of the world and mankind of type 2. In type 1, which in principle does not include a relationship between man and spirits of the dead or ancestral spirits (apart from exceptional cases) there are instead the so-called *assistant spirits*, as described in ch. 9.9.

The previous chapter concluded by pointing out that the difference between ancestral spirits and assistant spirits is of such a fundamental nature that the respective specialist or go-between, conceptually appointed, employs a characteristically different procedure when making contact with them: in *type 1* (animism without explicit veneration of ancestors) it is *the shaman*, in *type 2* (animism without veneration of ancestors) it is *the medium*.

14.3   The Shaman as the Representative of Type 1 Animism

Despite various attempts at an explanation the origin of the term shaman is not yet clearly defined. According to Zinser (1991:17), the etymologist with the most probable answer, it comes from Tungusic, a language of Northern Asia. Kortt on the other hand (1991:46) records that it might come from the Sanskrit term for "monk". Bystrina (1991) and Linke (1999) each name another possible etymological derivation.

Shamans are men and women of status in their kinship group or local community. The status derives from the office that they perform, and which was passed on to them because at some point it became evident that they had a special capacity for it. They possess greater intelligence or more personal charisma (mana!) than the other members of the group. Sometimes events have occurred in their life story which had to be interpreted as signs that spirit beings had chosen them and destined them. There will be more detail on this later.

The fact that the individuals who become shamans are those with above-average intelligence and personality, prominent among their kinship group or local community, can be explained by the way the animistic concept of man is structured, as described in ch. 3. The assumption is that shamans, unlike ordinary people, do not possess just one dream ego, but several. These have either had an early positive influence on the development of that person's intellectual and emotional abilities, including the development of his SEIC, or they have caused these abilities to emerge particularly strongly at a certain age. At all events it is his dream egos which essentially establish his status as a shaman. The Asheninca of Peru, who believe that the heart forms both the seat of the emotions and the intellect as well as the abode of the dream ego when the body is awake, hold the following notions in this connection.

Normally both animals and humans have just one heart. However, there are people who possess more than one. Such people indicate this by special intellectual qualities, impressive feats of memory, perspicacity or the ability to see events in advance in dreams, and acquire access to hidden knowledge. Such a person can have several hearts with corresponding intelligence and memory performance, as an Asheninca explained to me with conviction (Käser 1995). He or she is thus specially equipped to acquire knowledge available in the beyond, and is qualified for the office of shaman.

The notion that shamans possess several dream egos is also found among other South American ethnic groups, e.g. the Krahó (Carneiro da Cunha 1981:163), and the Ugrian of Western Siberia.

An Asheninca shaman can possess up to *four hearts*. A proportionate number of dream egos accompany him throughout his earthly life, and it is they who actually enable his work as a shaman.

14.4   Notions Concerning the Shaman's Dealings with Spirit Beings

People living in a society with shamanistic background assume that the shaman can perceive, have dealings with and communicate with all kinds of spirit beings not only in a state of trance but also when awake, something which is denied to ordinary people. The spirit beings he is involved with when awake include the dream egos of the members of his kinship group or local community known to him, because they live in his immediate vicinity. What the dream egos are doing, how they are faring and where they happen to be at any moment is also known to him from his dreams.

Sometimes it happens that a person's dream ego has lost its way, has been abducted by other spirit beings, or commanded to take part in one of their enterprises in the beyond. In such a case the shaman must take action, for the absence of the dream ego from the body can increase the danger of that person becoming ill and dying. The shaman is expected to go looking for the missing dream ego. He can only do that if he sends one of his own dream egos on a so-called *journey into the beyond*.

In ethnological writings this journey is usually termed *soul journey*, sometimes also heaven journey and underworld journey, depending on its purpose or destination. It constitutes one of the essential features of a shaman's activity. Since it is combined with the notion that it involves at least one of the shaman's dream egos leaving his body, taking itself away from him, it is also called *ecstasy* (Greek 'being outside of oneself'). If by contrast a spirit being (usually considered to be benevolent) enters a person's body, the term used is *enstasy* (Greek 'being inside').

14.5   How the Events Surrounding the Shaman's Journey into the Beyond Are Perceived

Ecstasy begins when the shaman, with the aid of one of the procedures described in ch. 12.6, has put himself into a state of trance. Once it starts all his dream egos are free to move. One of the dream egos – occasionally several – sets off to deal with the great variety of tasks involved in searching for an absent dream ego, especially in order to meet up with one of the shaman's assistant spirits and consult it. Assistant spirits are considered to be the actual source of all the knowledge that the shaman can acquire (cf. ch. 9.9). While one of his dream egos is on this journey, those that remain with him guard his body, for the latter is endangered by this situation. Malevolent spirit beings, regarding the journey as an invasion of their territory, could, for example, be angry enough to attack the shaman's body while he is in a trance, seize possession of it and kill it.

Only if a malevolent spirit being does take over the body of the shaman (or indeed of an ordinary person), can one in my opinion talk of *possession* in the negative European-Western sense, for this is a condition which neither he nor his society ever regard as worth striving for, but fear it and seek to avoid it, for understandable reasons.

Having now set off, the shaman's dream ego finds the journey to be a difficult undertaking. Its experiences resemble those of the spirits of the dead in type 2 animism who have to venture for the first time into the realm of the dead. It has to endure many exertions, traverse barren plains, impenetrable forests and frozen wastes, and survive combats. Malicious spirit beings hinder it, cannibalistic monsters seek to overcome it. Everywhere and all the time there are dangers lurking, as described in ch. 13.8.

In such situations help may be needed if the task is not to fail, and so right at the start of the journey the shaman's dream ego may be met by one of his guardian spirits and accompanied through to the end. This is especially the case with journeys to the underworld or to the depths of the ocean, or to one of the Lords of the animals, in order to beg pardon for its community because of people's wrong behaviour. For this purpose guardian spirits adopt the form of a riding animal in order to bring the shaman safely to his destination. It is better still, particularly for an Asheninca shaman, for the dream ego to change into a well-protected, aggressive *carnivore* for the journey, e.g. a jaguar. Among south American ethnic groups this animal is frequently regarded as the dream ego of a shaman on its journey into the beyond, so that it would be perilous to kill it. In the shamanism of North Eurasia it is thought that there is hardly any creature into which a shaman's dream ego could not transform itself. Among the Ugrian of Western Siberia shamans even resort to the strategy of sending their dream ego on their journey as a mosquito, exploiting the possibility that malicious spirit beings would not find it easy to detect.

Sometimes the journey into the beyond leads the shaman's dream ego over enormous distances into space, for the abode of its guardian spirits and other assistant spirits may be on a far distant star. Such distances can only be covered in a reasonable length of time by flying, so it has to take on the form of a bird. If one of the shaman's guardians or assistant spirits should have the form of a bird as part of its nature then he can rely on it to transport his dream ego to its destination. In this way the journey into the beyond becomes the *flight of the shaman*, as Linke (1999) has called it in his contribution to the shamanism issue. This is why among many ethnic groups shooting stars and bolts of lightning (Baer 1969) are held to be shamans on their interstellar flight to their assistant spirits on the various levels of the sky (cf. ch. 9.1).

They can also arrive there, if the notion is held, by ascending the trunk of the world tree (cf. ch. 4.3) whose branches support the various levels of the sky, or via the rungs of a spirit-like ladder between the sky and the earth, the location of which is known only to the shaman. In many ethnic groups his dream ego uses the rainbow as a bridge, a notion for which there is also evidence among the Germanic tribes.

In some societies the shaman whose dream ego is on a journey into the beyond is a *soul escort* or *psychopomp*, as it is termed in the literature. The trance is a fundamental aid to his fulfilment of this task. The perception is that he escorts the dream egos of the unborn or the newly born from the locations where they reside or originate to the sphere of their future kinship group or local community and into the body of their pregnant mothers. He may also – provided that this somewhat rare notion is present in connection with shamanism – escort the dream egos of the deceased to their final abode in the land of the dead (Linke 1999). Sometimes he has to release a dream ego that has fallen into a crevice, or fight on behalf of one that has been detained by a malevolent spirit being (Kortt 1991, Linke 1999).

In many societies shamans take dream egos from their own kinship groups or local communities with them on the journey into the beyond and must then be very careful that all of them get back unharmed (Kortt 1991:29).

When the shaman awakens from his trance this means that his dream ego has returned. This is the latest moment at which he can report on what he claims to have experienced, if he had not already done that during the trance. He is now in a position to begin to treat the illness, having learned about its cause and possible remedies from his assistant spirits, etc.

14.6   External Aspects of a Shamanistic Trance

For various reasons events of this kind take place mostly in the evenings. They usually involve and also interest the whole kinship group or local community, so everyone wants to take part, and this is only possible during the evening hours or at night, when no one is any longer doing any kind of work. Also the lighting effects produced by the drugs and the hallucinations of the shaman can only be fully perceived and achieve their impact in deep darkness. In some societies only a few persons are allowed to be present on such an occasion, and in others the shaman operates completely alone in a hut or a tent.

The information on the length of the trance, together with the journey into the beyond during the hallucination, varies considerably. It can take between 10 minutes and 24 hours. In some societies the shaman remains motionless during the whole trance, in others he or she stands up from time to time and climbs up a ladder into the upper floor of the house, to hold a monologue with the assistant spirits or communicate with them in a singing voice.

The process of a shamanistic *séance*[46] contains a fairly large number of ritually determined elements, which can vary greatly depending on the ethnic

---

[46] This is the usual term for the event in ethnological literature (from the French for conference, assembly, performance, presentation).

group. Not all of them are important for understanding the underlying conceptual structure of such events, and so do not need to be discussed here in detail.

The office of shaman involves special *attire* and certain *items of equipment*. When performing a ritual he wears clothing on which a stylised skeleton is visible. The latter can be interpreted in various ways, e.g. as a depiction of some kind of "skeleton soul" (cf. ch. 11.7), as a symbol of the shaman's involvement with people's death, but also as a symbol for game animals whose bones have to be returned to the Lord of the animals (or his female counterpart) through the shaman. Mirrors attached to his clothing are for scaring away malevolent spirits, who take fright and run when they see their own hideous face. In many ethnic groups shamans wear a so-called antler crown to indicate the nature of their particular assistant spirit (reindeer, elk, stag), or simply as an expression of the hunter-gatherer character of their culture. A drum is also widely used, and many shamans dance to its rhythms in their state of ecstasy. Many of them also carry a shaman's staff, a kind of sceptre.

However, this equipment is almost always found only in the so-called classical shaminism of the ethnic groups of northern Eurasia and North America in the Arctic Circle. In South American ethnic groups the external appearance of the shaman during the ritual is much less striking. This leads to a problem of terminology.

This has to do with the fact that the term shamanism is used for a variety of phenomena which are often only remotely connected with it. Sometimes healers are referred to as shamans, even though they are exclusively herbalists and only handle medicinal plants. Lay people also include here even priests, mystics, modern charismatics, ecstatics and prophets. This multiplicity distorts one's perspective on the real phenomenon. One should always bear in mind that the office of shaman comprises several functions, and that he is involved in activities for which he does not have to go into a trance and hence not embark on a journey into the beyond. Sometimes he is also a healer who exorcises malevolent spirit beings which have seized possession of a person's body, or he extracts harmful substances which have penetrated a person's body. In other societies he is an oracle, predicting the future. His abilities can also be drawn upon in the search for lost items. He has to gather information to do with hunting, weather, good fortune in war, migrating herds of animals etc. (Buchta 1997/98). In societies where the accompanying forms of phenomena are absent or where only individual parallels are recognizable one should speak of *animism with shamanistic elements* (Linke 1999). However, two of these elements must on no account be missing if a combination of phenomena is to be correctly designated as shamanism. These are the *trance*, or altered state of consciousness, and the *journey into the beyond*, for which the trance is a prerequisite.

14.7   The Work of the Shaman as a Personal Burden

In ch. 12.6 it was mentioned that the life of the shaman is not easy. Ritual deprivation, periods of fasting and the use of drugs as an emetic emaciate the body and have a detrimental effect on health. Hence many of them have a lower life expectancy than the other members of their community.

A particular strain of a psychic nature arises from the hallucinations in the trance of the journey into the beyond. The dangers he experiences and the frights he has to deal with continue to torment him even after the trance is over, giving him a lot to cope with. This is why he is not alone during the ritual. At the very least his wife assists him, and many shamans are even married to several wives for this reason.

The dramatic effects of hallucinating a journey into the beyond under the influcence of drugs have been described as follows by the ethnologist Gerhard Baer (1987:78) after an experiment on himself:

"We stretched out on the woven mats used for sitting and sleeping and waited. After a short time, about a quarter of an hour, I sensed the first effect, felt constricted, and sat up. It was as if I was being born on a strong current towards a waterfall; there was no escape. Fear gripped me. Even before the threshold of the trance was reached I found it hard to breathe. My chest seemed to be compressed. ... The hallucination began to produce sounds which reverberated in my ears. In this state I wanted to ask Jonas (one of the Piros) for support, but I couldn't move, and simply said: 'now, now.' Then I was on the threshold of the trance. An unbelievably piercing light, like an actual flash of lightning, went through me. It illuminated a nocturnal ocean of cloud, a stormy sea. A fear that my innermost being would be loosed from me blotted out for a moment all other sensations. I saw myself (or this innermost being) as a tiny ball, exposed in a nocturnal landscape lit up by the lightning. Then came hallucinations of colour and space. Cobwebs made of rows of coloured spots swayed to and fro, forwards and backwards; contours continually dissolved. Despite the greatest of efforts I found it impossible to focus on any part of the interior of the house and hold it in vision. These hallucinations kept coming back in waves, receding after about an hour, but the feeling of constriction (shortness of breath), headache, a trembling throughout the whole body, violent spasms of yawning and over-sensitivity of the eyes remained for a long time. The tiniest light was painful."

14.8   The Shaman as a Threat to His Community

As depicted so far the shaman appears almost exclusively as a benefactor. This impression needs to be qualified when one considers his activity in the wider context of his community. There is no question that his function in dealing with crises does indeed mitigate tensions in the life of the community and produces a harmonious effect. However, that is only one aspect of the reality.

Experience has shown that even in the case of minor medical problems his procedures of diagnosis of illness and subsequent therapy with the aid of dreams, trance and assistant spirits lead to mistreatments which have devastating consequences for the patients (cf. ch. 8.5). Diseases such as tuberculosis, meningitis or acute appendicitis cannot be cured by sucking on the patients body, blowing on the site of the pain, or massage techniques.

In addition in many societies where shamanism is practised there is the notion that the shaman can also engage his abilities to bring calamity. It is believed that he can swallow the dream egos of people he hates in order to make them physically ill and kill them. Crocker (1985:136) reports that among the Bororo of Brazil an overweight shaman was suspected of acquiring his obesity by consuming too many dream egos. It is also assumed that he misuses his control over influential spirit beings for his own advantage and to gain power, by threatening to use his abilities to harm individuals and groups opposed to his intentions and decisions. This would appear to equate shamans with witches and sorcerers, who are admittedly accepted as part of society, but are also regarded with mistrust (Crocker 1985:237).

In ethnic groups living in a modern state system this kind of misuse of power sometimes leads to tensions. Shamans who hold political office as representatives of their community can use their position, and the expectations their community has of them, as mediators between this world and the beyond, in their own favour. The fear of opposing the will of the shaman in secular political debate is calculated to have considerable influence on democratic decisions and sometimes to corrupt internal ethnic relations in a dramatic way. However, people usually assume that it is only from shamans who belong to other kinship groups and communities that such nastiness is to be expected.

14.9   The Shaman's Call to Office and the Development of His Career

The simplest way of becoming a shaman is when one of the members of his kinship group or local community *designates* one of their members, someone considered to be suitable, to undertake this task. Some individual, or even that person himself, dreams that he should become a shaman. His suitability may derive from the fact that he is known to dream a great deal, and his dreams reveal that he already possesses the experience and knowledge marking him out as an expert in matters to do with the beyond. Perhaps he has foreseen an accident, announced the location of a missing person, or discovered where to find an abundance of game or fish. Sometimes an elderly shaman may pass on the office to his son or daughter. Maybe one of them has learned in a dream that this is the desire of an assistant spirit.

There is also *self-vocation* or *self-appointment*, e.g. among the Jivaro and the Matsigenka of South America (Baer/Snell 1974).

In many societies those who attain the office of shaman have *distinguishing features*. These can be of a physical or purely bodily nature, for example extra fingers or toes. People with the characteristics of both sexes, so-called hermaphrodites, are considered to be particularly suitable to be shamans (and mediums!). If the Supreme Being and subordinate deities are perceived as bisexual, regarded as uniting both sexes in one person in symbolic perfection, it is presumed that people with such characteristics are more in tune with the divine and hence particularly suited to such offices.

If someone has an *illness* which brings him close to death but from which he is unexpectedly cured, this is often taken as a sign that spirit beings have chosen him as a future shaman. A person's epileptic fits can be interpreted by the community as appropriation by assistant spirits who wish to make that person into a shaman.

In this case also one might speak of possession in a European-Western sense. If one does, one should understand quite clearly that the society in question perceives nothing demonic or occult in it, for assistant spirits are held to be benevolent and constitute no threat to them.

The complexity of such a calling is evident in a detail described by Crocker (1985:101) in his account of the Bororo of Brazil: a child has had an epileptic fit. The event is interpreted as the loss of his dream ego which has been taken away by benevolent spirit beings (*aroe*) with the intention of making it acquainted with the spirit world. In this way the child can later become a shaman.

In somewhat rare cases a Supreme Being, for example a Lord (or female counterpart) of the animals, calls someone to be the future shaman.

Both men and women qualify for the office on (almost) equal terms. Sometimes women are barred from the trance and the subsequent journey into the beyond during menstruation, because according to female informants her body odour repels benevolent spirit beings and lures malevolent ones.

Older women no longer have this problem. In many ethnic groups of East Asia female shamans are in the majority (Linke 1999:190).

The selection often begins when the future holder of the office develops *an aversion to certain foods*, e.g. those with a strong smell and with a salty or sharp taste. Spirit beings, in this case his assistant spirits, feel repelled by them.

Accounts of the preparations for the office of shaman indicate that the future holder leaves his community for a period of time, demonstrates inexplicable and occasionally odd behaviour, undertakes symbolic cleansings, observes rules of hygiene and fasting dictates, and practises sexual abstinence. In a state of hallucination he experiences the injury, dismemberment or skeletisation of his body, and his death and resurrection, an event which he later continues to re-enact symbolically each time he goes into a trance and returns from that state of ecstasy.

The Bororo of South America expect a shaman candidate to cope with a situation in which he has to resist sexual temptation. He is forced to ingest maggot-infested food, take hold of a gigantic toad full of suppurating wounds, walk through a ball of fire etc. (Crocker 1985:204-205).

Shamans must *learn* the proficiencies of their office from a specialist. This can demand a lot of time. The material to be studied includes the production of medicines, knowledge of plants, procedures for retrieving absent dream egos, for inducing rain and sunshine etc. If they have to practise dances for the pleasure of the assistant spirits then they need to add musical and choreographical talents to the requirements they need to possess.

It is particularly important for them to be familiar with the *topography and geography of the world beyond*, termed mythical geography in ch. 4.3. A multi-layered cosmos with its travel routes and inhabitants, the great variety of guardian spirits and other assistant spirits, all this sometimes requires a long-lasting process of study. Sometimes shamans have to learn extremely cunning procedures to help them create an opening beneath the line of the horizon in order to get through into the space beyond (Buchta 1997/1998:13).

During the initiation phase they experience a *period of emotional trauma*, a kind of crisis, which usually concludes with the start of their official duties as shaman.

Often future shamans are not candidates or applicants in the usual sense of the term, for their calling may happen *against their will*. This results in personal conflict. If they refuse, they are threatened by sanctions on the part of their potential guardian spirits and other assistant spirits, who sometimes vigorously insist that they be ready to take on the office. Their revenge can be life-threatening (Buchta 1997/98).

Carrying out the duties of the office is no mean task. Shamans continually fear making mistakes, producing wrong diagnoses, being attacked by powerful malevolent spirit beings and overall endangering their kinship group or local community. Then there is the journey into the beyond, a special source of stress, as Baer's description quoted above demonstrates. They are also afraid of damaging or losing the insignia of the office, as a result of which they can become ill and even die (Crocker 1985:210).

14.10 Neo-Shamanism

A growing number of contemporaries interested in shamanistic techniques and procedures are presently engaged in trying to integrate aspects of the thought, techniques and methodology into the European-Western context, above all in medicine. This would only be possible in a very limited way, since the state of ecstasy, one of the central elements in the whole practice of shamanism, only has any real connotation where those involved recognize a particular, indispensible concept of the world and of man as a valid social reality.

Clearly this is not the case in European-Western societies, because all the symbolism that characterises shamanism arose from the experiences of the hunter-gatherer and cattle-breeding societies in the tundra and taiga (on this cf. Zinser 1991:23-25). In other words, the nature and significance of shamanism cannot be sought outside of its particular social environment, but logically inside that framework (Kortt 1991:28). The European-Western way of thinking and acting distils certain elements from the overall complex nature of shamanism, prefers for example to regard the journey into the beyond as a journey into the underworld, shifts its meaning, adds other emphases and absolutises it in terms of its function. For a pertinent publication which particularly claims to promote a so-called shamanist consciousness see Harner 1982.

Neo-shamanism is increasingly termed New Age shamanism. For the best information on it see Zinser 1988.

14.11 Summary

Shamans are conveyors of knowledge presumed to be available in the beyond, and which serves as a guide to coping with all kinds of crisis situations. This knowledge is ascertained by the shaman via his assistant spirits and redeployed to his community in this world. Central to it is the notion that the shaman or his dream ego *visits the beyond* in order to acquire the missing knowledge. In the process there is no direct contact between the people bene-fiting from this knowledge and the spirit beings who make it available (in contrast to the work of the medium).

The amount of academic and scientific literature on the subject of sha-manism has now become almost too vast to comprehend. The study by Eliade 1975 is regarded as a classic standard work.

14.12 In the Next Chapter

There is a special notion concerning the form of the shaman's ecstasy, ac-cording to which one or more of his assistant spirits take the place of his dream ego, the latter having left his body during the trance. It might seem that the shaman is still conscious, not lying down but standing up, moving around and speaking (Crocker 1985:203). Since the explanation of this be-haviour is that a spirit being not belonging to his person has taken possession of him, people refer to such instances as *possession-shamanism*.

However, it is not strictly speaking shamanism, for in such instances the ecstasy of the shaman-dream ego is diminished in its significance by the *en-stasy*[47] of an external spirit being, indeed overlaid and, as it were, substituted by it. Enstasy is nevertheless a fundamental element in the work of the *me-dium*, which is the theme of the following chapter.

The following sources contain more on the theme of this chapter:

Baer, Gerhard: Ein besonderes Merkmal des südamerikanischen Schamanen. Zeit-schrift für Ethnologie 94.1969:284-292.

Baer, Gerhard; Snell, Wayne W.: An Ayahuasca ceremony among the Matsigenka (Eastern Peru). Zeitschrift für Ethnologie 99.1974: 63-80.

Baer, Gerhard: Peruanische ayahuasca-Sitzungen – Schamanen und Heilbehandlun-gen. In: Dittrich/Scharfetter 1987:70-88.

Buchta, Brigitte: Aspekte des Schamanismus in der aktuellen Psychosomatik. MA Freiburg Br. WS 1997/98.

Bystrina, Ivan: Das Erbe des Schamanismus im alten Palästina. In: Kuper 1991:181-212.

Carneiro da Cunha, Manuela: Eschatology among the Krahó: reflection upon soci-ety, free field of fabulation. In: Humphreys/King 1981:161-174.

Crocker, Jon Christopher: Vital souls. Bororo cosmology, natural symbolism, and shamanism. Tucson, Arizona 1985.

---

[47] A number of researchers refer to the phenomenon as *alien spirit possession*.

Dittrich, Adolf; Scharfetter Christian (Hrsg.): Ethnopsychotherapie. Psychotherapie mittels außergewöhnlicher Bewusstseinszustände in westlichen und indigenen Kulturen. Stuttgart (Ferdinand Enke) 1987.

Eliade, Mircea: Schamanismus und archaische Ekstasetechnik. Frankfurt am Main (Suhrkamp) 1975.

Harner, Michael: Der Weg des Schamanen. Ein praktischer Führer zu innerer Heilkraft. Interlaken 1982.

Humphreys, S. C.; King, H. (eds.): Mortality and immortality: the anthropology and archaeology of death. London 1981.

Käser, Lothar: Kognitive Aspekte des Menschenbildes bei den Campa (Asheninca). *asien afrika lateinamerika* 23.1995:29-50.

Kortt, Ivan: Die soziale Bindung des sibirischen Schamanen. In: Kuper 1991:27-43.

Kuper, Michael (Hrsg.): Hungrige Geister und rastlose Seelen. Texte zur Schamanismusforschung. Berlin 1991.

Linke, Bernd Michael (Hrsg.): Die Welt nach der Welt. Jenseitsmodelle in den Religionen. Frankfurt am Main 1999.

Linke, Bernd Michael: Der Flug des Schamanen. Fahrten ins Jenseits. In: Linke 1999: 173-199.

Zinser, Hartmut: Traumreisen und Schamanisieren. Beobachtungen zum "New-Age"-Schamanismus. In: Materialdienst der EZW 51.1988.9:249-260.

Zinser, Hartmut: Zur Faszination des Schamanismus. In Kuper 1991:17-26.

Chapter 15
Contacts between the Living and Spirit Beings (2): The Work of the Medium

This chapter explains what aspects in the concept of the world and of man are important for the work of mediums, the ways in which mediums are employed, the basic conceptual difference between the work of the shaman and that of the medium, how a medium's séance is conducted, how one becomes a medium, and the significance of mediums for their society.

15.0   Introduction

Everything said in ch. 14.0-2 about the prerequisites, circumstances and conditions for the work of the shaman applies also to the medium. To help the reader to compare directly the commonalities and differences in their functions, statements made in ch. 14 will be summarised in ch. 15 and repeated word for word where there are important parallels.

Here also one of the fundamental assumptions is a perspective on the world which assumes that the beyond with its spirit objects and inhabitants, where mana, power and knowledge are limitlessly available, is superior to this world, and that one can compensate for the imperfections of this world by making contact with the beyond.

15.1   Causes of the Need for Contacts

Societies where there are mediums see themselves confronted with the same problems of safeguarding their existence as those where there are shamans, and hence both of them have to a large extent developed the same procedures for solving those problems.

Advice and help are needed in problem situations which arise because of the vulnerability of all human undertakings, making one aware that one's knowledge is fragmentary and hence not adequate for finding solutions and providing hope in the face of an uncertain future.

In contrast to societies with type 1 animism, where the notions of the beyond assume the presence of guardian spirits and other assistant spirits which are only accessible to the shaman, in the notions of the beyond in societies with the various features of type 2 animism there exist spirit beings, i.e. *spirits of the dead* and *ancestral spirits*, which are not only considered to be benevolent but are also much closer to people. Although they are essentially no different from the guardian spirits and other assistant spirits of the shaman, the care and attention which can be expected from ancestral spirits are by rights founded on the *kinship solidarity* or *perceived localised vicinity* of these spirit beings to the people in this world who are relying on help from the beyond. This means that they can be much more directly addressed and approached for help by their kinship group or local community. However, in this case also a go-between is required.

15.2   Procedures for Gaining Knowledge Perceived to Be Available in the Beyond

Spirits of the dead and ancestral spirits are available in dreams to give help and advice, and this opportunity is open to everybody individually. But if a problem situation has to be solved quickly and effectively, then the specialist is needed to make direct contact with them, whether consciously or in a state of trance, i.e. the *medium*.

15.3   The Medium as the Representative of Type 2 Animism

The origin of the term, unlike that of "shaman", is secure, being from the Latin. In Latin *medius* and its neuter form *medium* mean the middle one, that which stands in the middle.

The terms used for the medium in various languages are instructive. Among the Chuuk Islanders the different terms signify *means of transport*, *riding animal*, or *vehicle of the spirits* (*waatawa, wáán énú*). The concrete notions connected with these are described in section 15.6. Other terms for the medium indicate additional tasks which are carried out, e.g. *specialist in spirit beings* (*sowuyénú*), *in sacrifices* (*sowuwósoomá*), *in retrieving absent dream egos* (*sowuwamwééngún*) and *dance master* (*sowupwérúk*).

With regard to the personality of the medium, whether man or woman, almost everything said about the shaman in 14.3 also applies here. Detailed information on how the Chuuk Islanders perceive the personality make-up of their mediums can be found in section 15.8.

15.4   Notions of the Medium's Dealings with Spirit Beings

It must first be pointed out that mediums do not need to be in any special physical or psychic condition in order to be able to perceive, associate or communicate with all kinds of spirit beings. No other preparations are required beyond observing the appropriate taboos. Spirit beings can visit a medium at any time and in any place. It happens without ordinary people noticing anything. This type of contact is described as friendly and cooperative, characterised by mutual trust.

As a rule mediums make themselves understood during such informal contacts with spirit beings not by speaking with them but in the form of a *thought dialogue*, so that no one can listen to it.

The Islanders believe that there must be an infinitely large number of spirit beings, and so the medium can only really get to know some of them. If he wants to identify a particular spirit being, he has to know the person it belongs to or used to belong to. This means that basically the medium only has dealings with the benevolent spirit beings in the area of his own experience, those of his kinship group, local community, village or region, i.e. both with their dream egos and with the spirits of the dead that emerged from them. These are the ones closest to him, to which he himself has a quite personal relationship. Above all he is familiar in detail with the circumstances which prevail within the sphere of responsibility of the relevant spirit beings, and knows the extent of that sphere. Hence the medium of a village or island is also available on a regular basis to the local high-ranking spirit being, and to the village or island community subordinate to it, for making mutual contact. The medium looks after the place of sacrifice, the *faar*, ensures that the necessary offerings are brought, and that the requirements of that high-ranking spirit being are met. It is also indeed assumed that a medium is aware of what the spirit beings of his narrower social environment are intending, where they are gathering and what they are doing.

A medium can probably liaise in direct conversation between a benevolent spirit of the dead and the living members of its group when both parties are unknown to him, but this may well be a theoretical possibility.

Contacts with so-called unfamiliar spirit beings, as is known from African societies[48] (Streck 1997), remain an exception on Chuuk, and the Supreme Being never reveals himself and his will via a medium. This is similarly the case in other societies. It is rare for the Lord of the animals or his female counterpart to make use of a medium to address human beings directly.

The Old Testament figure of Balaam (Numbers 4:22-24) is of interest in this connection. He seems to have been a medium, or at least to have had the

---

[48] One example of possession by unfamiliar spirits is the so-called *Zar cult*, a form of religion rooted in folk belief and prevalent throughout North East Africa and Islamic societies in the Near and Middle East, in which healing of diseases with the help of ritual possession by spirits called Zar play a central role.

characteristics of one, via whom high-ranking deities and even Yahweh addressed human beings (Schüle 2001).

Since it is completely pointless and dangerous to make contact with malevolent spirit beings a medium deals exclusively with spirit beings which his culture and society consider to be benevolent. Only they have the capacity to communicate, the need to do so, and the knowledge which renders contact with them necessary.

In addition the medium is also aware of what the spirit beings within his purview are doing, how they are and where they happen to be, through his dreams.

So it is possible, for example, for a medium to encounter the weeping dream ego of a living person he knows, and to discover that the reason why it is crying is because that person must shortly die. In this way the medium is able to prophesy a person's imminent death. If someone incurs symptoms of disease which can be traced to the absence of his dream ego one can inquire of the medium whether he knows the whereabouts of the dream ego. It is quite possible that the latter has given the medium notice of its departure and indicated why it is absent, where it has gone and when it intends to return. It leaves such information behind so as not to let the group worry if one of their members should show related symptoms.

If a person's dream ego has disappeared without any trace the medium will ask a high-ranking spirit of the dead or another dream ego to search for its vanished fellow-member and, if it finds it, to persuade it to return. Otherwise the only possibility left is to fetch it back by means of a medicinal ritual (cf. ch. 11.6).

The medium even has the potential of asking the dream ego of a recently deceased child to delay its metamorphosis into a spirit of the dead until the mother has given birth again, so it can accompany the newborn for the duration of its life.

If a person's death is imminent many dream egos take their leave of the medium, letting him know whether they want to continue to regard him as their medium or not. In such a case they inform him later about how things are with them, when they have become spirits of the dead.

In the Islanders' thinking contacts between medium and dream ego play a somewhat subordinate role. *His contacts with spirits of the dead are much more significant.*

Spirits of the dead or ancestral spirits visit their medium to converse with him, to impart news of other spirits of the dead, and to convey the wishes they desire to pass on to the living. Reciprocally a medium can request the spirits of the dead on behalf of the living to provide food, give information in special situations, to assist etc. He can also, however, pass on warnings from the benevolent spirits of the dead to members of the family whose lifestyle threatens to call forth the wrath of a high-ranking spirit being and thereby endanger the community.

A close emotional relationship can develop between the spirit beings and their medium, similar to that among friends, whereby the spirits of the dead of his kinship group or local community appear as the medium's confidants. This rapport is imbued with a feeling which has a special part to play in the inter-personal relationships of the Islanders, summed up in the word *ttong*. The emotional relationship it refers to can be very intensive and enduring. Many spirits of the dead remain loyal to their medium for the whole of his life. The more such devoted spirit beings cultivate relationships with a medium, and the more high-ranking ones there are among them, the more important his fame and his authority as the medium of mighty spirit beings can become. One can in fact assume that the latter will do all they can to make their pronouncements via their medium appear pertinent and reliable.

It can be that after the death of their medium spirits of the dead, in their state of mourning, do not look for another and are consequently forgotten. However, as a rule they do seek out a new medium, particularly the more important, high-ranking spirits of the dead.

The activities described so far present the medium's way of proceeding when passing on information between the living and the spirits of the dead as rather informal, with minimal ritual, or none at all. These somewhat indirect options involve little effort or expense for those taking part.

In terms of the characteristic features of informal dealings with spirit beings there would seem to be very little difference between the medium and the shaman. However, there is one feature where they vary significantly.

There are indeed many societies which believe that a medium who has to look for information for dealing with a problem can also send his dream ego into the beyond in order to associate with spirit beings. Normally, however, the journey into the beyond is not regarded as standard procedure for a medium; the latter himself receives a *visit from the beyond* by a spirit being.

The basic concept of the work of the medium is consequently diametrically opposite to the basic concept of the work of the shaman.

15.5   Notions of the Course of Events Surrounding Direct Contact between People and Spirit Beings Via the Medium

Mediums become involved when a particular problem situation has to be dealt with at once and on the spot, with the kinship group or local community wanting to learn how to solve the issue.

The affair can be quite simple in nature. A spirit being is to be conciliated, and one is trying to find out what its wishes are. The matter is more difficult if one of the ancestral spirits of a family group wants to talk to them because it is not satisfied with their behaviour, or because it wants to reinforce a demand made to them in a dream but not yet complied with. Having said this, many spirit beings simply want to make contact with their relatives from time to time by personally letting themselves be heard.

The following are some particular problem situations. A case of illness in the family cannot be alleviated by the usual means or is of such a new kind that the necessary remedy is unknown. One then has to find out via the medium whether the cause of the illness lies in some evil deed that has been concealed, who the guilty person is and how long the unfortunate situation will last. If the illness is of a new type a spirit of the dead with medical knowledge can name a remedy for it, another can be asked where the possibly absent dream ego of a sick person may be residing, and what may persuade it to return. One can ask the appropriate spirits of the dead where missing relatives have disappeared to, how they are getting on and whether they will return.

Matters of general importance for a larger social group might involve clarifying whether the dream ego of a recently deceased person has become a high-ranking ancestral spirit, what his name now is etc. Those holding political office use the medium to get help in decision-making and information on how a dispute can be settled. The listing of the possible reasons for a direct conversation between the living and the spirits of the dead could go on for as long as one might wish.

The contact takes place during a *séance*, during which those present expect that a spirit being classified by them as benevolent will *take possession of a medium* for a limited period of time in order to communicate with them, answer their questions, itself put questions to them and receive their answers. It is also possible that no reciprocal conversation is taking place. In such a case only the spirit being speaks, and those present accept its words as a message from the beyond, without making any comment.

In this form of séance the medium appears to those present to be fully conscious. However, it can be that the medium himself is not aware of being fully conscious. At the conclusion of the event many mediums know what happened and what was said, and others do not (cf. also Fuhrmann 2001).

In some societies the mediums have to put themselves into the condition of trance using the means described in ch. 12 before a spirit being can take possession of them and let itself be heard. Such a medium is then either only partly conscious, or even not at all. In qualification it should be mentioned that only in exceptional cases do mediums make use of drugs to induce the state of trance.

Those taking part can explain the unconscious state of the medium in terms of the departure of his dream ego from the body, or of one of them if he has several. In such a case it is assumed that another spirit being wishing to enter into contact with the group takes the place of the dream ego in the medium's body, *incorporating* itself, and using the body's sense organs, vocal cords and auditory functions in order to let itself be heard (cf. again Fuhrmann 2001). *In such cases the temporary state of ecstasy of the dream ego is replaced by the enstasy of a spirit of the dead, ancestral spirit or unfamiliar spirit.*

However, as we have already seen, some societies believe that a person's dream ego exists permanently outside the body and only has to be nearby for the person to retain all his faculties. When a spirit being "takes possession" of a medium the associated expectations are somewhat different. The best way to recognize these expectations is to observe how a séance unfolds, such as those normally practised among the Chuuk Islanders of Micronesia before their Christianisation.

15.6   Basic Structures of a Mediatorial Séance on Chuuk

Preliminary observation: one should by no means expect all mediatorial séances in type 2 animism to follow the structure described in the following example. This is a model from Oceania. On the other hand the parallels to the description of a mediatorial séance by the African historian and ethnologist Mbiti (1974) are striking. This is hardly surprising, for like the societies of Oceania those of Africa are counted broadly among those with an animistic concept of the world of type 2, including an emphasis on veneration of ancestors.

The preparations for a mediatorial séance on Chuuk – for the sake of simplicity I am going to describe them in the present tense – usually begin with an initial request. If this comes from members of the kinship group or local community who are wanting to speak to one of their ancestral spirits then the appropriate medium is asked to be available at a particular time and location. If the request comes from a spirit being the medium can also summon the group.

Making contact is not tied to a particular time of day, but usually takes place in the evening when all those involved have finished the day's work and can attend. There are also no special rules about the location. In many societies, e.g. in south East Asia and in Africa, mediatorial activities can be observed openly throughout the day, sometimes in markets, and especially on public occasions of a local festive nature, including processions, where mediums can display their activities.

On Chuuk it is rare to gather in the open air for this purpose. Most people's homes do not have sufficient space for everyone, and so the participants usually move to the *wuut*, the big community house. In the case of a high-ranking spirit being responsible for a village or an island proceedings normally take place in the *wuut*, where his place of offering, the *faar*, is located. This is a kind of suspended altar, its central part forming a table-like platform hanging by a rope from one of the beams. This platform can also be in the form of a double boat.

Several days before the event the medium begins his physical preparations. He observes the taboos regarding food and sex, which at other times do not have to be kept so strictly. He avoids any work which would bring him into contact with forbidden foods or strong odours. For example he no longer slaughters an animal. A pig's gall bladder with its bitter contents could keep away the spirit beings he needs to invoke.

His preparations include intensive care of his body. The medium bathes himself several times and makes generous use of fragrant liquids, turmeric and coconut milk, applied to his body. Shortly before the start of the event he puts on clean clothing and his jewellery. He has eaten nothing more since morning, so as to remain free from any food odours.

Making contact with a spirit of the dead is a spectacular event. While the medium is making final preparations numerous people have gathered, whether directly involved or not. At the place of offering fresh gifts have been hung, among them medicine of illumination (cf. ch. 10.3), for not only the medium but also the ancestral spirit to be invoked needs to have a "clear" SEIC when he speaks. However, a sacrifice is not perforce obligatory.

If famous and high-ranking spirit beings are to be invoked dances take place in their honour, but only in exceptional cases.

Those present are not required to observe the taboos so strictly, but have also adorned themselves in similar fashion, including an aura of perfume, and have taken their seats along the walls of the house.

The medium sits with legs tucked under on the *kiyeki* in the middle, a mat of woven pandanus leaves, so as to be visible to all. He waits till no more people are coming in, and there is calm. Eventually only whispers are allowed, for benevolent spirit beings are usually uneasy when there is noise and hence keep away from large crowds of people (cf. ch. 9.1). While the spirit being is present nothing must happen which could startle it and chase it away. Hence no percussion instruments are in evidence at such an event, in contrast to many other ethnic societies. Nor does the medium have to get into a state of trance or any other unusual emotional state. He sits there motionless and waits.

When all is calm, one of those present calls out the name of a spirit being and asks it to come. If its name is not yet known because it is the spirit of a recently deceased person the name used is the one it had as a human being. The calling is always done by the highest ranked man in the kinship group or local community which regards it as their ancestral spirit. If the spirit being is one guarding and governing a larger area the calling is done by the highest ranked political leader present. In no case does the medium himself call the spirit being.

It is assumed that the spirit of the dead or ancestral spirit that is called is residing close by and will not decline, because it is aware of the preparations that have been made. Sometimes it is already busy claiming and consuming the offerings that have been hung on its altar. If the spirit is indeed occupied with the gifts this can be detected by whether the altar is hanging still or already swaying. Sometimes the request to come must be repeated several times.

The moment when the invisible spirit makes contact with the medium cannot be precisely determined. If the medium begins to show signs of disturbance one knows that the spirit being is near him. At this point the medium pushes the fingers of both hands together as if to fold them, but then leaves them open and begins to tap the pandanus mat rhythmically with the palms of his hands. This rhythmic sound is claimed to have a stimulating effect on the spirit being. The medium maintains this behaviour until the end of the séance.

The signs of the medium's bodily agitation become gradually more intense. He begins to breathe more heavily, to tremble and to groan. If he sneezes or coughs, those present know that the spirit being has made physical contact with him and is about to *climb on to his shoulders*.

At this point the description of the séance must be interrupted briefly in order to draw attention to a notion that is often overlooked. European-Western observers normally expect that spirit beings making contact with a person take up residence *inside his body*. Typical descriptions of this expectation are mostly couched in the phrase, "a spirit entered him". Also when mediums are in a state of trance this is normally taken at face value to be a so-called *enstasy* (cf. ch. 14.4) Other possibilities of interpreting the event are hardly discussed or even perceived.

The Chuuk Islanders do concede that malevolent spirits responsible for causing internal diseases or unpleasant emotional states can penetrate a person's body. However, they can bring about their devastating effects through contact on the outside, by clinging to the person or gripping him with their teeth in the manner of an aggressive animal.

The Islanders also believe that benevolent spirit beings have no need at all to enter a medium's body in order to "speak from inside him". Normally ancestral spirits employing a medium even do this exclusively from outside his body. They either *descend on the medium from above* or climb over his back *on to his shoulders*, sitting astride with their legs dangling and directing the behaviour of the medium in this position. The event is manifestly understood as *possession* of the medium in the usual sense of the word, but with the qualification that it has to do with possession by a spirit being perceived on Chuuk as benevolent.

Such notions were also commonplace in Europe from the Middle Ages on into modern times. Traces of them remain in expressions such as "what the devil got into him", to convey that the person behaved in a particularly crazy manner.

❑ Suggestion for own investigations: find out how this procedure is expressed in the language you are working in. In Bible translations this can have decisive significance if the behaviour and operation of the Holy Spirit is to be "rightly" conveyed and understood, both linguistically and with reference to the culture: does he come "upon" people, "over" them or "into" them?

Back to the description of the séance. The moment when a spirit being makes ready to climb on the back of the medium indicates that the procedure has reached a critical moment, for no one knows exactly whether the spirit of the dead or ancestral spirit coming upon the medium is indeed the one which has been requested. The event does not only attract benevolent spirits of the dead but also many malevolent spirit beings who attempt to trouble the medium. However, he can count on his own dream egos together with other ancestral spirits of his family to keep such spirit beings away from him. If malevolent spirit beings do nevertheless come at the medium it is assumed that his guardians are not present or were not sufficiently alert. In such cases not only is the medium in extreme danger, but also all the other people present. If a malevolent spirit being has made physical contact with the medium the situation changes dramatically.

The *signs of physical agitation* that the medium experiences change abruptly. He gets goose pimples (cold body temperature of malevolent spirit beings!) and contorts his eyes. His *SEIC is dimmed*, and his behaviour takes on extreme forms. The medium gestures like a madman. He leaps up, rages, utters animal noises and screams at the assembled people, searches with contorted features and angry looks for a stick or knife to threaten the people with. The latter cry out and flee. A few courageous people finally succeed in overcoming the medium and helping him to shake off the evil spirit being. In the general confusion it is no longer possible to proceed with the event. All those involved regard this kind of possession as dangerous, destructive and not only undesired but also completely senseless, for malevolent spirit beings are neither capable of speech nor can they be approached for advice and help (cf. ch. 8).

At this point the description of the séance must again be interrupted in order to draw attention to a widespread misunderstanding. The taking possession of a medium by a malevolent spirit being leads to aspects of behaviour which partly coincide with those of so-called possessed people encountered in Christian communities in Europe and the West. According to Werner such behaviour is characterised by "anti-religious attitudes such as curses, obscenities, blasphemies, aversion to believers, hindrances to prayer and opposition to worship, as well as physical symptoms, e.g. disturbances of the senses and bizarre apprehensions, changes in face and voice, convulsions, screams, vomiting, self-harm, sprains, unconsciousness and eventually by unusual parapsychological phenomena such as telepathy, precognition, levitation and materialisation" (Werner 2001:73).

There is clearly a conceptual difference between the agents which determine the behaviour of a medium as described above and the agents which determine the behaviour of a person in the way Werner describes. The former has to do with malevolent spirit beings as understood in animism, the latter with Satan and his acolytes as understood in the Bible, i.e. demonic beings equipped with intelligence and desiring to plunge human beings to their doom. From an external perspective the parallels are obvious, but in terms of concept there are considerable differences.

It is therefore important to examine each individual case of possession in order to ascertain which explanation leads to a "right" understanding of such phenomena, and which does not. This is the only way to treat them correctly. Naïvely equating them all too often distorts the European-Western observer's perception of how differently phenomena of possession can be understood from an animistic point of view. (A description of what is meant by right understanding can be found in **FC** ch. 17.)

Back to the séance. If the spirit being which has made physical contact with the medium is not malevolent, but benevolent, then the signs of bodily agitation quickly disappear. The medium becomes calm, his features relax, his psychic condition is characterised by joy, contentment, equanimity, feelings of happiness, a gentle disposition and sensible demeanour. He remains seated with legs tucked under, swaying his upper body rhythmically to and fro. The typical movements of his hands continue.

His SEIC is always particularly clear and lucid when one of the ancestral spirits of his own immediate family climbs on to his shoulders, or when it is the benevolent spirit of a dead child, which mediums are especially glad to have dealings with.

Nevertheless even benevolent spirit beings can sometimes mean physical exertion for the medium. One can perceive clearly from his physical bearing if the spirit of a dead adult is on his shoulders, pressing him down with its weight. The medium can bear the spirits of children with his upper body erect. In the case of spirits of adults you can hear him groan and see how he begins to perspire (warm temperature of benevolent spirit beings!). It can also happen that the medium may stand up with a spirit being on his shoulders and perform dancing steps to those present which the spirit wishes to teach them.

Many spirit beings wait a fairly long time before climbing on to the medium. If need be the speaker who initially called them will have to encourage them to climb up.

The actual conversation between the speaker and the spirit being cannot begin until the latter has taken its place on the medium's shoulders. Only then is the medium "possessed" in the sense of the term.

It has still not spoken a word. But the moment has come when the speaker can ask the ancestral spirit to declare its name, by asking it who it is. Sometimes the question has to be put to it several times.

If the spirit being already has a name known to those present, then once it is declared they know to which former person it refers. The spirit of a deceased person which is getting in touch via a medium for the first time must declare what its name was as a human being if it is different from its name as a spirit of the dead. If it is identified in this way it is commanded to speak by the person who called it.

The command to speak is never directed to the medium, but always to the spirit being. However, the latter always recognizably employs the mouth and vocal cords of the medium. In all other respects in this situation the two of them form one psychic and mental unit. The medium uses the first person when the spirit being lets itself be heard.

The latter first of all delivers a formal oration using all the polite phraseology which is normal for the Islanders. This includes thanks for the offerings, for the honour of the invitation etc. Apart from the somewhat unusual metaphorical idioms which are customary when conversing with spirits of the dead there is no special language used. However, there are societies where mediums and other specialists in the religion have to use a special language when communicating with spirit beings, e.g. the Ngaju of South East Asia (Kuhnt-Saptodewo 1993:40).

Many spirit beings on Chuuk speak Japanese or English, but only in rare cases. This is also a way of testing whether the medium is practising deception. For example, if the deceased person knew English, then his spirit must be speaking it, too.

One may ask it to speak clearly so that all can understand. This changes the voice of the medium to such an extent that the deceased person can be recognised in it, particularly if it is the spirit of a child.

The more clearly and plausibly a spirit of the dead speaks, the more high-ranking it is considered to be. Of course the ultimate proof only comes later on, if its prophesies come true or pass later examination, i.e. if the game animals it predicted in a certain place are indeed found, or if the medicine made according to the formula it was asked for actually proved to be effective. A high-ranking spirit being does not lie. It has a supreme love of the truth. Hence its prophesies are held to be particularly reliable. Since children have not yet learned the art of lying, their spirits are held to be more reliable than all others, and so they possess special status.

Spirits of the dead do not only speak. Many of them sing and teach the listeners a new song. Others weep, e.g. when the report that a member of the community who has disappeared will not be coming back.

One can usually count on a spirit of the dead speaking in a friendly, calm and sensible manner, and answering all the questions put to it. However, it can also get cross if its wishes are not carried out, or if it has to relate that someone has committed an evil deed. Then it angrily requires those present to change their behaviour, and threatens reprisals if its demands are not complied with. In such cases spirit beings which are fundamentally benevolent can behave like malevolent ones.

If those present have no more questions to ask, the event rapidly reaches its conclusion. The speaker expresses his admiration for the knowledge of the spirit being, thanks it for the readiness with which it has imparted its knowledge and formally requests it to depart. The spirit being can also state that it has nothing more to say and has no more questions to put and no more wishes to convey.

The length of time such contacts with a spirit being last can vary, but they are seldom longer than two hours. It can happen that several are called, one after the other. This depends among other things on the stamina of the medium, for whom the event means considerable strain.

One can tell visibly from the medium's body, that the spirit being has descended from his shoulders. His movements eventually cease completely.

15.7   The Medium's Personality

Both *men* and *women* are equally qualified to be mediums. In selecting their mediums the spirit beings take account of *aesthetic considerations*. They prefer those with a *beautiful* and *stately appearance*. People who are elderly, frail and ugly have little prospect of becoming mediums.

It is noteworthy that globally there are clearly more women who are either operating as mediums, occasionally go into a trance, or show symptoms of possession by an unfamiliar spirit being. This is above all true of women in societies in which men have the dominant role and women are expected to be subordinate. The phenomena of possession is particularly apparent in women who are in crisis, whether personal or domestic, and seek to induce by this behaviour a possible explanation of their plight, drawing attention to it and hoping for some expression of care and concern for their situation and its surrounding effects.

The *sex of the spirit beings* plays no part in how they choose their medium. Female spirit beings can choose men as their mediums and vice versa. However, women suffer from the disadvantage of not being able to function during their monthly period. On the other hand there is no need to decline because of being pregnant.

Although one medium is sufficient for a kinship group or local community there is often a woman as well as a man in the role.

The need to convey knowledge presupposes that the medium should be of *above average intelligence*. Normal capabilities are not sufficient. Among the Chuuk Islanders it is assumed as a matter of course that no spirit being would consider someone as a medium if he were not to some extent its equal in terms of psychic and intellectual competence. Psychically conspicuous, fragile people or epileptics are out of the question for this office. A medium's personality profile also requires a degree of maturity and experience of life. This means that younger people below thirty years are ruled out simply for this reason, because one cannot be confident of their ability to observe the sometimes very strict taboo concerning sexual activity over a fairly lengthy period.

One essential aspect of the personality profile of the medium is contained in the notion that a person's conspicuously positive psychic and intellectual qualities are related to the possession of more than one dream ego, a principle we have already noted in connection with the shaman. At the same time having several dream egos also implies extended opportunities for information about what is happening in the beyond. Although the medium cannot usually dispatch his dream egos himself to get such news, they can go on their own initiative. For example they can accompany a deceased's dream ego to the location of its metamorphosis (of its SEIC) (cf. ch. 13.7), taking on the function of a psychopomp, just as we have seen with the shaman. However, the medium is no more able to hold direct conversation with his own dream egos than ordinary people can.

His dream egos are important guardians against attempts by malevolent spirit beings to disturb the medium when he is carrying out his mediatorial functions. If the medium begins to show symptoms related to the absence of his dream egos he can fetch them back himself.

The medium's intelligence, the knowledge he possesses which is inaccessible to ordinary people, and his functions as a medium not only signify the prestige and status of his person but also a special position of power, which he can use to his own advantage, particularly if he exercises his office in parallel with that of the political leader.

15.8   The Medium's Call to Office and the Development of His Career

On Chuuk the selection of medium is basically determined by the spirits of the dead themselves, i.e. at least one of them. In certain cases the initiative can come from people, but it must still be confirmed by the spirit beings. This happens in various ways. An elderly medium, whether awake or in a dream, learns from the beyond that following his death a particular younger man or younger woman is to take over his office. Such news can also come to no matter whom in a dream. Sometimes a spirit of the dead pronounces the name of a future medium through a medium currently practising. And finally someone can try on their own initiative to become a medium by making the appropriate preparations and observing the relevant taboos. In this case the group designates one of their members who seems suitable to them and fulfils the necessary preconditions.

Such a case applies when the group wishes to make contact with the dream ego of a recently deceased person in order to find out if his metamorphosis has already taken place and what possibilities are available to it to bring advantages to those left behind.

In principle a medium must regard himself as the go-between for all conceivable benevolent spirit beings, and as a rule may not give preference to any single one of them, even if a particular one among them is especially agreeable. The spirit being chooses the medium, not the other way round. Spirit beings may feel inclined or disinclined towards a medium. No medium can oblige a spirit being to have dealings with him. In other words they are not at his command and so he cannot regard them as his personal possession. They can select another medium at any time. By contrast a spirit being regards the medium he prefers as his property. Sometimes this can mean that mediums (and shamans) are exposed to the arbitrariness of their owners.

A sure sign that spirits of the dead desire or accept a particular person as their medium is of a physical nature. The person involved suddenly senses an unusual aversion to every kind of food, for days and weeks feels extreme nausea at the very thought of eating anything and can only drink coconut milk. During this time he loses a considerable amount of body weight.

This aversion to all kinds of food is caused by the spirits of the dead in order to liberate the future medium from all the food odours that they themselves reject, i.e. those which in future will be taboo for that person. A long period of nausea is also a sign that the future medium must from now on avoid sexual intercourse if he is not to endanger his selection. He can decline it by disregarding these taboos, and rubbing himself with orange peel or water which has been used to wash fermented breadfruit. However, in so doing the designated future medium is opposing the will of the spirit beings and risking their wrath.

After some days of imposed fasting the chosen person begins to perceive the spirit doubles of objects, people's dream egos, and other spirit beings around him. He is also addressed by them. In this he is indeed fully conscious, but appears to be "absent-minded", because he is not paying attention to what is going on in life around him. He is fully aware of what is happening to him and can give account of it, e.g. that a particular spirit of the dead has come to him, designated him as its medium and informed him that any time soon he will have to talk about it to those of his group who are alive and remain. Or the future medium reports that the dream ego of a certain living person has let him know that that person's body will soon die and that after its metamorphosis into a spirit of the dead it would like to have him as its medium. This person's dream life also becomes more intensive, and later his dreams, with their knowledge of events in the beyond, gain special importance for the fulfilment of his tasks.

Those around the future medium remain unaware of all these happenings. His psychic condition reveals nothing unusual and he does not fall into any trance, apart from the fact that he appears absent-minded because he is not focusing on what is going on in the material world around him. Moreover it never happens that a benevolent spirit of the dead which the medium is involved with unexpectedly comes upon him, so he cannot suddenly appear to be "possessed". Only spirit beings held to be malevolent ambush a person in this way.

After a certain time the nausea disappears, for it cannot be the intention of the spirit beings to let their chosen medium starve to death. From then on he can have himself inducted by an experienced colleague in the field into the necessary knowledge, specialised vocabulary and mediatorial procedures. In addition, as a future psychopomp, he has to learn how to prepare the medicine for dream egos who are unwilling to return, and as a future dance master make himself more closely familiar with the relevant knowledge.

His selection can be retracted at any time by the participating spirit beings deciding to distance themselves from him. Usually the guilt for this lies with him. He has not observed the prescribed taboos, or incurred guilt through wrong behaviour, and will be punished by the spirits of the dead by completely losing his mediatorial skills.

15.9   Special Cases

The person of the medium and his activities provide the numerous societies where mediatorial work is practised with a rich source of possibilities for extending the various concepts and notions, including cultural overlays. At the same time it is true that there is no society which has exhausted and fully realised all the possibilities.

There are some very specific types of medium. Some are so limited in their field of activity that they can only perceive spirit beings when awake. They could be termed *seers*. The Chuuk Islanders are also familiar with this kind, calling him *móngupwi*. His ability to perceive spirit beings only relates to those which are still dream egos. Other spirit beings are invisible to him. Nor can the seer hold any kind of conversation with them or let himself be used as a medium by them. In all other ways he is no different from ordinary people.

15.10   The Significance of the Medium for His Society

Mediums, together with shamans, are the most important sources of understanding about what is happening in the beyond, and of the knowledge believed to be available there. Such sources are of use not only to the members of those societies but also to ethnologists.

In the view of the Chuuk Islanders and many other societies all traditional knowledge was once unknown, and gradually revealed to people from the beyond via the mediums. This includes not only knowledge such as the diagnosis and healing of diseases, improvements in providing food etc., which are necessary for solving the problems of daily life. It comprises also the means of satisfying aesthetic needs such as dances and songs, which the people ultimately attribute to origins in the beyond. Hence the mediums (and in many ways also the shamans) must be given the credit for being *a key factor in innovations inside their cultures.*

Of course the work of the mediums and shamans provides them with the opportunity of *staging* séances aimed at impressing their clients, manipulating them, and satisfying their expectations. In many societies it appears that it is by no means rare for mediums and shamans to have to defend themselves against the accusation that they are deceivers and want to control their society, and that is the real reason why they claim that what they say is true. Status, prestige and also the chance to gain material advantage for themselves and their group corrupt them and easily seduce them into misusing their power.

There exists no scientific demonstration which could confirm the objective reality of the experiences of mediums and shamans in trance, any more than there is for the existence of spirit beings and their activity. An extremely rigorous presentation of the subjectivity of the content and perceptions of animistic concepts of the world and of man can be found in a dissertation entitled "Der Schamane sieht eine Hexe, der Ethnologe sieht nichts" ("The shaman sees a witch, the ethnologist sees nothing" (Reimann 1998).

15.11 Summary

In simple terms, the medium is normally a mediator for bilateral contacts between the living members of a social group and those benevolent spirit beings understood to be the continuation of the personality of deceased members of that group. The medium has a relational connection with these spirit beings at the same time as they are still assigned to living persons as their dream egos. A medium can also perceive all kinds of spirit beings while awake and converse directly with them, something which for ordinary people is only possible in dreams and is consequently indirect. In this way he conveys the wishes of persons in this world to the world beyond, and vice versa.

The medium also functions as the expert for the diagnosis and healing of diseases, particularly those which are caused by the absence of the dream ego from the living person's body.

15.12 In the Next Chapter

The above analysis of the medium is the concluding aspect of the animistic concept of man and of the world. There remains the question of whether, despite its enormous complexity, it is possible to put together a brief and succinct definition of animism as a concept. Ch. 16 is an attempt to do so.

The following sources contain more on the theme of this chapter:

Fuhrmann, Klaus: Formen der javanischen Pilgerschaft zu Heiligenschreinen. Diss. Freiburg 2001.

Kuhnt-Saptodewo, Sri: Zum Seelengeleit bei den Ngaju am Kahayan. Auswertung eines Sakraltextes zur Manarung-Zeremonie beim Totenfest. München 1993.

Mbiti, John S.: Afrikanische Religion und Weltanschauung. Berlin, New York (Walter de Gruyter) 1974.

Reimann, Ralf Ingo: Der Schamane sieht eine Hexe – der Ethnologe sieht nichts. Menschliche Informationsverarbeitung und ethnologische Forschung. Frankfurt (Campus) 1998.

Streck, Bernhard: Fröhliche Wissenschaft Ethnologie. Eine Führung. Wuppertal 1997.

Schüle, Andreas: Israels Sohn – Jahwes Prophet. Ein Versuch zum Verhältnis von kanonischer Theologie und Religionsgeschichte anhand der Bileam-Perikope (Num 22-24). Münster, Hamburg, London (LIT) 2001.

Werner, Roland: Transkulturelle Heilkunde. Der ganze Mensch. Heilsysteme unter dem Einfluss von Abrahamischen Religionen, Östlichen Religionen und Glaubensbekenntnissen, Paganismus, Neuen Religionen und religiösen Mischformen. Frankfurt am Main 2001.

Chapter 16
So what Is Animism?

This chapter gives a brief summary of the conclusions of the previous chapters.

16.1 Conclusions

The abundance of individual aspects which together comprise the various forms of animistic religions do not permit one to come up with a simple and handy definition of what animism is.

It is clear from what has been presented in the previous chapters that the long-standing conventional term "animism" can only be a makeshift solution.

Belief in souls or spirits, terms which often appear in popular definitions in reference works, are of no use, for they take no account of what is essential, but instead allow partial aspects of the edifice that is animism to appear central.

The complex array of perceptions and actions which, in the light of the lack of a more apt term, I will also continue to call animism, rests first and foremost on a *concept of the world which appears to have its origins in a totally subjective, practical view and experience of reality*.

In this concept of the world the cosmos is made up of the totality of objects and beings existing in two forms, a material form and a spirit form.

According to animistic perceptions *spirit objects and beings* appear to be in the majority in the cosmos. Collectively they form an *almost ideal world* in which, apart from exceptions, there is in principle *no mortality*. From the perspective of European-Western thinking this spirit world can be understood as the other side or the beyond.

Material objects and beings, existing alongside spirit ones, and in the same cosmic space, form by contrast a *vulnerable and transitory world*. From the perspective of European-Western people this material world can be understood as this side or the here and now.

Without a complementary spirit counterpart the ability of material objects and beings to exist is limited. They can only be fully functional if their spirit counterpart is at least close to them and on hand.

The basic elements of such an animistic concept of the world with its theory of the nature of all that exists gives rise to a characteristic concept of man. People consist of a material body and at least one spirit counterpart.

This means that they live simultaneously both on this side and in the beyond. After the death of the body their existence continues only in the beyond.

Between this side and the beyond there are many kinds of connections. Since a person lives simultaneously in both spheres he has (conditional) access to what is happening in the beyond. He can share its life and experiences in dreams. *Access to the beyond requires the involvement of specialists.* The most important are shamans and mediums.

Effects and influences passing from the beyond over to this side are evidently more frequent and lasting than in the other direction. The most effectual of these include actions of spirit beings which as ancestral spirits impose sanctions on their living kinship groups and local communities when their members infringe ethical and social norms. Hence "sin" in this sense only has consequences for a person's form of existence on this side, i.e. for his body, which can be punished for such sin with disaster, illness and death. *People do not have to account for their actions during this life in the life beyond.* As a rule the notion of a hell has no place in animistic concepts of the world.

The animistic world view is essentially oriented towards life on this side. Human behaviour which is determined by animistic ways of thinking, including especially religious practices, is aimed first and foremost at *safeguarding existence in the here and now.*

16.2   In the Final Chapter

People who have to read a lot of books usually follow a system. This might include scanning the list of contents if the book picked up is an unknown work. The orderly list of chapter headings reveals whether the book is worth reading or not. At the same time some chapters appear more worthwhile than others at first glance. This can sometimes tempt readers to start with a different chapter from the first one.

This seems to have been the case with a number of readers of **FOREIGN CULTURES** (bibliographical details about it in the introduction!). There the title of the final chapter is "Ethnology – some less serious moments". Most readers start with this chapter, the last one, as they quite happily admit to me in conversation.

A similar ending will now be given to **ANIMISM**. Some readers may find that inappropriate, bearing in mind the seriousness and grimness of the demonic which they link with the topic, and which it does have in some places. It is indeed not without significance that its humorous aspects are not at all as abundant as is the case in other areas of human culture. I also confess that I do not attach this last chapter with the same unconcern as I did with **FOR-EIGN CULTURES**. I nevertheless do so, in the knowledge that even to people whose life is imbued with animism nothing that is human is alien, including the comic, the weird, and the ludicrous aspects of their world view and the actions it can lead to.

As for you dedicated readers who on picking up this book have perhaps begun with the first chapter and laboriously and seriously worked through the material: you have reached the end of your labours! So let all the strain fall away and enjoy the frivolousness of the last chapter.

Chapter 17
Animism and the Occult – Some Less Serious Moments

This chapter describes some of the strange offshoots that animistic notions can give rise to among people, whether they live in pre-literate societies or in Europe and the West.

As with all things human, throughout the world religious practice also has its light-hearted, comic and quirky side. Members of religious communities occasionally tend to believe quite seriously in the truth of quite fanciful doctrines, obstinately defending them, if necessary even in the civil courts. The more trivial the issues that are dealt with in such court cases, the more amusing the verdicts turn out to be, with their arid legal diction and deadly seriousness.

Heinrich Stader, himself a lawyer, has recorded a selection of cases which did indeed come to court, publishing them (2001) in a slim volume. Among other things we discover how to reach a correct legal decision when ground radiation, despite mattresses having been 'dowsed', was not adequately blocked; what the legal situation as regards copyright is when spirit beings from the beyond convey information to those living on this side; whether theologians should evaluate hallucinations during fasting as a practical component of a student's course. The publishing house which issued this amusing read also includes in its listing a number of similar releases on quite different topics. Here are two of them:

In their "exercises in logical decision-making in the higher morality" (subtitle) the authors Lehner, Meran and Möller (1980), parodying sociological and theological style, establish that "traditional dogma is incapable of adequately comprehending the interdependent atonement-sin transmission mechanism."

Unequivocal animistic dimensions are achieved by Mummendey in a draft which appeared in the same series (1982), entitled "A social psycho-physiological study of acute vampirism", a tongue-in-cheek account of the notions of vampires (Dracula) biting people in their sleep, drawing off blood and by the same bite managing to turn them also into vampires. Here is a quote from the concluding summary (1982:7): "At the heart of the investigation is the creation of two-dimensional electro-odontograms during the very act. A detailed discussion taking into account theoretical perspectives relating to the emotions and actions involved, and a brief prognosis of the future, are appended".

It is no secret that while working in the field ethnologists have more frequent experiences involving the exotic environment than other "travellers" do. After returning from a research trip it can be fun to build up an impression with stories of adventures of this kind, especially if a certain amount of romanticising of the memories lends the report a hint of the typical sailor's yarn. Occasionally such experiences go far beyond pub talk and turn into a professional ethnographic account of high quality, as e.g. in the following case.

From 1986 the ethnologist Karl-Heinz Kohl stayed several times in Belogili, a remote village on the East Indonesian island of Flores, investigating the religion from an ethnological perspective. Although (like myself) he was not all that keen on football, he could not escape the local outbreak of football fever in the wake of the fifty year jubilee celebrations of the Indonesian Republic. The team of Belogili, where he was doing his research, was to play against the team of the neighbouring village of Waiklibang.

Right from the start the event was clouded by heavy omens. From early times, when head-hunting was still carried on in the region, until into the 1960s there had been related conflicts between the two villages, and the hostility was still smouldering.

What is interesting is that the violence which characterised the earlier fighting has now been sublimated into the sporting contest. Even more interesting is Kohl's discovery that the animistic practices which originally accompanied and prepared the events surrounding head-hunting also still play a central part today in football matches, albeit with objectives which are tailored and altered to fit this modern form of conflict.

From his description of the jubilee events we learn how a football can be "fed" in such a way as to enable goals to be scored more easily, and we discover what protests are triggered by a healer ("sorcerer") who has placed himself behind the opponents' goal in order to use his mana to discompose the goalkeeper. How the whole thing eventually degenerates into a chaotic brawl, during which even the girls of the two villages run wild, how the resulting shambles is brought to an end by means of "calming" salvos from the village policeman's machine pistol over the heads of the rival factions, what parallels there are between an enemy's skull and the gaining of a football trophy, and what ethnological conclusions (to be taken seriously!) can be drawn from it all, this can all be read with pleasure in Kohl (2000).

The following sources contain more on the theme of this chapter:

Kohl, Karl-Heinz: Beim Fußball helfen die Geister. Spiel, Krieg und Ritual in Ostflores. In: Neumann/Weigel 2000:101-112.

Lehner, Hansjörg; Meran, Georg; Möller, Joachim: De statu corruptionis. Entscheidungslogische Einübungen in die Höhere Amoralität. Litzelstetter Libellen Nr.1. Abteilung Handbüchlein und Enchiridia. Konstanz-Litzelstetten (Faude) 1980.

Mummendey, Hans Dieter: De Vampyris. Auf dem Wege zu einer sozialen Psychophysiologie des akuten Vampirismus. Litzelstetter Libellen Nr.2. Abteilung Handbüchlein und Enchiridia. Konstanz-Litzelstetten (Faude) 1982.

Neumann, Gerhard; Weigel Sigrid (Hrsg.): Lesbarkeit der Kultur. Literaturwissenschaften zwischen Kulturtechnik und Ethnographie. München 2000.

Stader, Heinrich: "Das Feuer im Beichtstuhl ging offensichtlich von selbst aus ..." Prozesse um Religion und anderes Okkultes. Ein Vademecum für Juristen und leicht gläubige Laien. (Libelle Verlag,) Lengwil am Bodensee 2001.

Bibliography

Adegbola, E. A. Ade (ed.): Traditional religion in West Africa. Ibadan 1983.

Adler, Matthias: Ethnopsychoanalyse: das Unbewusste in Wissenschaft und Kultur. Stuttgart, New York (Schattauer) 1993.

Albers, Irene; Franke, Anselm (Hrsg.): Animismus. Zürich 2012.

Århem, Kaj: Into the realm of the sacred: an interpretation of Khasi funeral ritual. In: Cederroth/Corlin/Lindstrom 1988:257-288.

Auffahrt, Christoph; Bernhard, Jutta; Mohr, Hubert (Hrsg.): Metzler Lexikon Religion Bd. 1. Stuttgart und Weimar (Metzler) 1999.

Augsburger, David W.: Pastoral Counseling Across Cultures. Philadelphia, Pennsylvania 1986.

Augustyn, Prisca: The semiotics of fate, death, and the soul in Germanic culture. The christianization of Old Saxon. New York et al. (Peter Lang) 2002.

Badenberg, Robert: The body, soul and spirit concept of the Bemba in Zambia. Bonn 2002, 2nd ed. (edition iwg, mission academics, Band 9). Verlag für Kultur und Wissenschaft).

Badenberg, Robert: Sickness and healing. A case study on the dialectic of culture and personality. Nürnberg 2008, 2nd ed. (edition afem – mission academics, Band 11). VTR Publications.

Badenberg, Robert: Das Menschenbild in fremden Kulturen. Ein Leitfaden für eigene Erkundungen. Handbuch zu Lothar Käsers Lehrbuch Animismus. Nürnberg Bonn 2007. (French edition: La conception de l'homme dans les cultures étrangères. Guide d'investigation personnelle. Charols/France 2011. English edition: The Concept of Man in Non-Western Cultures: A Guide for One's Own Research. Handbook to Lothar Käser's Textbook *Animism – A Cognitive Approach.* VTR Publications 2014).

Baer, Gerhard: Ein besonderes Merkmal des südamerikanischen Schamanen. Zeitschrift für Ethnologie 94.1969:284-292.

Baer, Gerhard; Snell, Wayne W.: An Ayahuasca ceremony among the Matsigenka (Eastern Peru). Zeitschrift für Ethnologie 99.1974: 63-80.

Baer, Gerhard: Die Religion der Matsigenka (Ost-Peru). Monographie zu Kultur und Religion eines Indianervolkes des Oberen Amazonas. Basel (Wepf) 1984.

Baer, Gerhard: Peruanische ayahuasca-Sitzungen – Schamanen und Heilbehandlungen. In: Dittrich/Scharfetter 1987:70-80.

Bahuchet, Serge; Thomas, Jacqueline M. C. (éds.): Encyclopédie des Pygmées Aka. Paris (SELAF) 1991.

Barley, Nigel: The Dowayo dance of death. In: Humphreys/King 1981:149-159.

Barthel, Thomas S.: Ethnolinguistische Polynesienforschung. Anthropos 59.1964: 920-926.

Baumann, Hermann: Das doppelte Geschlecht. Ethnologische Studien zur Bisexualität in Ritus und Mythos. Berlin 1955 [Neudruck 1980].

Bertholet, Alfred: Dynamismus und Personalismus in der Seelenauffassung. Tübingen 1930.

Bettez Gravel, Pierre: The malevolent eye. An essay on the evil eye, fertility and the concept of mana. New York et al. (Peter Lang) 1995.

Bird-David, Nurit: "Animism" revisited. Personhood, environment, and relational epistemology. Current Anthropology 40. Supplement.1999:67-91. Auch in Albers/Franke 2012.

Black, Peter: Psychological anthropology and its discontents: Science and rhetoric in postwar Micronesia. In: Kiste/Marshall 1999:225-253.

Blacking, John (ed.): The anthropology of the body.. New York 1977.

Bleibtreu-Ehrenberg, Gisela: Der Leib als Widersacher der Seele. Ursprünge dualistischer Seinskonzepte im Abendland. In: Jüttemann/Sonntag/Wolf 1991:75-93.

Bloch, Maurice; Parry, Jonathan (eds.): Death and the regeneration of life. Cambridge et al. 1982.

Boddy, Janice: Spirit possession revisited. Beyond instrumentality. Annual Review of Anthropology 1994.23:407-434.

Bolz, Peter: Oglala. In: Müller 1983: 422-449.

Bourguignon, Erika (ed.): Religion, altered states of consciousness, and social change. Columbus, Ohio 1973.

Boyer, Pascal (ed.): Cognitive aspects of religious symbolism. Cambridge 1993.

Bremmer, Jan: The early Greek concept of the soul. Princeton University Press 1983.

Brewster, Thomas E.; Brewster Elizabeth S.: LAMP. Language acquisition made practical. Colorado Springs 1977 (oder später).

Brown, Michael F.: Ropes of sand: order and imagery in Aguaruna dreams. In: Tedlock 1987:154-170.

Buchta, Brigitte: Aspekte des Schamanismus in der aktuellen Psychosomatik. Magisterarbeit Freiburg im Breisgau WS 1987/1988.

Buggle, Franz; Westermann-Duttlinger, Hilde: Animismus als alternative Weise des Welterlebens. Theoretische Überlegungen und empirische Forschungsergebnisse. Forschungsberichte des Psychologischen Instituts der Albert-Ludwigs-Universität Freiburg i.Br. Nr. 41. Freiburg 1987.

Burkhardt, Helmut; Swarat, Uwe (Hrsg.): Evangelisches Lexikon für Theologie und Gemeinde. Wuppertal et al. 1992.

Burling, Robbins: Garo beliefs in the afterlife. In: Cederroth/Corlin/Lindström 1988:31-38.

Burnett, David: World of the spirits. A Christian perspective on traditional and folk religions. London (MonarchBooks) 2000.

Cain, Horst: Aitu. Eine Untersuchung zur autochthonen Religion der Samoaner. Wiesbaden (Franz Steiner) 1979.

Cancik, Hubert; Gladiger, Burkhard; Kohl, Karl-Heinz (Hrsg.): Handbuch religionswissenschaftlicher Grundbegriffe. Stuttgart et al. (Band 1) 1988; (Band 2) 1990; (Band 3) 1993; (Band 4) 1998; (Band 5) 2001.

Carneiro da Cunha, Manuela: Eschatology among the Krahó: reflection upon society, free field of fabulation. In: Humphreys/King 1981:161-174).

Cederroth, Sven; Corlin, Claes; Lindström Jan (eds.): On the meaning of death. Essays on mortuitary rituals and eschatological beliefs. Uppsala 1988.

Cederroth, Sven: Pouring water and eating food: On the symbolism of death in a Sasak community on Lombok, Indonesia. In: Cederroth/Corlin/Lindström 1988:39-61.

Chagnon, Napoleon: Yanomamö. Fort Worth et al. (Harcourt Brace College Publishers) 1992 (4. Auflage).

Chapin, Mac: Muu Ikala: Cuna birth ceremony. In: Young/Howe 1972:59-65.

Chelhod, Joseph: La baraka chez les Arabes ou l'influence bienfaisante du sacré. In: Revue de l'histoire des religions. T.148. Paris 1955:68-88.

Corlin, Claes: The journey through the Bardo. Notes on the symbolism of Tibetan mortuary rites and the Tibetan Book of the Dead. In: Cederroth/Corlin/Lindström 1988:63-75.

Crawley, A. Ernest: The idea of the soul. London 1909.

Crawley, A. Ernest: "Doubles". In Hastings 1911, 4:853-860.

Crocker, Jon Christopher: Vital souls. Bororo cosmology, natural symbolism, and shamanism. Tucson, Arizona 1985.

Cunningham, Scott: Mana. Magie und Spiritualität auf Hawaii. Berlin, München, Wien (Scherz, O. W. Barth) 1994.

D'Andrade, Roy: The development of cognitive anthropology. Cambridge University Press 1995.

De Heusch, L.: Why marry her? Society and symbolic structures. Cambridge 1971.

Demandt, Alexander: Die Träume der römischen Kaiser. In: Holzhausen 1998:200-224.

Denoon, Donald; Firth, Steward; Linnekin, Jocelyn; Meleisea, Malama; Nero, Karen (eds.): The Cambridge history of the Pacific Islands. Cambridge University Press 1997.

Descola, Philippe: Leben und Sterben in Amazonien. Bei den Jivaro-Indianern. Stuttgart 1996.

Dieterlen, Germaine: Les âmes des Dogons. Paris 1941.

Dilley, Roy M.: Dreams, inspiration and craftwork among Tukolor weavers. In: J□drey/Shaw 1992:71-85.

Dittrich, Adolf; Scharfetter, Christian (Hrsg.): Ethnopsychiatrie. Psychotherapie mittels außergewöhnlicher Bewusstseinszustände in westlichen und indigenen Kulturen. Stuttgart (Ferdinand Enke) 1987.

Dracklé, Dorle (Hrsg.): Zur kulturellen Konstruktion von Kindheit und Jugend. Berlin 1996.

Eliade, Mircea: Schamanismus und archaische Ekstasetechnik. Frankfurt am Main (Suhrkamp) 1975.

Errington, Shelly: Embodied Sumangé in Luwu. Journal of Asian Studies XLII, No. 3, 1983:545-570.

Fartacek, Gebhard: Begegnungen mit □inn. Lokale Konzeptionen über Geister und Dämonen in der syrischen Peripherie. Anthropos 97.2002/2:469-486.

Fasching, Gerhard: Phänomene der Wirklichkeit. Okkulte und naturwissenschaftliche Weltbilder. Wien, New York (Springer) 2000.

Feest, Christian F.: Beseelte Welten. Die Religionen der Indianer Nordamerikas. Freiburg, Basel, Wien (Herder) 1998.

Firth, Raymond: Essays on social organization and values. London 1964.

Firth, Raymond: The analysis of Mana: an empirical approach. In: Harding/Wallace 1970:316-333.

Fischer, Hans: Studien über Seelenvorstellungen in Ozeanien. München 1965.

Fischer, Hans (Hrsg.): Ethnologie. Eine Einführung. Hamburg 1983.

Fischer Hans: Gräber, Kreuze und Inschriften. Ein Friedhof in Neuguinea. Berlin (Reimer) 2002.

Fischer-Lichte, Erika; Horn, Christian; Umathum, Sandra; Warstat, Matthias (Hrsg.): Wahrnehmung und Medialität. Tübingen, Basel 2001.

Frank, Barbara: Ron. In: Müller 1983:204-227.

Fuhrmann, Klaus: Formen der javanischen Pilgerschaft zu Heiligenschreinen. Diss. Freiburg 2001.

Galling, Kurt (Hrsg.): Die Religion in Geschichte und Gegenwart. Band 1. Tübingen 1957.

Galling, Kurt (Hrsg.): Die Religion in Geschichte und Gegenwart. Band 5. Tübingen 1961.

Gelfand, M.: Shona religion. Cape Town, Wynberg, Johannesburg 1962.

Gladigow, Burkhard; Kippenberg, Hans G. (Hrsg.): Neue Ansätze in der Relgions-wissenschaft. München (Koesel) 1983.

Gladwin, Thomas; Sarason, Seymour B.: Truk: Man in paradise. Viking Fund Publications in Anthropology Nr. 20. New York 1953.

Götz, Nicola H.: Obeah – Hexerei in der Karibik – zwischen Macht und Ohnmacht. Frankfurt am Main (Peter Lang) 1995.

Goodenough, Ward Hunt: Cooperation in change. New York 1963.

Goodenough, Ward Hunt: Under heaven's brow. Pre-Christian religious tradition in Chuuk. Philadelphia 2002.

Greenbaum, Lenora: Societal correlates of possession trance in Sub-Saharan Africa. In: Bourguignon 1973:39-57.

Greschat, Hans-Jürgen: Mana und Tapu. Die Religion der Maori auf Neuseeland. Berlin 1980.

Guenther, Matthias G.: Buschmänner (Nharo). In: Müller 1983:75-107.

Haekel, Josef: Religion. In: Trimborn 1971:72-141.

Hahn, Eberhard: Erster und zweiter Thessalonicherbrief. Edition C: B, Bibelkommentare zum Neuen Testament Bd. 17. Neuhausen-Stuttgart (Hänssler) 1993.

Hambruch, Paul; Sarfert, Ernst; (Damm, Hans): Inseln um Truk. Ergebnisse der Südsee-Expedition 1908-1910. II. Ethnographie: B. Mikronesien, Bd. 6. 2. Halbband. Thilenius, Georg (Hrsg.) Hamburg 1935.

Harding, Thomas G.; Wallace Ben J. (eds.): Cultures of the Pacific. New York 1970.

Harner, Michael: Der Weg des Schamanen. Ein praktischer Führer zu innerer Heilkraft. Interlaken 1982.

Harvey, Graham (ed.): Indigenous religion. A companion. London, New York 2000.

Harvey, Graham: Art works in Aotearoa. In: Harvey 2000:155-172.

Hasenfratz, Hans-Peter: Die toten Lebenden: eine religionsphaenomenologische Studie zum sozialen Tod in archaischen Gesellschaften. Leiden (Brill) 1982.

Hasenfratz, Hans-Peter: Seelenvorstellungen bei den Germanen und ihre Übernahme und Umformung durch die christliche Mission. Zeitschrift für Religions- und Geistesgeschichte (Köln) 38.1986/1.2:19-31. [a]

Hasenfratz, Hans-Peter: Die Seele: Einführung in ein religiöses Grundphänomen. Zürich 1986. [b]

Hasenfratz, Hans Peter: Die religiöse Welt der Germanen: Ritual, Magie, Kult, Mythus. Freiburg (Herder) 1992.

Hastings, James (ed.): Encyclopaedia of religion and ethics. Edinburgh 1911.

Hauschild, Thomas: Der böse Blick. Ideengeschichtliche und sozialpsychologische Untersuchungen. Hamburg 1979, Berlin 1982 (2. überarbeitete Auflage).

Hauschild, Thomas: Religionsethnologie: Dekonstruktion und Rekonstruktion. In: Schweizer, Thomas et al. 1993:305-330.

Hauser-Schäublin, Birgitta: Abelam. In: Müller 1983:178-203.

Heintze, Dieter: Bilder des Menschen in fremden Kulturen. Stuttgart 1973.

Heintze, Beatrix: Besessenheits-Phänomene im mittleren Bantu-Gebiet. Studien zur Kulturkunde Band 25. Wiesbaden 1970.

Herrmann, Ferdinand: Symbolik in den Religionen der Naturvölker.Stuttgart 1961.

Hirschberg, Walter (Hrsg.): Wörterbuch der Völkerkunde. Stuttgart 1965.

Hirschberg, Walter (Hrsg.): Neues Wörterbuch der Völkerkunde. Berlin 1988.

Hochegger, Hermann: Die Vorstellungen von "Seele" und "Totengeist" bei afrikanischen Völkern. Anthropos 60.1965:273-339.

Hollan, Douglas W; Wellenkamp, Jane C.: Contentment and suffering. Culture and experience in Toraja. New York 1994.

Holthaus, Stephan; Müller, Klaus W. (Hrsg.): Die Mission der Theologie. Festschrift für Hans Kasdorf zum 70. Geburtstag. Bonn 1998.

Holzhausen, Jens (Hrsg.): Psyche – Seele – anima. Festschrift für Karin Alt zum 7. Mai 1998. Stuttgart und Leipzig 1998.

Homiak, John: The mystic revelation of Rasta Far-Eye: visionary communication in a prophetic movement. In: Tedlock 1987:220-245.

Hsu, Francis L.: Psychological anthropology. Cambridge, Mass. 1972.

Hülsewiede, Brigitte: Die Nahua von Tequila. Eine Nachuntersuchung, besonders zu Struktur und Wandel der Familienfeste. Münster und Hamburg 1992.

Hüwelmeier, Gertrud; Krause, Kristine (eds.): Traveling spirits: migrants, markets and mobilities. New York et al. 2010.

Humphrey, Caroline with Urgunge Onon: Shamans and elders. Experience, knowledge and power among the Daur Mongols. Oxford 1996.

Humphreys, S. C.; King, H. (eds.): Mortality and immortality: the anthropology and archaeology of death. London 1981.

Iwawaki, Saburo; Kashima, Yoshihisa; Leung, Kwok (eds.): Innovations in crosscultural psychology. Amsterdam 1992.

Jacobsen, T. W.; Cullen, Tracey: A consideration of mortuary practices in Neolithic Greece burials from Franchti Cave. In Humphreys/King 1981:79-101.

Jensen, Adolf Ellegard: Hainuwele: Volkserzählungen von der Molukken-Insel Ceram. Frankfurt 1939.

Jensen, Adolf Ellegard: Das religiöse Weltbild einer frühen Kultur. Stuttgart 1948.

Jensen, Adolf Ellegard: Mythos und Kult bei Naturvölkern: Religionswissenschaftliche Betrachtungen. München 1992.

Jedrej, M. C.; Shaw, Rosalind (eds.): Dreaming, religion and society in Africa. Leiden, New York, Köln 1992.

Jilek, W. G.: Veränderte Wachbewusstseinszustände in Heiltanzritualen nordamerikanischer Indianer. In: Dittrich/Scharfetter1987:135-149.

Jüttemann, Gerd; Sonntag, Michael; Wulf, Christoph (Hrsg.): Die Seele. Ihre Geschichte im Abendland. Weinheim 1991.

Käser, Lothar: ... und bliebe am äußersten Meer. Bad Liebenzell 1972.

Käser, Lothar: Der Begriff "Seele" bei den Insulanern von Truk. Diss. Freiburg 1977.

Käser, Lothar: Die Besiedlung Mikronesiens: eine ethnologisch-linguistische Untersuchung. Berlin 1989.

Käser, Lothar: Durch den Tunnel. Die Geschichte der Übersetzung des Alten Testaments in die Sprache der Truk-Inseln in der Südsee. Bad Liebenzell 1990(a).

Käser, Lothar und Gisela: Die Campa-Indianer. ethos (Berneck/Schweiz) 3.1988:6-13.

Käser, Lothar: Pauti. Mit einer Missionarin der Schweizer Indianermission unterwegs bei den Campa-Indianern in Peru. Berneck/Schweiz 1989, [2]1990(b).

Käser, Lothar: The concepts "sin" and "curse" on the Islands of Chuuk/Micronesia. NAOS (University of Pittsburgh, PA) 10.1-3(1994):29-32.

Käser, Lothar: The concept "The Sacred" in the islands of Truk. In: NAOS (University of Pittsburgh, PA) 7.1-3(1991):33-36.

Käser, Lothar: Kognitive Aspekte des Menschenbildes bei den Campa (Asheninca). *asien afrika lateinamerika* 23.1995:29-50.

Käser, Lothar: Fremde Kulturen. Eine Einführung in die Ethnologie für Entwicklungshelfer und kirchliche Mitarbeiter in Übersee. Bad Liebenzell und Erlangen 1997.

Käser, Lothar: Der Begriff "Himmel" als Bibelübersetzungsproblem in den austronesischen Sprachen Ozeaniens und Südostasiens. In: Holthaus/Müller 1998:152-161.

Karabila, Abdelkhalek: Die Welt der ☐inn und der Heiler. Eine volkskundliche Untersuchung in der Provinz Nador (Marokko). Diss. Mainz 1995.

Kasch, Regina: Zur kulturellen Variabilität der Lua in Nordwestthailand. Magisterarbeit Freiburg 1998.

Keesing, Roger: Rethinking Mana. Journal of Anthropological Research 40.1984:137-156.

Khoury, Adel Theodor (Hrsg.): Lexikon religiöser Grundbegriffe. Judentum, Christentum, Islam. Graz, Wien, Köln 1987. UB: LS Rel 30/8.

Kiste, Robert C.; Marshall, Mac (eds.): American anthropology in Micronesia. An assessment. University of Hawaii Press 1999.

Köhler, Ulrich: Das Modell des Kosmos im zeremoniellen Leben der Tzotzil von San Pablo. Indiana 9.1984:283-303.

Köhler, Ulrich: Kosmologie und Religion. In: Köhler 1990:221-240.

Köhler, Ulrich (Hrsg.): Altamerikanistik. Berlin 1990.

König, Franz; Waldenfels, Hans (Hrsg.): Lexikon der Religionen: Phänomene – Geschichte – Ideen. Freiburg im Breisgau; Basel; Wien 1992.

Kohl, Karl-Heinz: "Fetisch, Tabu, Totem". In: Gladigow/Kippenberg 1983:59-74.

Kohl, Karl-Heinz: Der Tod der Reisjungfrau: Mythen, Kulte und Allianzen in einer ostindonesischen Lokalkultur. Stuttgart 1998.

Kohl, Karl-Heinz: Beim Fußball helfen die Geister. Spiel, Krieg und Ritual in Ostflores. In: Neumann/Weigel 2000:101-112.

Kortt, Ivan: Die soziale Bindung des sibirischen Schamanen. In: Kuper 1991:27-43.

Krämer, Augustin: Truk. Ergebnisse der Südsee-Expedition 1908-1910. II. Ethnographie: B. Mikronesien, Bd. 5. Thilenius, Georg (Hrsg.). Hamburg 1932.

Krämer, Augustin: Inseln um Truk (Centralkarolinen Ost). Ergebnisse der Südsee-Expedition 1908-1910. II. Ethnographie: B. Mikronesien, Bd. 6, 1. Halbband. Thilenius, Georg (Hrsg.). Hamburg 1935.

Krasberg, Ulrike (Hrsg.): ... und was ist mit der Seele? Seelenvorstellungen im Kulturvergleich. Frankfurt am Main 2009.

Kriss, Rudolf; Kriss-Heinrich, Hubert: Volksglaube im Bereich des Islam. Wiesbaden 1960 (Band 1), 1962 (Band 2).

Kuhnt-Saptodewo, Sri: Zum Seelengeleit bei den Ngaju am Kahayan. Auswertung eines Sakraltextes zur Manarung-Zeremonie beim Totenfest. München 1993.

Kuper, Michael (Hrsg.): Hungrige Geister und rastlose Seelen. Texte zur Schamanismusforschung. Berlin 1991.

Labouvie, Eva: Zauberei und Hexenwerk. Ländlicher Hexenglaube in der frühen Neuzeit. Frankfurt (Fischer) 1991.

Lauby, Heiko: Tötung und Regeneration – Zum Verständnis archaischer Weltbilder. Beispiele aus der jägerischen Glaubenswelt. Magisterarbeit Albert-Ludwigs-Universität Freiburg 2000.

Laubscher, Matthias: Religionsethnologie. In: Fischer 1983:231-256.

Laufer, P. Carl: Das Wesen des Menschen im Denken der Gunantuna (Neubritannien). Wiener völkerkundliche Mitteilungen 5.1957.2:127-160.

Lehmann, Friedrich Rudolf: Mana. Eine begriffsgeschichtliche Untersuchung auf ethnologischer Grundlage. Dresden 1915.

Lehmann, Friedrich Rudolf: Mana. Der Begriff des "außerordentlich Wirkungsvollen" bei Südseevölkern. Leipzig 1922.

Lehmann, Friedrich Rudolf: Die polynesischen Tabusitten. Eine ethnosoziologische Untersuchung. Veröffentlichungen des Staatlich-sächsischen Forschungsinstituts für Völkerkunde in Leipzig, Bd. 10. Leipzig 1930.

Lehner, Hansjörg; Meran, Georg; Möller, Joachim: De statu corruptionis. Entscheidungslogische Einübungen in die Höhere Amoralität. Litzelstetter Libellen Nr.1.
Abteilung Handbüchlein und Enchiridia. Konstanz-Litzelstetten (Faude) 1980.

Leonard, Anne P.: Spirit mediums in Palau: Transformations in a traditional system.
In: Bourguignon 1973:129-177.

Linke, Bernd Michael (Hrsg.): Die Welt nach der Welt. Jenseitsmodelle in den Religionen. Frankfurt am Main 1999.

Linke, Bernd Michael: Der Flug des Schamanen. Fahrten ins Jenseits. In: Linke
1999: 173-199.

Linke, Bernd Michael (Hrsg.): Schöpfungsmythologie in den Religionen. Frankfurt
am Main (Otto Lembeck) 2001.

Lorenz, Sönke; Bauer, Dieter R. (Hrsg.): Hexenverfolgung. Beiträge zur Forschung –
unter besonderer Berücksichtigung des südwestdeutschen Raums. Würzburg 1995.

Lutz, Catherine: Emotion words and emotional development on Ifaluk Atoll. Ph.D.
dissertation, Harvard University 1980.

Mahony; Frank J.: A Trukese theory of medicine. Ph.D. Dissertation Stanford University 1970.

Mandunu, Joseph Kufulu: Das "Kindoki" im Licht der Sündenbocktheologie. Frankfurt am Main 1992.

Mbiti, John S.: Afrikanische Religion und Weltanschauung. Berlin, New York
(Walter de Gruyter) 1974.

Mehringer, Jakob: Pajonal-Asheninca (Campa-Indianer). Ihre kulturelle Stellung im
Rahmen der ostperuanischen Proto-Aruak-Stämme. Hohenschäftlarn 1986.

Mendonsa, Eugene. L.: The journey of the soul in Sisala cosmology. Journal of
Religion in Africa (Leiden) 7.1975.1:62-70.

Merill, William: Rarámuri stereotype of dreams. In: Tedlock 1987:194-219.

Middleton, John: Lugbara death. In: Bloch/Parry 1982:134-154.

Mischung, Roland: Religion und Wirklichkeitsvorstellungen in einem Karen-Dorf
Nordwest-Thailands. Frankfurt am Main1984.

Molla-Djafari, Hamid: Gott hat die schönsten Namen ... Islamische Gottesnamen,
ihre Bedeutung, Verwendung und Probleme ihrer Übersetzung. Frankfurt am
Main et al. 2001.

Molleson, Theya: The archaeology and anthropology of death: what the bones tell
us. In: Humphreys/King 1981:15-32.

Mommensteeg, Geert: Allah's words as amulet. Etnofoor 3.1990:63-76.

Morice, R.: Psychiatric diagnosis in a transcultural setting: The importance of lexical categories. British Journal of Psychiatry 1978.132:87-95.

Mühlmann, Wilhelm Ernst: Artikel "Animismus". In Galling 1957:389-391.

Müller, Klaus E. (Hrsg.): Menschenbilder früher Gesellschaften: ethnologische Studien zum Verhältnis von Mensch und Natur. Gedächtnisschrift für Hermann Baumann. Frankfurt/Main 1983.

Müller, Klaus E.: Der gesprungene Ring: wie man die Seele gewinnt und verliert. Frankfurt am Main 1997.

Müller, Klaus E.: Wortzauber. Eine Ethnologie der Eloquenz. Frankfurt/Main 2001.

Müller, Klaus W.: Kurs 330 – Südseemissionare unterwegs. Bad Liebenzell 1975.

Multhaupt, Tamara: Hexerei und Antihexerei in Afrika. München 1989.

Mummendey, Hans Dieter: De Vampyris. Auf dem Wege zu einer sozialen Psychophysiologie des akuten Vampirismus. Litzelstetter Libellen Nr.2. Abteilung Handbüchlein und Enchiridia. Konstanz-Litzelstetten (Faude) 1982.

Murray Thomas, R. (ed.): Oriental theories of human development. Scriptural and popular beliefs from Hinduism, Buddhism, Confucianism, Shinto, and Islam. New York et al. (Peter Lang) 1988.

Muth, Robert: Träger der Lebenskraft. Ausscheidungen des Organismus im Volksglauben der Antike. Wien 1954.

Nabofa, M.Y.: Erhi and eschatology. In: Adegbola 1983.297-316.

Neumann, Gerhard; Weigel, Sigrid (Hrsg.): Lesbarkeit der Kultur. Literaturwissenschaft zwischen Kulturtechnik und Ethnographie. München (Wilhelm Fink) 2000.

Neumann, Wolfgang: Der Mensch und sein Doppelgänger. Alter ego-Vorstellungen in Mesoamerika und im Sufismus des Ibn-Arabi. Wiesbaden (Steiner) 1981.

Neumann, Wolfgang: Tuareg. In: Müller 1983:274-292.

Neuman, Wolfgang: Schöpfungsmythen nordamerikanischer Indianer. In: Linke 2001:147-172.

Oduyoye, Modupe: Man's self and its spiritual double. In: Adegbola 1983:273-288.

Okazaki, A.: Living together with "bad things": the persistence of Gank, notions of mystical agents. In: Tomikawa 1985.

Omyajowo, J. Akin: What is witchcraft? In: Adegbola 1983:317-336.

Panoff, Michel; Perrin, Michel: Taschenwörterbuch der Ethnologie. (Hrsg. v. Justin Stagl) Berlin ³2000.

Paproth, Hans-Joachim: Studien über das Bärenzeremoniell. Uppsala 1976.

Pfeffer, Georg: Seelentausch bei den Gadaba. In: Laubscher 1991:51-92.

Piaget, Jean: Das Weltbild des Kindes. Stuttgart 1926 und 1978.

Platvoet, Jan G.: Rattray's request: Spirit possession among the Bono of West Africa. In: Harvey 2000:80-96.

Potter, Jack M.: Wind, water bones and souls: the religious world of the Cantonese peasant. Journal of Oriental Studies (Hong Kong) 8.1970:139-153.

Psota, Thomas: Waldgeister und Reisseelen: die Revitalisierung von Ritualen zur Erhaltung der komplementären Produktion in Südwest-Sumatra. Berlin 1996.

van Quekelberghe, Renaud: Klinische Ethnopsychologie. Einführung in die transkulturelle Psychologie, Psychopathologie und Psychotherapie. Heidelberg 1991.

Rahm-Mottl, Ursula: Die magisch-religiöse Bedeutung des Beduinenschmucks im Negev. In: Der Arabische Almanach 2002/03. Zeitschrift für orientalische Kultur. 13. Jahrgang (Berlin, Nov. 2002):33-37.

Reichardt, Anna Katharina; Kubli, Erich (Hrsg.): Menschenbilder. Bern et al. 1999.

Reichmayr, Johannes: Einführung in die Ethnopsychoanalyse. Geschichte, Theorien, Methoden. Frankfurt am Main 1995.

Reimann, Ralf Ingo: Der Schamane sieht eine Hexe – der Ethnologe sieht nichts. Menschliche Informationsverarbeitung und ethnologische Forschung. Frankfurt (Campus) 1998.

Reis, Horst: Die Vorstellung von den geistig-seelischen Vorgängen und ihrer körperlichen Lokalisation im Altlatein. Eine Untersuchung mit besonderer Rücksicht auf den Gebrauch der bezüglichen Substantive (animus – anima – cor – pectus – mens – ingenium – indoles). 2 Bände. München 1962 (Münchener Studien zur Sprachwissenschaft, herausgegeben von Karl Hoffmann und Helmut Humbach, Beiheft E, 1. und 2. Teil).

Renner, Egon: Die kognitive Anthropologie. Aufbau und Grundlagen eines ethnologisch-linguistischen Paradigmas. Forschungen zur Ethnologie und Sozialpsychologie 12. Berlin 1980.

Riede, Ursus-Nikolaus: Die Macht des Abnormen als Wurzel der Kultur. Der Beitrag des Leidens zum Menschenbild. Stuttgart, New York (Georg Thieme) 1995.

Ritchie, Mark Andrew: Spirit of the rainforest. A Yanomamö shaman's story. Chicago (Island Lake Press) 1996.

Ritchie, Mark Andrew: Spirit of the rainforest. A Yanomamö shaman's story. Chicago (Island Lake Press) 1996.

Roser, Markus: Hexerei und Lebensriten. Zur Inkulturation des christlichen Glaubens unter den Gbaya der Zentralafrikanischen Republik. Erlangen 2000.

Rothenbühler, Heinz: Abraham inkognito. Einführung in das althebräische Denken. Rothenburg (Selbstverlag) ²1998.

Rousseau, Jérôme: Kayan religion. Ritual and religious reform in Central Borneo. Leiden 1998.

Ruppert, Hans Jürgen: Okkultismus. Geisterwelt oder neuer Weltgeist? Wiesbaden und Wuppertal 1990.

Sautter, Gerhard: Artikel "Animismus" in Burkhardt/Swarat 1992:75-76.

Schlatter, Adolf: Die Briefe an die Thessalonicher, Philipper, Timotheus und Titus. Erläuterungen zum Neuen Testament Bd. 8. Stuttgart (Calwer Verlag) 1987.

Schlatter, Gerhard: Artikel "Animismus" in: Cancik 1988:473-476.

Schlatter, Gerhard: Animismus. In: Auffahrt/Bernhard/Mohr 1999:61.

Schlehe, Judith: Die Meereskönigin des Südens, Ratu Kidul. Geisterpolitik im javanischen Alltag. Berlin 1998.

Schneider, Jürg: From upland to irrigated rice. The development of wet-rice agriculture in Rejang Musi, Southwest Sumatra. Berlin 1995.

Schnelle, Udo: Neutestamentliche Anthropologie. Jesus – Paulus – Johannes. Neukirchen-Vluyn 1991.

Schnepel, Burkhard: Ethnologische Betrachtungen zur Wahr-Nehmung und Wahr-Machung von Träumen. In: Fischer-Lichte/Horn/Umathum/Warstat 2001:233-253.

Schönhuth, Michael: Das Einsetzen der Nacht in die Rechte des Tages. Hexerei im symbolischen Kontext afrikanischer und europäischer Weltbilder. Münster und Hamburg 1992.

Schüle, Andreas: Israels Sohn – Jahwes Prophet. Ein Versuch zum Verhältnis von kanonischer Theologie und Religionsgeschichte anhand der Bileam-Perikope (Num 22-24). Münster, Hamburg, London (LIT) 2001.

Schweizer, Thomas; Schweizer, Margarete; Kokot, Waltraud (Hg.): Handbuch der Ethnologie. Berlin 1993.

Sell, Joachim: Der schlimme Tod bei den Völkern Indonesiens. S'Gravenhage 1955.

Severi, Carlo: Talking about souls: the pragmatic construction of meaning in Cuna ritual language. In: Boyer 1993:165-181.

Shaw, Rosalind: Dreaming as accomplishment: Power, the individual and Temne divination. In: Jędrej/Shaw (eds.) 1992:36-54.

Stader, Heinrich: "Das Feuer im Beichtstuhl ging offensichtlich von selbst aus ..." Prozesse um Religion und anderes Okkultes. Ein Vademecum für Juristen und leicht gläubige Laien. (Libelle Verlag,) Lengwil am Bodensee 2001.

Stahl, Georg Ernst: Theoria Medica Vera. Halle 1737.

Stein, R. A.: Tibetan civilization. London 1969.

Sterly, Joachim: "Heilige Männer" und Medizinmänner in Melanesien. Köln 1965.

Steyne, Philip N.: Gods of power. Houston TX (Touch Publications) 1990. Deutsch: Machtvolle Götter. Eine Untersuchung über Glaube und Gebräuche des Animismus, wie er von Naturvölkern praktiziert wird, und wie er heute in allen religiösen Bewegungen vorkommt. Bad Liebenzell 1993.

Stöhr, Waldemar: Die altindonesischen Religionen. Handbuch der Orientalistik. Leiden 1976.

Strathern, Andrew: Witchcraft, greed, cannibalism and death: some related themes from the New Guinea Highlands. In: Bloch/Perry 1982:111-133.

Strathern, Marilyn: The gender of the gift: problems with women and problems with society in Melanesia.. Berkeley (University of California Press) 1988.

Streck, Bernhard: Fröhliche Wissenschaft Ethnologie. Eine Führung. Wuppertal 1997.

Tauchmann, Kurt: Kankanaey (u. Lepanto). In: Müller 1983:222-247.

Tedlock, Barbara (ed.): Dreaming. Anthropological and psychological interpretations. Cambridge et al. 1987.

Thiel, Josef Franz; Doutreloux, Albert (Hrsg.): Heil und Macht. Approches du sacré. St. Augustin 1975.

Thiel, Josef Franz: Ahnen – Geister – Höchste Wesen. Religionsethnologische Untersuchungen im Zaïre-Kasai-Gebiet. St. Augustin 1977.

Thiel, Josef Franz; (Museum für Völkerkunde Frankfurt): Was sind Fetische? Frankfurt 1986.

Thiel, Josef Franz: Religionsethnologie. Grundbegriffe der Religionen schriftloser Völker. Berlin 1984.

Thiel, Josef Franz: Trauerriten in "Naturreligionen". In: Linke 1999:201-210.

Thiel, Josef Franz: Tod in der Gemeinschaft. Sterben und Trauer bei den Bantu in Zentralafrika. In: Linke 1999:211-223.

Tomikawa, M. (ed.): Sudan Sahel Studies I. Tokio 1985.

Tomikawa, M. (ed.): Sudan Sahel Studies II. Tokio 1987.Topley, Marjorie: Chinese rites for the repose of the soul, with special reference to Cantonese custom. Journal for the Malayan Branch of the Royal Asiatic Society 25.1952:149-160.

Trimborn, Hermann (Hrsg.): Lehrbuch der Völkerkunde. Stuttgart 1971.

Tschesnow, Jan W.: Historische Ethnographie der Länder Indochinas. Berlin 1985.

Tworuschka, Udo: Heilige Wege. Reise zu Gott in den Religionen. Frankfurt am Main (Lembeck) 2002.

Tyler, Stephen (Hrsg.): Cognitive anthropology. New York 1969.

Tylor, Edward Burnett: Primitive culture. Researches into the development of mythology and philosophy, religion, art and custom. 2 vols. London 1871.

van der Weijden, Gera: Indonesische Reisrituale. Basel 1981.

Vitebsky, Piers: Shamanism. In: Harvey 2000:55-67

Vorgrimler, Herbert; Bernauer, Ursula; Sternberg, Thomas: Engel. Erfahrungen göttlicher Nähe. Freiburg, Basel, Wien (Herder) 2001.

Wachs, Marianne: Seele oder Nicht-Ich: von der frühvedischen Auseinandersetzung mit Tod und Unsterblichkeit zur Nicht-Ich-Lehre des Theravada-Buddhismus. Frankfurt am Main, Berlin, Bern, New York, Paris, Wien 1998.

Wagner, Fritz: "Gezählt, gewogen und zu leicht befunden" (Daniel 5,25-28). Bemerkungen zum Motiv der Seelenwägung. In: Holzhausen 1998:369-384.

Walker, Sheila, S.: Ceremonial spirit possession in Africa and Afro-America. Forms, meanings and functional significance for individuals and social groups. Leiden 1972.

Warneck, Johannes: Die Religion der Batak. Ein Paradigma für die animistischen Religionen des Indischen Archipels. Leipzig 1909.

Watson, James L.: Of flesh and bones: The management of death pollution in Cantonese society. In: Bloch/Parry 1982:155-186.

Werner, Roland: Transkulturelle Heilkunde. Der ganze Mensch. Heilsysteme unter dem Einfluss von Abrahamischen Religionen, Östlichen Religionen und Glaubensbekenntnissen, Paganismus, Neuen Religionen und religiösen Mischformen. Frankfurt am Main 2001.

Whorf, Benjamin Lee: Sprache, Denken, Wirklichkeit. Reinbek 1997 (und später).

Wiesemann, Ursula (Hrsg.): Verstehen und verstanden werden. Praktisches Handbuch zum Fremdsprachenerwerb. Lahr 1992.

Wiesemann, Ursula: Besprechung von Käser, Lothar: Fremde Kulturen. Eine Einführung in die Ethnologie für Entwicklungshelfer und kirchliche Mitarbeiter in Übersee. Bad Liebenzell und Erlangen 1997. In: evangelikale missiologie 14.1998.2:75.

Wiher, Hannes: Shame and guilt. A key to missions. Bonn 2003.

Willerslev, Rane: Soul hunters. Hunting, animism, and personhood among the Siberian Yukaghir. Berkeley (University of California Press) 2007.

Williams, F. E.: Orokaiva society. Oxford 1930.

Willoughby, W. C.: The soul of the Bantu. A sympathetic study of the magicoreligious practices and beliefs of the Bantu tribes of Africa. Garden City, N.Y. 1928, reprinted 1970.

Wolf, Hans-Jürgen: Hexenwahn. Hexen in Geschichte und Gegenwart. Bindlach (Gondrom) 1994.

Wolters, Gereon: Darwinistische Menschenbilder. In: Reichardt/Kubli 1999:95-115.

Woodburn, James: Social dimensions of death in four African hunting and gathering societies. In: Bloch/Parry 1982:187-210.

Woodward, Mark R.: Gifts for the sky people: Animal sacrifice, head hunting and power among the Naga of Burma and Assam. In: Harvey 2000:219-229.

Wulf, Christoph: Präsenz und Absenz. Prozess und Struktur in der Geschichte der Seele. In: Jüttemann/Sonntag/Wulf 1991:5-12.

Yamada, Takako: An Anthropology of Animism and Shamanism. Budapest 1999.

Young, Philip; Howe, James (eds.): Ritual and symbol in native Central America. University of Oregon Anthropological Papers. No. 9, 1976.

Zinser, Hartmut: Traumreisen und Schamanisieren. Beobachtungen zum "New-Age"-Schamanismus. In: Materialdienst der EZW 51.1988.9:249-260.

Zinser, Hartmut: Zur Faszination des Schamanismus. In Kuper 1991:17-26.

Index

The Concept of Man in Non-Western Cultures
A Guide for One's Own Research

by Robert Badenberg

Handbook
to Lothar Käser's Textbook
Animism – A Cognitive Approach

If we want to understand the animistic cognitive system we must focus particularly on its concept of man. Access to it can only be achieved by proceeding systematically. A basic prerequisite for this is a knowledge of the language spoken by the people whose culture is shaped by such an animistic system of thought. Incidentally acquired knowledge is not enough to give the outsider, whether missionary, teacher, doctor or nurse, the necessary insights for operating effectively within a society governed by an animistic cognitive framework.

Why a textbook and a handbook on the same subject? A textbook seeks to address foundational issues and to ask general questions. A handbook on the other hand is concerned to deal with qualitative and quantitative research. This book is the companion volume of Lothar Käser's textbook on Animism – A Cognitive Approach and provides the interested researcher a tool to guide one's own research into the cognitive aspects of a particular dimension of animism, namely, the concept of man.

Robert Badenberg, qualified in mechanical engineering, trained at the Theological Seminary of the Liebenzell Mission (1982-1987). Further study at the Columbia International University (CIU), German Branch, Korntal, awarded M.A. in Missiology (1999). Doctorate in Missiology at the University of South Africa (2001). As author, missionary (he worked in Africa from 1989 to 2003) and mission ethnologist he commands much experience in this field.

Pb. • pp. 116 • £ 9.80 • $ 15.99 • € 12.80
ISBN 978-3-95776-115-6

VTR Publications • Gogolstr. 33 • 90475 Nürnberg • Germany
info@vtr-online.com • http://www.vtr-online.com

Foreign Cultures

by Lothar Käser

An Introduction to Ethnology
for Development Aid Workers and Church Workers Abroad

In recent decades foreign cultures have not just loomed large for Europeans seeking holiday destinations. Since the 1960s increasing numbers of professionals such as teachers, doctors, agronomists, and other professional workers and missionaries from Europe and America have been partnering local churches in Africa, Asia and Latin America whose fellowships are often very differently organised. When preparing these specialists, development agencies and missions often overlook the knowledge and insights that ethnology and cultural anthropology have to offer, help that makes it easier for professionals to take their bearings, to be well integrated, and to go about their work more effectively. This book deals with such issues.

For future theorists dealing with foreign cultures (ethnologists, anthropologists, etc.) there is now a whole range of brilliantly written textbooks. However, for development aid practitioners, whether secular workers or church workers, these introductory works are overloaded with theory and are thus difficult to digest. What has been missing until now is a simple introduction to the basic concepts which could enable a European working in foreign surroundings to come to terms with the ethnological literature relevant for his activities overseas, to recognise these essential concepts woven into the daily cultural reality of life and work, and to work with them and to bring to bear his or her own analysis. This book is a simplified introduction along these lines, not just written for the target readers just mentioned, but also for students of ethnology/cultural anthropology and for those who frequent ethnological museums.

The author is a professor of anthropology with relevant experience of the issues. He spent five years working in the South Pacific, and has visited Africa, Asia and South America on many occasions for research.

Pb. • pp. 290 • £ 22.50 • $ 37.50 • € 29.95
ISBN 978-3-95776-113-2

VTR Publications • Gogolstr. 33 • 90475 Nürnberg • Germany
info@vtr-online.com • http://www.vtr-online.com